*Taking
the Wheel*

Taking the Wheel

Women and the Coming of the Motor Age

VIRGINIA SCHARFF

THE FREE PRESS
A Division of Macmillan, Inc.
NEW YORK
Collier Macmillan Canada
TORONTO
Maxwell Macmillan International
NEW YORK   OXFORD   SINGAPORE   SYDNEY

The Free Press
A Division of Macmillan, Inc.
866 Third Avenue, New York, N.Y. 10022

Collier Macmillan Canada, Inc.
1200 Eglinton Avenue East
Suite 200
Don Mills, Ontario M3C 3N1

Printed in the United States of America

printing number
1   2   3   4   5   6   7   8   9   10

Library of Congress Cataloging-in-Publication Data

Scharff, Virginia
    Taking the wheel : women and the coming of the motor age /
Virginia Scharff.
        p.   cm.
    ISBN 0–02–928135–0
    1. Women automobile drivers—History.   2. Automobiles—Social
aspects.   3. Women's studies.   I. Title.
TL 152.52.S3   1991
305.42—dc20   90–49507
                                                                   CIP

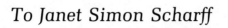

To Janet Simon Scharff

Contents

Acknowledgments   ix

1 The Lady and the Mechanic   1
2 From Passenger to Driver   15
3 Femininity and the Electric Car   35
4 Power and Comfort   51
5 Spectacle and Emancipation   67
6 Women Drivers in World War I   89
7 Corporate Masculinity and the
  "Feminine" Market   111
8 Women at the Wheel in the 1920s   135
9 Reinventing the Wheel   165

  Notes   177
  Index   213

Acknowledgments

From the time I began looking into this topic, many people have helped me with research. I would like to thank Ruth Dickstein, women's studies specialist at the University of Arizona library. The Interlibrary Loan department at the University of Arizona offered impressively prompt and meticulous work. Research librarians at the University of California at Los Angeles, Arizona State University, the Arthur and Elizabeth Schlesinger Library at Radcliffe College, the Henry Ford Museum and Greenfield Village, the Arizona Historical Society, and the Houston Public Library have offered generous assistance. I would particularly like to thank the Schlesinger Library for giving me permission to use materials from the Mary E. Dillon Collection, and Heather Hatch and Barbara Bush, photograph librarians at the Arizona Historical Society, for their assistance with photos.

I have been fortunate to receive financial aid from various sources. The Department of History and the Women's Studies Program at the University of Arizona provided assistance, as did the Woodrow Wilson National Fellowship Foundation, Fran and Jack Swift, and Janet Scharff. As head of the history department at the University of New Mexico, Jonathan Porter has offered enthusiastic encouragement and professional guidance.

Numerous people have read and commented on portions of this work as it progressed. I would like to thank Michael Berger, Corlann Gee Bush, Ruth Schwartz Cowan, Mark Foster, Patricia Nelson Limerick, Eric Monkkonen, Emiliana Noether, Paula Petrik, Richard Tedlow, and Mary Jo Wagner for their insights and criticisms. Conversations with Scott Bottles and Joseph Interrante helped me to think and rethink about women and cars. Robert Krantz offered expert advice on automotive questions both technical and historical. Melanie Gustafson and Autumn Stanley provided a wealth of often obscure material and many helpful comments.

It is my great fortune to be a part of a community of feminist scholars. Katherine Jensen and Mary Aickin Rothschild introduced me to the intellectual excitement, camaraderie, and immense joys of women's studies and women's history. Myra Dinnerstein has shown me what can be accomplished by great imagination, encompassing intellectual curiosity, and boundless energy. Barbara Babcock, Janice Harris, Betsy Jameson, Tessie Liu, Valerie Matsumoto, Casey Miller, Janice Monk, Beverly Seckinger, Jane Slaughter, and Kate Swift have provided stimulating ideas, collegiality, and models to emulate. I want also to thank Noralee Frankel and the members of the Committee on Women Historians of the American Historical Association, particularly Alice Kessler-Harris and Judith Walkowitz, for all I learned from them as graduate representative to the committee, and for their dedication to the advancement of women in the historical profession.

I have saved for last the pleasure of thanking those to whom this piece of work owes much of what merit it has, who are in no way responsible for its defects. Paul Carter stands as proof that scholarship need (and indeed must) not dull the imagination or the spirit, and I thank him for his interest and encouragement. I owe William H. Sewell a great intellectual debt for his careful reading of my work, and for serious and enjoyable conversations about language, history, and theory. I find it hard to estimate my indebtedness to Martin Wachs, who has not only read and offered essential comments on this study, but has opened his research files to me, encouraged me professionally, and proven to me that cooperation is possible among those who work on similar topics. Likewise, I cannot express sufficient gratitude to Leonard Dinnerstein, who has valued and aided my work and who is as astute a critic of prose and of argumentation as I have known.

Karen Anderson's brilliant mind, meticulous research, breadth of knowledge, and dedication to a better world have inspired me on a daily basis. She has read carefully and criticized insightfully more of my work than I have had any right to ask her to do. If I am in any position to judge, she has somehow managed to balance the professionalism of the teacher with the unstinting warmth of the true friend. I cannot imagine that most students are as lucky as I was in finding a mentor.

Few scholars have an editor as involved and insightful as Joyce Seltzer. She has made this a much better book than it would have been without her help.

Finally, I want to thank Peter Swift for his always useful and refreshing insights and criticisms, his skill as mechanic and father, his laughter, and his kindness. Too, without Sam and Ann Swift, it would have been difficult for me to appreciate the historical forcefulness of the joys and exigencies of motherhood.

CHAPTER 1

The Lady and the Mechanic

Picture the affluent American woman of 1900, poised to go out to do some shopping. Girded in corsets and petticoats and forty pounds of underskirts and overskirts, cloak, and formidable hat, she is clad in immobility. The embodiment of ladyhood, she makes her way to the street. If she is very wealthy, her coachman helps her into her carriage. Otherwise, she is likely to walk. Her garments trail in mud and dirt, picking up traces of the inevitable byproducts of horse traffic (much to her disgust). Once she makes her purchases and asks the store clerk to have them delivered to her house, she walks home. Or maybe she is tired enough from the outing, and sufficiently well-to-do, to hire a hack. The American lady is, after all, a delicate creature. Instead of subjecting herself to the rigors of public traffic, she belongs behind closed doors.

Perhaps she lives in a larger city, far enough from her destination that she will need to take a streetcar to get to the store. She waits on a corner, hot or cold, wet or windblown according to the season. When the trolley finally comes (late as usual) the car is so crowded that she has to stand, crushed among motley riders. A child runs across the tracks. The trolley lurches and screeches to a stop. Pitched against a neighboring strap-hanger, she loses her new hat. A raucous young man, boarding the car, shouts in her ear and steps on the hat. Buying things is pleasant, but there are limits to one's endurance. The conditions on the trolley assail propriety as certainly as her too-proximate fellow passengers endanger her millinery.

Victorian experts—doctors, professors, ministers, politicians—conceived of the American lady as thus frail, timid, easily shocked, and quickly exhausted, physically and temperamentally incapable of mastering the demands of public life. Born to the weak sex, biology consigned her to lifelong inactivity and immobility. During her monthly menstrual periods, said one prominent doctor, "the ordinary occupations are to be suspended. . . . Long walks, dancing, shopping, riding and parties should be avoided at this time of the month invariably and under all circumstances."[1] Too much schooling would surely overtax such a fragile organism. Citing such scientific authorities as Charles Darwin and Herbert Spencer, Dr. Edward Clarke of the Harvard Board of Overseers argued in 1873 that stimulating women's brains would enfeeble their reproductive organs. It was both cruel and unnatural to expect them to study alongside men. "Identical education of the two sexes," he wrote, "is a crime before God and humanity that physiology protests against and that experience weeps over."[2]

Even while they enjoyed apparent good health, women were supposed to lack the intellectual capacity to handle such cerebral matters as politics or business. One need not (and, some experts held, ought not) vote to be a good mother; how much less suited women were to practicing public professions. As one politician opposed to woman suffrage explained:

> A woman's brain evolves emotion rather than intellect; and whilst this feature fits her admirably as a creature burdened with the preservation and happiness of the human species, it painfully disqualifies her for the sterner duties to be performed by the intellectual faculties. The best wife and mother and sister would make the worst legislator, judge and police.[3]

Whether considering education, politics, business, or the professions, prominent men registered their fears about the consequences of women's emergence from the private world of home into the public realm. Their tone was protective and proprietary. They worried that women would neglect their housekeeping, ignore their children, undermine proper relations between the classes and races, and degrade their morals if involved in public life. Invoking the fragility of women's bodies, the feebleness of their brains, or the frailty of their characters, Victorian experts admonished women to stay home. Their notion of woman's place was hygienic, political, economic, and spatial as well as symbolic. An antisuffragist Florida congressman put the matter quite starkly: "I do not wish to see the day when the women of my race in my state shall trail their skirts in the muck and mire of partisan politics."[4] Women could only dirty themselves by venturing beyond the front door, into the hectic and unpredictable crush of public traffic.

Victorian Americans were hardly original in distrusting women's movements in public spaces. For centuries, the Chinese had bound women's feet to keep them from straying too far from home. Ancient Rome apparently solved the problem of city traffic congestion by prohibiting women from driving chariots.[5] Yet the language Americans use tells us much about the grounding and transformation of popular perceptions. The commonplace word "traffic" has an interesting history, intimately connected with the question of women's movements and activities in public spaces. The word originally referred to transportation, to goods to be exchanged, to trade between people, or more ominously, to relations between those aspiring to be good and the forces of corruption. The *Oxford English Dictionary* lists definitions including "the transportation of merchandise for purposes of trade;" "the buying and selling or exchange of goods for profit;" "intercourse, communication; dealings, business" (exemplified by a 1560 usage, "that secret trafficke that thou haste with infidels," or the 1727 usage "a traffick intercourse with Satan"), and "goods or merchandise in which trade is done."[6] Yet another early definition of traffic, "a prostitute" (ex-emplified by the 1561 usage, "these trafickes, these common truls I mean, walk abroad,") suggests that goods traded might include sexual favors.[7] In the seventeenth century the word was used to present a gendered image of trade "often with a sinister implication," and women's status as sexual trade goods or traders was equally open to question, as in the 1628 verse, "The world doth build without, our God within; He traffics goodness, she traffics sin."[8]

Beginning in the nineteenth century, a period of vast change in transportation technology, "traffic" came to mean "the passing to and fro of persons, or of vehicles or vessels, along a road, railway, canal, or other route of transport."[9] Yet even as this meaning of traffic gained wider and wider currency, "traffic" continued to refer to dealings "in a disparaging sense, or said of dealings considered improper," as in the 1854 usage, "Beauti-ful and dissolute females, trafficking in their charms."[10] After four centuries of common use, the word implied not simply trade or the manipulation of commodities but, often, illicit trade involving women maneuvering in community spaces. It reso-nated with suspicion of women's presence in public, with ques-tions about their freedom of movement, and with misgivings about female control over portable, alienable (if sexual) property. Women's independent access to public spaces and to trade goods posed a triple threat, to public life, to property, and to women themselves.[11]

By the opening of the twentieth century, American women expanded their claims to new prerogatives and places. The Pro-gressive movement, born in the nation's growing cities, provided them with a political medium for expression and a wide set of possibilities. In search of education, employment, justice, and self-expression, they invaded the university and the courtroom, established settlement houses and social services, exposed cor-ruption, and displayed the products of their creativity. In the name of women's rights, they even took to the streets. These turn-of-the-century bourgeois women followed their less privi-leged sisters into public places. In the nineteenth-century urban United States, working-class women had made themselves both threatening and vulnerable by laying claim to a boisterous neighborhood life that offered survival, pleasure, profit, danger, and diversion. In the streets of America's big cities, women bought and sold everything from fish to flowers, hawking their wares at top volume. They gossiped, fought, taunted men and one another, hollered at their children, paraded new clothes bought with hard-earned wages, flirted with young swells.[12] More privileged urban women were slower to venture into the streets, and generally more restrained when they did so. Yet their potentially greater access to property, their power as consumers, added a dimension to the problem of public womanhood. Might they use their purchasing power to claim other kinds of authority? Would the woman who felt the jingle of coins in her pocket, and the urge to explore new territory, buy a ticket to an uncharted destination?

The fear that women might stray too far from home had a particular urgency in the waning years of the Gilded Age. The notion that middle- and upper-class American women ought to confine their actions to the bounds of "woman's sphere" remained strong, but that sphere was expanding geographically as the result of innovations in transportation. For wealthy women, access to carriages and hacks had long meant the chance to travel greater distances from home than less affluent women could. In the second half of the nineteenth century, American cities had also begun to develop public transportation systems.

No lawful or social standards governed relations between women and men on municipal transport. Though transit companies came to discriminate quite openly and lawfully against African-Americans, they would make no such legal distinction according to gender.[13] Thus public transit became a setting for confusion and struggle over proper relations between the sexes. As whites of different classes mingled on the cars (African-Americans of both sexes were expected to sit in the back of such public conveyances as they were permitted to use at all, or relinquish their seats to whites), no one was quite certain whether men ought to practice chivalry and offer their seats to women of all classes on crowded cars, or whether housewives and shoppers owed exhausted workingmen the courtesy of a place to rest their weary bones. Despite misunderstandings and occasional confrontations, middle-class women boarded the horse cars in significant numbers, and for their own reasons. The city surveyor of Philadelphia, commenting in 1866 on the success of horse-drawn railways in that municipality, noted that "our ladies attend to their shopping and visiting by the cars."[14]

The availability of cheap public transportation, coupled with the growing population of cities, suburbanization, and the increasing distance between household, shopping, and industrial workplace, encouraged women to range further from home than they had in earlier times.[15] As electric-powered trolleys replaced horse cars, women passengers in many cities used the streetcar as a regular means of getting around town on errands, social calls, and pleasure trips. Wilhelmina Emery, a Boston woman who moved to Los Angeles in 1905 and kept a diary of her first two years in Southern California, wrote matter-of-factly of frequent trolley trips, some to shop at department stores in the heart of the city's commercial district, others on sightseeing excursions around Los Angeles. The trolley gave Emery the chance to see the city for herself.[16]

At the same time, depending on public transportation meant putting up with crowding, unreliable schedules, inflexible routes, and a general lack of privacy. Wilhelmina Emery recorded one crowded and terrifying ride on the streetcar that included an encounter with a runaway horse and a woman who caught her dress on the steps "and nearly tore the skirt right off."[17] If the annoyances, inconveniences, and dangers of public transportation afflicted male passengers, they seemed particularly daunting factors for women. The tribulations of the trolley therefore occasioned frequent complaint, and sometimes even sparked organized protest. In New York in 1907, a group of women formed the Society for the Protection of Passenger Rights, an organization concerned with conditions in the city's public transportation system. The group criticized the subway system as filthy, "crowded to the point of indecency," and dangerous, saying that "there is altogether too much rowdyism in the cars and that women are annoyed and insulted by young ruffians without interference from the conductors." Members of the Society promised to investigate not only the subways, but also surface roads, elevated roads, "the matter of transfers," and taxis.[18]

As female ridership grew, muckraking newspapers crusaded against the physical and moral dangers posed by grasping traction monopolies like the Pacific Electric and Los Angeles Railway in Los Angeles. A reporter for the *Los Angeles Record* painted a grim picture of streetcar conditions in 1912:

> Inside the air was a pestilence; it was heavy with disease and the emanations from many bodies. Anyone leaving this working mass, anyone coming into it . . . force the people into still closer, still more indecent, still more immoral contact. A bishop embraced a stout grandmother, a tender girl touched limbs with a city sport, refined womens' faces burned with shame and indignation—but there was no relief. . . . It was only the result of public stupidity and apathy. It was in a Los Angeles streetcar . . . [any] old day you are a mind to board a city street car between the hours of 5 and 7 in the afternoon.[19]

Little wonder that politicians in cities like Chicago and Los Angeles, facing transit funding issues, found it expedient to declare themselves protectors of female virtue imperiled by inadequate transportation services.[20] Beneath the welter of political conflicts, there lurked the idea that the very character of mass transit set it on a collision course with bourgeois ladyhood. The trolley was simply too public a vehicle for the female personification of privacy. How, then, might a woman preserve her temper, her reputation, her constitution, and her gown, and still manage to get around town?

∞

As the lady tried to map her passage into mobile womanhood, some Americans set themselves to solve the nation's transportation problems. In sheds and barns and machine shops, muscular men tinkered. Garbed in filthy, comfortable overalls, their heavy boots thudding on hard-packed ground and concrete floors, they wrestled with the engrossing challenge of how to make a carriage move without benefit of a horse. Their fingernails rimmed with black grime, they wielded hacksaws and wrenches, pencils and T squares, tire irons and calipers. Before them were workbenches spread with grease-covered bits of metal, with mechanical diagrams smudged by many erasures, perfectly baffling to the uninitiated. They put things together and took them apart, lifted heavy assemblages of parts again and again, cursing the mistakes, celebrating what worked, arguing deep into the night. Sometimes, brothers worked and fought together. Sometimes, a man's whole life bent toward achieving success in a freezing shed, toward the moment when an ungainly wheeled contraption was rolled out the door, pushed down the road, and sparked miraculously into life.

In 1876, engineer George B. Brayton displayed a two-cycle internal combustion engine at the Philadelphia Centennial Exposition. Fascinated American inventors and mechanics soon came to wonder how the engine might be adapted to power a highway vehicle. Others, meanwhile, began to think about steam and electricity as power sources for a horseless buggy. These men were, for the time, unusual, since travel on the wretched American road system held limited appeal for most people. They would, however, get a boost from bicycle enthusiasts of the 1880s and 1890s. Cyclists led the way in lobbying governmental agencies to improve the nation's highways. The better the roads, the more likely people would be to use them.[21] The bicycle business did more than generate public enthusiasm for good roads. It also served as a training ground for some of the nation's earliest automobile makers, from the White brothers of Cleveland, who manufactured steam cars, to Colonel Albert E. Pope of Hartford, Connecticut, who became first the nation's largest bicycle producer, and then its earliest large-scale auto manufacturer, concentrating on electric cars.

In 1893, as members of the League of American Wheelmen pressed Congress to appropriate $10,000 to study road improvement, Charles and Frank Duryea, brothers raised on an Illinois farm, ushered in the American gasoline motor era. The Duryeas made their living as bicycle mechanics in Chicopee, Massachusetts. Europeans like Karl Benz, Gottlieb Daimler, and Emile Constant Levassor had already built horseless carriages, and were taking steps toward commercial production of motor vehicles as custom-built playthings for the wealthy. The Duryeas had read about Benz's work in an 1889 issue of *Scientific American*, and by 1892 were at work on their own motor buggy. The following year, Frank hitched their one-cylinder, gas-powered motor carriage behind a horse, dragged it to the edge of town, spun the flywheel (again and again), and the engine caught. Finally, he coaxed the vehicle to move more than two hundred feet under its own power.[22]

The Duryea car, now in the Smithsonian institution, was a high, open, spindly affair. The phaeton carriage body, mounted on slender wooden wheels with rubber tires, resembled a couch mounted on a curved platform and fitted with a collapsible awning. It had two speeds (forward and reverse), and Frank steered it by means of a tiller bar. The heart of its originality, the source of self-propulsion, was shelved under the body, protruding slightly to the rear, rather like, as one historian noted, a bustle. It weighed in at only 750 pounds. Virtually the minute he drove it, Frank was dissatisfied with the design, and began working on a more substantial two-cycle model. By 1895, he would drive his car to victory in the nation's first automobile race, a fifty-five mile round-trip between Chicago and Evanston sponsored by the *Chicago Times-Herald*, featuring six vehicles, only two of which finished the course. A year later, the brothers went to England, where Frank would win a race from London to Brighton. Soon enough, however, they began to argue over which of them deserved credit for their invention, igniting a bitter lifelong enmity. Theirs was the first, but by no means the last such feud in the history of the contentious and competitive American auto business.[23]

In the remaining years of the nineteenth century, while women stepped up their campaign for the vote, set up urban enclaves from Hull House in Chicago to Henry Street in New York, and took up the sport of bicycling, the American motorcar industry began to take shape. Many of the men who entered the automotive competition, like the Apperson brothers of Kokomo, Indiana, were self-taught mechanics who had little patience with the niceties of engineering theory. Such men possessed a willingness to tackle the risky, quirky problems of designing and fabricating horseless carriages which might at least fail to move, and might at worst burst into flame. College graduate Elwood Haynes, who designed a gas-powered car in 1894, hired the Appersons to build it, and the brothers soon fell out with Haynes over the issue of who really designed the 820-pound car that traveled Pumpkinvine Pike in Kokomo at a speed of some six miles an hour on July 4, 1894.[24] The conflict between the erudite Haynes and the unlettered Appersons symbolized more than a clash of personalities. It also reflected the mechanic's disdain for book-learning and distrust of those who valued brains over brawn. Only a few American automobiles had been produced, but already car makers had begun to forge a concept of rough-hewn, muscle-bound masculinity central to the industry's developing self-image.

The figure of the automotive pioneer, like that of the bourgeois lady, was a selective portrait. Historians of the business, often Detroit insiders themselves, have depicted the industry's forefathers as men of burly practicality, independent and quarrelsome, schooled in the machine shop rather than classroom or boardroom.[25] Such an image derived from the time when men designed and assembled automobiles one at a time, with their own hands, claiming the workingman's identity. Yet even in the earliest days of the American auto industry, those who made cars were remarkable less for their common origins than for the qualities they brought out in each other. To later auto industry tycoons, more comfortable with spread sheets than with socket wrenches, these first American car makers seemed "original, forceful, strong charactered, ambitious fellows" with "strong appetites for excitement."[26] In early factories like the Olds Motor Works of Detroit, college boys like Michigan graduate Roy D. Chapin and workingmen like Jonathan D. Maxwell discovered common ground grappling with machines on the shop floor. Wrapped in coveralls, drenched with grease, swearing at the same recalcitrant gear or gasket, or at each other, businessmen's sons and poor farm boys developed rough camaraderie.

The fellowship of wrenches notwithstanding, the moment inventors turned from creating prototypes to producing for a market, they had to put on ties and collars and head off to find backers. The most successful among them transformed themselves, however reluctantly, from grease-stained inventors into corporate trustees, wheeling and dealing with bankers, business-men, and lawyers. Ransom E. Olds, a tinker par excellence, first built a steam car in 1887. By 1895, he would be working on a gasoline car, but would not be able to complete it in time to enter it in the landmark race sponsored by the *Chicago Times-Herald*. The following year, Olds visited Detroit and deployed his considerable talents as a salesman and promoter to convince copper millionaire Samuel L. Smith to back him in a venture to produce cars in quantity. Smith contributed $199,600 and got ninety-five percent of Old Motor Works stock. For an invest-ment of $400, Olds got to build cars.

Olds's success story reads like one of Horatio Alger's dime novels, the hero triumphant through pluck and luck. When his factory burned in 1901, all that remained was a single model of a low-priced runabout. Betting the company's future on the sole remaining car, Olds ordered Roy Chapin to drive the car from Detroit to New York, an unprecedented stunt that would make the Oldsmobile the hit of the Madison Square Garden auto show. Soon immortalized in popular song, the "Merry Oldsmo-bile," a small, light, open buggy with a one-cylinder engine and a curved dash, would be the first automobile in the world to be manufactured in quantity. In 1901, Olds produced six hundred cars; in 1904, the company built five thousand vehicles. Ransom Olds, the mechanic, had become a millionaire.[27]

But though Olds continued to prosper as a car maker, he would soon stand in the shadow of that dominant figure of the automobile business, Henry Ford. Among auto pioneers, Ford most perfectly embodied the transformation of mechanic into magnate, and none more carefully preserved and embellished the car manufacturer's manly image. His often-told life story has come to stand as a primal tale of both the developing automo-bile business and of American masculine entrepreneurial character.[28] There was something legendary in Ford's career, his stunning rise to power and wealth as a man of the people, his self-destructive reincarnation in the 1920s and 1930s as tyrant and dangerous crank. His devotion to the common man, his disdain for the dead hand of history, his pragmatic vision, and his virulent prejudices have appeared as essential components of Ford's extraordinary ability to express the normal, the uncomfortably archetypal, in American manhood. To his admirers, Ford personified inventive energy and bright-eyed ingenuousness; to his critics he was the soul of boundless egotism and unwitting evil. All these qualities were supposedly latent in every American farm boy of his time, the "every boy" who, people supposed, might grow up to be President. In Ford, it appeared that the volatile American frontiersman had exchanged buckskins for overalls.

As an auto mechanic, Ford's impatience with the weight of tradition fired him with a passion for speed. Like other early American auto manufacturers, he proved his legitimacy as a car maker not by producing custom cars tailored to the carriage trade, as European manufacturers did, but by racing. He would make his reputation once and for all in 1902 with the huge and powerful 999, a four-cylinder, seventy-horsepower vehicle, almost ten feet long and the fastest car of its day.[29] The story of 999 became a kind of masculine creation myth for the industry. The car took shape piece by piece in an unheated room above a machine shop, where, according to legend, Ford and swashbuckling draftsman C. (for Childe) Harold Wills literally fought off the cold while they worked. When the chill got too much for them, it was said, "they would put on boxing gloves and flail each other until they felt warm."[30] The 999 was so difficult to drive that only a daredevil would attempt the feat, and Ford found such a man in impecunious cyclist Barney Oldfield, who accepted the job with the observation that he "might as well be dead as dead broke." Ford's car won handily.[31]

Ford became the most successful American automaker of the pre-World War I period, and the most celebrated American of his time. But even as he built one of the largest corporations in the world, Ford continued to treasure an image of himself as he had been at the turn of the century: the humble-farm-boy-turned-mechanic, mastering the machine with sweat and ingenuity, scraping his knuckles bare, and jettisoning anyone or anything that came between him and the car. Looking backward, other auto industry pioneers would be seized with nostalgia for the era of the horseless carriage, of muscular genius, mechanical mishaps, personal enmities and fraternity in overalls. They decried the ease with which callow neophytes—women even—could take the wheel. The earlier days "were strenuous days," wrote M.I.T. graduate and bicycle-mechanic-turned-auto-manufacturer Hiram Percy Maxim,

> in which only the fit and young survived. But they were intensely enjoyable. The thrill of feeling the pull of a well-adjusted gasoline-engine fired one's blood. . . . One wore old clothes and carried a full assortment of tools and spare parts when one ventured forth in horseless-carriage days; today we wear our evening clothes and do not know where the tools are kept. Only the mechanically self-reliant ventured forth in horseless-carriage days. Today we see thousands of mechanically uninformed women undertaking journeys running into thousands of miles.[32]

In the first years of the new century, as these combative men struggled to give birth to the industry that would transform the nation's economy and landscape, many American women began to explore new terrain, to venture on their own beyond the front door and into city and countryside. Some of them, both affluent and adventuresome, looked to the motorcar with intense curiosity and excitement. If, as Dolores Hayden has pointed out, "women have never explicitly demanded the *droit de la ville,* the medieval right to the freedom of the city that distinguished urban citizens from feudal serfs," the auto had the potential to help some women claim that right, most without ever demanding it.[33] But the auto was born in a masculine manger, and when women sought to claim its power, they invaded a male domain. As women stepped up to take the wheel, they had to overcome their own lack of confidence and combat both subtle and overt resistance.

2

From Passenger to Driver

"Tʜᴀᴛ the motor girl is willing to make any sacrifice for the sport she so loves is plainly shown in the new automobile face protectors," wrote a fashion columnist of 1903.[1] The writer assuredly was not kidding. The well-to-do people who embraced the auto in its earliest incarnations had to dress for duress. Motoring was dirty work (or play, as the case often was). Though males of the business class had developed a fastidious and elaborate office costume that needed to be kept clean, they shared a masculine identity with men who customarily donned practical protective clothing for certain kinds of jobs. Machinists wore coveralls; firefighters wore slickers; coal miners wore hard hats; the managers of industrial enterprises put on appropriate garments when they visited plant or mine. When male automobilists, as they were sometimes called, donned heavy coats, goggles, and sensible hats, they affirmed manliness. Feminine dress exhibited less utility. Unless they were either too poor to pay attention to fashion or too bold to worry about outraging public opinion, women coped with dirt in household, field, and factory in skirts. At most, one resorted to a scarf or sun hat, or to ruffled dust cap and pinafore. The idea of wearing clothing for practical rather than decorative purposes flew in the face of standards of femininity, particularly for middle- and upper-class women. As the protagonist of a comic sketch titled "The Frivolous Girl Goes Motoring" put it, "I can't bear to see anyone all muffled and bundled in an auto. If I had a dozen autos I shouldn't ever want to rig out the way motoring women do. They look hideous."[2]

A turn-of-the-century female motorist, getting ready for a ride in a Merry Oldsmobile, had her work cut out for her. She had, after all, to preserve feminine decorum. The street and the trolley posed threat enough to her costume and complexion. A speedy turn in the open, high-riding, smoke-spewing motor vehicles of the brand-new century meant establishing a series of redoubts in defense of sartorial order. First, the duster, or motoring coat. It might be made of leather or rubber or fur; in all cases, it was hot and heavy, adding yet more poundage to her already heavily freighted body. Then there were a host of devices to protect face, eyes, hair, and hat. These ranged from simple, if cumbersome, goggles and heavy veils to more elaborate contraptions. On rainy days, the motoring woman might choose a waterproof rubber hood and shoulder cape, looking rather like someone who planned to take a shower with all her clothes on. An all-weather motoring mask for women approximated a large bucket inverted over the head. Made of mica with a translucent linen veil, it closely resembled the protective head covering worn by modern workers who handle plutonium.[3]

The automobile thus presented the women who hurried to try it out with a problem in style and, more broadly, in self-presentation. "There is nothing secretive about the motor car," wrote fashion columnist Grace Margaret Gould. "It says, in effect, as it takes its whirling way, 'If you want to see the latest thing out, look at me and look at my passengers.' "[4] Whether they drove or not, whether they wished to be noticed or not, motoring women made themselves conspicuous. Some courted the public eye and found the automobile a handy device to attract attention. Others, less interested in notoriety than in mobility, tried to invade the masculine domain of the automobile without exciting comment. They had to fail. Simply getting into a motor vehicle made women too prominent to escape notice; actually taking the wheel made them too astonishing to escape controversy. For women, the journey from back to front seat, from passenger-hood to control of a vehicle deeply identified with men, began in public and entailed repeated confrontations with popular manners, morals, and expectations.

The first women to challenge the masculine monopoly of the auto had the advantages of wealth and social status. In 1900 a few cars could be had for under $300, but most sold for $1,000 or more, making them too expensive for families of moderate means. Woodrow Wilson, then president of Princeton, thought the motorcar such a symbol of conspicuous consumption that it would incite the masses to revolution.[5] A society columnist for William Randolph Hearst's newly established *Motor* magazine ("The National Monthly Magazine of Motoring") allowed that "motoring and money have a way of always whisking by together," and names like Morgan, Whitney, and Vanderbilt routinely appeared in *Motor*'s pages.[6] To people like Wilson, who agreed with social philosopher Thorstein Veblen's stinging critique of leisure class ostentation, the combination of rich women (themselves objects for the display of capitalists' wealth) and fancy automobiles presented a decadent spectacle. Imagine how Veblen might have reacted to the sight of

> Mrs. George J. Gould, with jeweled tiara and large ropes of pearls— each strand a gift from her husband when a child was born— . . . regal when the door of her motor car opens . . . and other magnificent women resplendent as the Queen of Sheba, alighting from luxurious motor cars to go up the crimson-carpeted stairway to equally luxurious opera boxes.[7]

As the case of Mrs. Gould suggests, not all automobilists were drivers. The earliest motorists in the United States often possessed enough wealth to claim the advantages of owning an automobile without necessarily taking on the task of learning to drive one. Accustomed to having servants do physical work for them, wealthy women and men alike often left the driving to paid chauffeurs. Some car owners simply instructed their coachmen to move from looking after employers' horses and carriages to taking care of their automobiles. Others sought to hire this new type of servant in accustomed ways, contacting employment agencies or advertising in newspapers. Either way, the chauffeur's employer entered a paradoxical relation of spatial intimacy with a "strange" man who was, at once, the employer's social and economic inferior, and also utterly in control of her or his physical comfort and safety, sometimes in locales far removed from family and friends.

While Woodrow Wilson worried about the elite monopoly on the automobile, less democratic observers feared that the new social phenomenon of automobility might lead to disorderly and dangerous cross-class familiarities, particularly between passenger-owners and their chauffeurs. After all, in the infancy of the motor age, even those who availed themselves of the relative passivity and comfort of the *tonneau*, the enclosed rear seating compartment common in early auto design, demonstrated daring, or at least a desire to portray themselves as adventurously modern. Would not such people be precisely the type to forget the obligations of class in the heat of thrill-seeking? On the other hand, for the rich, entrusting oneself to the coachman had always required a faith that he would remain deferential despite his potential advantage as occupant of the driver's seat.[8] Once the coachman became chauffeur, however, that relation of trust had literally to be extended and reinforced to contain a much larger geographical area and a powerful mechanical advantage on the chauffeur's part.

The term "chauffeur" itself carried overtones of the ambivalent relation between auto owners and those who would be given the power to drive them around. Many commonly used automotive terms were adopted from the French. Originally derived from the French verb *chauffer*, "to heat," the noun "chauffeur" also meant "to stoke up, fire up, a boiler, an engine," a meaning which extended plausibly to cover persons responsible for operating conveyances powered by internal combustion engines. The word was also used in the colloquial phrase *"chauffer une femme,"* meaning "to make hot love to a woman."[9] As male chauffeurs and their purportedly sensation-seeking female passengers sped away from public surveillance, many wondered which fire would be stoked.

C. P. Berry, an early authority on automobile law, linked chauffeurs not only with threats to persons, but with perils to property. He noted that the term referred to "a member of the bands of outlaws during the 'Reign of Terror' in France who roamed over the northeast part of the country. . . . They were called chauffeurs because they roasted the feet of men and women to compel them to disclose hidden treasure."[10] In 1927, a feature in *Popular Mechanics* repeated this derivation of the term, expanding in commenting that "These men seized travellers, carried them into captivity, and burned their feet in order to compel them to tell the hiding place of their money."[11]

Contemporary newspaper sources revealed uneasiness about the chauffeur-employer relationship, and combined class tensions with ethnic conflicts. When the New York City YMCA opened a chauffeur training school in 1904, the *New York Times* noted the "alleged carelessness and dishonesty of many of the men who drive motor cars." The YMCA declared its intention to train "Americans" and "Christians" instead of "imported chauffeur[s]," insisting that "the young men who wish to supplant the foreigners will have the natural desire to avoid running over Americans."[12] Valentine Koch, president of a chauffeur's club, argued that not all chauffeurs were "grafters, drunkards, moonlight excursionists, and incompetents." Nonetheless, the image of the chauffeur as moral degenerate and safety threat prompted E. T. Birdsall of the American Automobile Association to reassure the public that training schools "emphasize the moral side of a chauffeur's duty."[13]

Clearly, the cultural gap between social status and control of technology provoked substantial confusion and concern. Employers learned rather quickly that they could not count on chauffeurs to carry out orders with deferential manner and good cheer. In 1906, the *New York Times* reported that "hundreds of chauffeurs have suddenly been raised to places of responsibility from humble and inferior positions. . . . Employed by men of wealth, but who are totally ignorant of the intricacies of automobiling, these chauffeurs quickly become the boss in every sense of the word." Some chauffeurs agreed that relations between employer and driver were different from those customary between masters and servants. The Professional Chauffeurs' Club objected to livery and other signs of servant status; garage owners claimed that chauffeurs ordered them around; owners complained that their drivers were refusing to do such menial tasks as washing the car. Advocates of the training schools, eager to place their students, argued that the schools produced a "better class" of chauffeurs, individuals who were presumably both competent and compliant.[14] For those who were paid to transport other people in what were at the time called "pleasure cars," moral and mechanical trustworthiness were twin job requisites. They were expected to provide, rather than partake of, the leisurely joys of motoring. By 1913, applicants for chauffeurs' licenses in New York had to "have good moral character, be sober, and possess a good record."[15]

Chauffeurs' technological power over male employer-passengers and their automotive property stirred public concern and strained class (and sometimes ethnic) relations. However, more potentially threatening conflicts proliferated when the passenger was female. The American public was titillated and alarmed by the question of what kind of relations rich women had with their chauffeurs, servants whose sexual power as men (particularly as working-class men) complicated a job that required physical intimacy with leisure-class women.[16] Automobile manufacturers made it possible for owners to maintain hierarchical physical separation from drivers when they incorporated the tonneau, or rear seating compartment, into their automotive design, sheltering the passengers and leaving the driver's seat open to the elements. But not all models were so constructed. And in any case, automobiles by their very nature made it possible for drivers and passengers to go where no one else might observe whether a vehicle's occupants were keeping to their appropriate places.

The popular press thus sometimes treated the woman passenger as a sexually suspect figure all too vulnerable to the erotic power of her driver. "The Wonderful Monster," a 1905 serial syndicated by William Randolph Hearst and published in *Motor* magazine, warned of the power of both cars and male drivers to awaken incendiary urges in women.[17] The pseudonymous

authors related the mysterious and melodramatic story of Lady
Dorothy Beeston, wife of Sir Wilfred Beeston, a woman "enthusiastically fond of motoring."[18] The very thought of her car brings
a "soft" smile to her lips:

> To think of "The Monster," as she called it, was to long for it.
> That great living, wonderful thing with its passion for motion
> seemed to call and claim her as a kindred spirit. She wanted to
> feel the throb of its quickening pulses; to lay her hand on lever
> and handle and thrill with the sense of mastery; to claim its
> power as her own—and feel its sullen-yielded obedience answer
> her will.[19]

Lady Beeston both fears and desires to be alone with the
Monster. However, her desire for "mastery" is complicated by
the fact that she has a partner in her "motor-mania," chauffeur
Pierre Cassagnac, a hunchback Frenchman of uncertain birth,
mechanical genius, and menacing madness. Sir Wilfred mistrusts
Pierre and frets over Lady Beeston's "smoldering fire" for fast
driving. Lady Beeston, evidently intending to be reassuring, tells
her husband that she is simply a product of modern life; "We
can't take life temperately, easily, as our forefathers did. We
exhaust ourselves in getting any pleasure, and no pleasure is
worth getting unless it holds excitement or danger."[20]

Strange things begin to happen. Lady Beeston becomes secretive and distracted. She and Pierre appear to have some terrible
bond. Sir Wilfred and some of the Beestons' friends agree that
Lady Beeston must be protected from Cassagnac and the car.
Shortly after midnight on Christmas night, the possessed lady,
the crazy chauffeur, and the demonic car are discovered missing.
However, class relations will be put to rights; the deluded chauffeur will get his comeuppance. In the midst of a "frenzied journey" at "a delirious speed in which both [Pierre and Lady
Beeston] exult," Cassagnac stands erect and is thrown from the
car and killed. Lady Beeston's fire is not quite quenched even
when she is tossed into a snowdrift, where "fear wrestled with
her torturing desire," and "a delicious ecstasy possessed her."
Fortunately, Sir Wilfred will redeem his wife from "the

madness of a passion untamed, the infidelity of her secret
pleasure."[21] He retrieves her from the snowdrift with "manly
tenderness," lamenting her victimization by the deluded chauffeur and "the frivolous pleasures, the follies and vices of the
new century." Lady B. confesses that "I still thrill in the memory
. . . of feeling the Monster obeying the slightest twitch of my
hand until the madness of Pierre seemed to pervade the machinery of the Monster and change it from a willing slave to a fiend
bent on death and destruction." But, terrified by her brush with
oblivion, she begs her husband's forgiveness, promising never,
ever, to drive a car again.[22]

"The Wonderful Monster" takes an unequivocal stand
against the automobile's capacity to disturb properly hierarchical
class relations. The story also has a clear message for and about
women. Lady Beeston sins by trying to grasp the modern pleasure
of automotive speed, which gives her an illegitimate and explo-
sively sexualized power over time and space.[23] She has also
erred by succumbing to the hypnotic suggestions of her chauffeur,
thus abrogating her status as a "lady" in charge of socially inferior
males. Who, after all, was driving the Monster? The question
is never really answered. Was the car a demon that drove itself
on an errand of death? Was the insane Pierre in the driver's
seat, figuratively if not literally? In the end, the author concludes
that Lady Beeston's own lust for fast driving is to blame; a character remarks, "There may be latent in every woman some tragic
passion, which, once awakened and uncontrolled, may rob a
man of her love and a house of its mistress."[24] In the car culture,
such a passion might attach itself to man or motor; combining
the two, according to some observers, would overwhelm feminine
frailty.

∞

Whether they took the wheel themselves, or rode as passengers, motoring women asserted not only their intention to conquer
distance, but also their right to control a costly piece of property
they might not even own outright. Little wonder that observers
of the time saw something incongruous, something fundamentally disruptive, in the spectacle of women on wheels. Women
in automobiles entered public space at a time of unprecedented

debate over women's right and capacity to step into public life with regard to the ballot box and the university.[25] Such an inroad could not escape notice in a context where the distinction between public and private places served as a boundary defining proper masculine and feminine roles. When New Jersey passed an auto operators' licensing law in 1906, the fact that more than one hundred women applied for such licenses, and that several New Jersey women claimed to have driven thousands of miles, seemed surprising enough to merit a story in the *New York Times*.[26]

The auto attracted affluent women of all kinds, the famous as well as the anonymous. Edith Wharton, that acute chronicler of the lives and troubles of women of the American upper classes, first rode in an automobile on a spring day in 1903, while touring in Italy. After a windy, dusty fifty-mile ride, an exhilarated Wharton "swore then and there that as soon as I could make money enough I would buy a motor; and so I did."[27]

So avidly did Wharton take to automobiles that her friend Henry James claimed he always identified her with a shiny new motorcar. By the spring of 1904, Wharton and her husband, traveling in England, arrived at James's Lamb House in Rye in their newly purchased Panhard-Levassor, a French "motor-car of moderate speed and capacious dimensions." As they cruised through the Sussex countryside, Wharton informed James that she had purchased the car with some of the earnings from her novel, *The Valley of Decision*. James, in Wharton's words "forever contrasting his [friends'] supposed opulence and self indulgence with his own hermit-like asceticism," at length replied that with the proceeds from his own last novel (*The Wings of the Dove*) he had "purchased a small go-cart, or hand-barrow, on which my guests' luggage is wheeled from the station to my house. It needs a coat of paint. With the proceeds of my next novel, I shall have it painted."[28]

Henry James accompanied Edith Wharton on many auto trips, but he observed grumpily that Wharton's speeding about in her car seemed to him "such incoherence, such a nightmare of perpetually renewable choice and decision, such a luxury of bloated alternatives." Wharton, for her part, regarded the automobile as "an immense enlargement of life." With her longtime chauffeur Charles Cook, she undertook what she called "motor-flights" in Europe, the United States, and even Morocco. Always a curious mixture of enthusiasm for innovation and longing for the comforts of tradition, she exulted:

> The motor-car has restored the romance of travel. Freeing us from all the compulsions and contacts of the railway, the bondage to fixed hours and the beaten track, the approach to each town through the area of ugliness created by the railway itself, it has given us back the wonder, the adventure, and the novelty which enlivened the way of our posting grandparents. Above all these recovered pleasures must be ranked the delight of taking a town unawares.[29]

However much Wharton, and other motoring women, hoped simply to "take a town unawares," the open vehicles of the day, built chiefly by carriage-makers, were high-riding, sometimes doorless affairs that exposed all passengers to public scrutiny, and women seemed particularly to be on display. Autos were novelties that brought people out to gawk by the roadside. But more importantly, women like Wharton understood that automobility meant more than simply the chance to be displayed in all one's ostentatious and pointless hedonism. Such modern females terrified traditionalists like James with their public exhibition of spending power, and with their refusal to see constraint as protection, choice as a "nightmare." Climbing into an automobile, a woman rejected the cloister, certainly, and potentially also the female sphere of hearth and home.

Conspicuous as early motorists made themselves, the auto was nevertheless a private possession. As such, it seemed to some women a perfect solution to the problem of gaining admission to public life, especially commercial and leisure activities, without exposing oneself to the vagaries and annoyances of public transportation. It opened up the possibility of independent mobility for those who used it. Extending that potential to women meant both expanding the private sphere into the realm of transportation and, paradoxically, puncturing woman's "sphere" by undermining the already strained notion that woman's place was in the home. Coming as it did in the Progressive Era, a time in which women's work, family roles, and political rights were the subject of considerable discussion and the locus of tremendous change, the auto represented a new, movable field upon which women's struggle for power and autonomy would be played.

Pricked by curiosity or ambition, some women, like some men, grew impatient as passengers in chauffeur-driven vehicles and sought to seize the wheel themselves. Surely, some Victorian spirits sniffed, no woman was temperamentally, physically, or socially suited to meet the manifold manly challenges of motoring? What sane man would hand over to a woman such a costly piece of property? And what woman of standing would risk her good name by deliberately exhibiting herself in the flow of traffic, would hazard being regarded as a trafficker herself? Apprehensive, the experts awaited her appearance, but not for long. In 1899, Mrs. John Howell Phillips of Chicago established herself as the first American woman to receive a driver's license.[30]

∞

In 1900, only 8,000 passenger automobiles had been registered in the United States; by 1905, the number of registrations had increased nearly tenfold, to 77,000.[31] Since so few states required drivers' licenses in this early period (as late as 1909, only eleven states required operators' licenses for drivers of motor vehicles), and since data on car ownership has been collected variously by municipalities, counties, and states, there is no way to say precisely how many drivers, male or female, were on the road in the first decade of the twentieth century.[32] Society columns from the period depict female motorists as a common sight at Newport, Southampton, and Saratoga, but fragmentary evidence from a slightly later time suggests that before 1920, women comprised at most a small minority of drivers.[33] The *Los Angeles County Automobile Directory* revealed that in 1914, fifteen percent of new cars registered in the county appeared under women's names.[34] A 1914 directory of automobile owners in Tucson, Arizona listed 425 car owners, only 23 of whom (or five percent) were women. The *Houston Automobile Directory* for 1915 listed 7732 auto owners, including 425 women (5.5 percent). Without doubt, given the common practice of registering autos in the husband's or father's name, some women not listed as owners did drive, but we cannot know how many.[35] Whatever their numbers, as more and more women learned to drive, the broader question of whether women in general could, or should, drive motorcars became the subject of patronizing advice, genteel reproof, feminist defense, humorous stories, and heated argument.

The case against women drivers has, of course, been a staple of American folklore.[36] Early critics of women drivers, much like their contemporaries who opposed women's entry into higher education and woman suffrage, cited three presumed sources of women's inferiority at the wheel: emotional instability, physical weakness, and intellectual deficiencies.[37] A humorous article titled "Why Women Are, or Are Not, Good Chauffeuses" in Outing magazine in May, 1904 featured a group of country club men who, upon hearing that "The Littlest Woman" plans to buy a car, express the fear that she will surely break her neck. Their disparaging comments bring a protest from "Miss Billy King," an obviously competent and very attractive sporting motorist who haughtily inquires, "Has one to be shorn of all feminine graces, then, to be a good chauffeuse?" Her admirers quickly deny that they meant anything of the sort, insisting that Miss King is different from most of womankind in general, and from "The Littlest Woman" in particular. "It's her temperament and her disposition and her very character," one explains.[38]

Women, the men point out, suffer from natural impulsiveness and timidity, inability to concentrate and single-mindedness, indecisiveness and foolhardiness, weakness and utter estrangement from things mechanical. Yet, as Billy King protests their description of female nature, they concede that they know some decisive, steady, confident women, and that such women, like Miss Billy, make capable drivers. The men agree that "Motoring, and indeed all outdoor pleasures are masters of iron, especially to a woman, who always, in a fashion, has to adopt them, while a man takes to them naturally," but they also admit that some women have indeed mastered such physically demanding activities. Even understanding auto mechanics, which they regard as wholly alien to women, is not out of the question: "A woman of intelligence to whom machinery is difficult can usually master the mechanism of her motor if she sets about it."[39]

Finally, the men concede that mechanical knowledge is not always necessary to good driving. Even the admirable Miss Billy King apparently knows little about her auto's quirky ignition system, yet that hardly keeps her from enjoying the delights of motoring. "I suppose," one man concludes ruefully, "that a woman never does learn to run a motor. She just plain gets around it, the way she does around anything she wants."[40] Soon enough, a nationwide network of commercial garages and professional mechanics, as well as more reliable vehicles, would enable drivers, male and female, to circumvent the problem of mechanical failure, albeit with some expense, inconvenience, and delay.

Some women drivers hastened to reassure male doubters and to claim all the advantages of automobility for themselves and for their sex. Mrs. A. Sherman Hitchcock of Providence, Rhode Island wrote an article for *Motor* in 1904, offering some practical and reassuring advice to women drivers.[41] Hitchcock insisted that "The first requisite . . . for the woman beginner is absolute confidence in herself," and asserted that experience would bring increased assurance.[42] Ignoring the question of physical strength, Hitchcock tackled the matter of mechanical aptitude. She conceded that "most men have some idea of mechanics, but to most women they are an unknown quantity." She believed, however, that "there are, no doubt, many women who possess an inherent ability for mechanics . . . [who] soon will be able to locate technical troubles and overcome them. If no inherent tendency exists, one can very likely be developed."[43] More generally, according to Hitchcock, the benefits of driving for women made "even the responsibility itself a fascination."[44] Women who learned to drive, she believed, gained confidence, courage, and the ability to think quickly, as well as a sense of empowerment:

There is a wonderful difference between sitting calmly by while another is driving and actually handling a car herself. There is a feeling of power, of exhilaration, and fascination that nothing else gives in equal measure. When the ponderous car begins to move and the motor seems a living, breathing thing responding to your slightest touch, easy to control and simple to manipulate, then comes the realization of "motoring" in its truest sense.[45]

Mary Mullett, another celebrant of the woman "whose slender hands are as steady on the wheel as is the iron grip of the trained chauffeur," pointed out that in 1906, by which time there were some 106,000 passenger cars registered in the United States, "in this country actually more automobiles are run by women now than were run by men a few years ago."[46] Mullett drew attention to the role that family politics played in discouraging women drivers. Many critics, she said, were husbands who complained about their wives' driving, whose testimony was suspect because "the man who is generous enough . . . to revel in his wife's superior skill with an auto is as rare as the one who thinks a woman knows how to poke the fire with anything like his own masterly discretion."

Mullett also noted that male drivers were evaluated as individuals, whereas females' performance at the wheel was attributed to the natural compulsions of sex. To those who harped on women's difficulties learning to drive, she replied that "any beginner is liable to these mental aberrations. . . . Yet if it's a woman who does anything of the sort, she must expect to be treated as if only a woman could have been guilty of such a lapse." On the one hand, women's competence at driving was often dismissed as luck; on the other, men sometimes tended to patronize women drivers by praising them for performing basic driving tasks.[47] Mullett proposed abandoning the double standard, claiming that as individuals, drivers' competence varied, but taken collectively, female and male drivers were more alike than different. Emphasizing human diversity over gender identity, Mullett advanced an argument which numerous women researchers in the social sciences were busy proving at the time, and which some woman suffragists continued to articulate. On the road, in classroom and laboratory, and at the ballot box, such women insisted on being judged in terms of individual talents and achievements.[48]

Joan Newton Cuneo, the first eminent woman race driver, understood why women might feel discouraged from driving. Instead of asking why women were bad motorists, she asked why there were so few of them.[49] Cuneo agreed that women generally lacked familiarity with mechanics and that most women (of the class able to afford a car) did not want to get dirty. But she also pointed out that women often encountered an "unpleasant attitude" on the part of male drivers, and that "automobile manufacturers are not building cars that are especially adapted to women's use," raising the question of the relationship between gender ideology and automotive design.[50]

Cuneo believed that such obstacles were surmountable, and were, in fact, "more imaginary than real." Where mechanical difficulties were concerned, she pointed out that numerous garages already dotted the countryside, and that other motorists were often happy to help out those in distress. True enough, Cuneo agreed, "not every woman is competent to drive an automobile," but there was no reason to believe that men and women were significantly different in this regard: "Neither is every man, for that matter." Women, according to Cuneo, might even be better drivers than men in some instances, since "caution should be the great watchword of all motor drivers, and . . . a man has more of a spirit of bravado than a woman." Like Hitchcock, Cuneo believed that motoring held great benefits for women.

> There is no good reason why thousands of women should sit quietly in the tonneau and let the men have the keenest enjoyment of the greatest sport of today. . . . If women could realize the exhilaration that comes from being able to handle a 60-horsepower touring car, the sight of a woman driver would be anything but a novelty.[51]

However unfair, given the growing numbers of competent women motorists, the woman driver stereotype persisted, and succeeding generations of women drivers, facing old arguments with new twists (sometimes presented from within their own ranks) had to reinvent themselves at the wheel. In 1913, *Motor* columnist Margaret R. Burlingame expounded on "the psychological ingredient that is missing in women drivers" in an article titled "When Woman Drives, Man Jumps."[52] Burlingame observed that male drivers generally gave an oncoming car plenty of room whenever they saw a woman at the wheel, and that motoring men did so not out of politeness, but because they justifiably felt endangered by the presence of women drivers.[53] Her reasoning, which *Motor*'s editor felt obliged to balance with a disclaimer at the head of the column ("it would be easy for any motorist to name numerous women drivers, possessed of far more of the qualities necessary to the successful motor car pilot, than an equal number of men"), drew on the arguments made by advocates of women drivers while subverting their aim.

Mary Mullett had pointed out that all women motorists were subject to criticism on the basis of each woman's errors; Burlingame, for her part, accepted such logic, and asserted that however much any woman "happens to be a sensible driver, . . . she belongs to the general class of 'women drivers' and as such the faults of the class fall on her." Contrary to Mullett's statement that husbands' egos prevented them from admitting that their wives were good drivers, Burlingame explained that she knew "a woman who thinks she drives like her husband, when, as a matter of fact, she drives recklessly without her husband's accurate knowledge of his machine and his years of experience."[54]

Burlingame went on to claim that "the average woman's mind has not been trained to quick action," and that "the muscles of a man have long been taught to obey instantly" while a woman's "untrained muscles cannot do the thing quickly enough to save her," cementing her case for male superiority at the wheel.[55] But then she chose to illustrate her claim that men were better drivers with an anecdote that cast doubt on her seriousness in advocating male superiority:

> I was driving with a man and his wife one evening. We were on a busy thoroughfare and it had been evident for some time that the man's mind was far away from his surroundings. However, he was such a good driver that we neither of us felt free to caution him about anything ahead or behind him. Both his wife and I saw a street car turning ahead of us, but supposing he saw it too, we said nothing. Just as the car was half way around the

turn and within 10 feet from us, he saw it. Instead of throwing on his brakes, he turned quickly and ran partly up the curb. . . . A mind used to instantaneous work and muscles used to perfect control had saved a serious accident. No woman would have thought of such a solution. . . . We just looked at him, too stunned to say anything, but he read our thoughts, and this is what he said: "No need to get frightened—I had three ways out of that: through the middle, over the top, or through the motorman."[56]

∞

Determined to discover an answer to the question "Do Women Make Good Drivers?" *Motor* sponsored a contest on the topic in 1914.[57] The magazine published essays variously emphasizing the static nature of womanhood, the vast possibilities for female advancement, and women's historical lack of access to public spaces. The prizewinning answer, entered by one E. W. Gardner of Webster, Iowa, was titled "Sex No Criterion." Dismissing the issue of physical strength ("all who are capable of walking, talking, or dressing themselves have strength to operate the modern motor car"), Gardner argued that nurture, not nature, made the motorist. Experience, he claimed, was the best driving teacher. Most women had been shielded from public life, and thus had little firsthand knowledge of road rules or mechanical and transportation problems. No wonder, then, that male drivers felt imperiled by female motorists, since "the life of the average woman unfits rather than fits her for safe motor car operation." Gardner added, however, that "if by individual effort or happy environment her handicap is removed or is not present—fine! As it is, however, give her the road."[58]

Jennie Davis of East Orange, New Jersey, offered "A Woman's Point of View." Citing the benefits of fresh air, exhilaration, and freedom from other cares, which "tone up the system to a point where medicines are unnecessary," Davis still held that women in general were too delicate to drive in heavy traffic or on extended journeys. Davis also made the point that "often the driving of an automobile is a woman's first responsible experience with the streets." Being sheltered from public life handicapped women drivers, since "what is only everyday, ordinary excitement for a man becomes a strain when attempted by a woman." With timorous optimism, she observed that "perhaps in the days to come, when her emancipation has become absolutely complete, woman may acquire the same habits of instinctive action that man now has. But that time is not yet."[59]

Some of those who expressed opinions on the woman driver question echoed arguments from both sides of the suffrage question. Louis A. Valdettaro of New York City insisted: "Discussing women's fitness for driving under varying traffic conditions is on a par with discussing her ability to use the ballot." Adding that women voters generally tended to be better informed and more responsible than their male counterparts, he also allowed that, since anyone in a given jurisdiction could vote, but "only those women who feel themselves perfectly competent to do so take charge of the wheel of a motor car," women drivers were generally better qualified than voters, male or female. Valdettaro also affirmed, on the basis of observation in "the worst traffic in New York," women's ability to handle the heaviest city traffic "with all the skill and nonchalance of a hardened taxi pilot."[60]

On the negative side, however, some commentators clung to the views of Victorian traditionalists. S. P. Foster of Elmer, New Jersey, reduced the question of female driving to biology, asserting that women, "as a whole, are utterly unfitted to pilot ships, command armies, or operate automobiles, through no fault of their own. They were born that way." He also invoked the kind of humorous, chivalrous argument commonly used to justify protecting women from the burden of suffrage.

> While we love them all, we'd rather not have any than a dead one, and believing them to be unfitted mentally and physically to operate motor cars safely under varying conditions of traffic, we would use our good offices to persuade them to keep away from the steering-wheel and, instead, to sit in the machine where they can tell us how to operate the car. They enjoy that better than running a car themselves, and we want them to have the biggest share of the pleasure of automobiling.[61]

By 1915, one writer declared definitively that women had taken their rightful place at the wheel.[62] Yet women's driving ability was by no means a closed subject. From the earliest days of the car culture, attempts to argue women out of first the tonneau, then the driver's seat took on the tone of the lost cause determined to inflict as many casualties as it could before surrender. If the female passenger appeared a plutocrat's parasite at least, a sexual and material threat at worst, the woman driver seemed always something less than a driver. Ridicule and discouragement are potent political weapons, and no doubt many women were deterred from driving in part because they or persons close to them believed that no woman could manage an automobile. Yet despite the amount of energy devoted to discouraging women from taking the wheel, millions persisted in learning to drive.

Defenders of women drivers have ever been as numerous as detractors. Given the potential market that women drivers represent, those supporters have, not surprisingly, included many people who produce and sell automobiles and automotive products and services. Coat and cloakmakers were so quick to see in motoring women a new market that already, by 1904, *Motor*'s fashion columnist had declared that "motor fashions have not been standing still. First, automobile togs were clumsy with no suggestion of graceful lines, then they evolved into garments of style. . . . They are always more useful and more practical than first glance discloses."[63]

Just as the fashion industry saw a chance to cash in on the automobile's increasing popularity, so some auto producers would set about tailoring their products to a growing female public. Clearly, women would insist on driving, just as they were demanding the right to broaden their horizons in other regards. It seemed just as clear to many of the men who made motorcars that differences between males and females would have to be taken into account, from the inside of the vehicle out, from engine to upholstery and paint. And so, while Henry Ford hunched over a drafting board, scheming up a car for Everyman, other entrepreneurs would seek profit in catering to the figure they imagined as Everywoman—to her tastes, her talents, her limitations.

3

Femininity and the Electric Car

WHILE American women chafed at their social, spatial, and political limitations, some car makers began to fashion new wheels to preserve the dainty domain of Victorian decorum. Colonel Albert A. Pope, president of the Pope Manufacturing Company of Hartford, Connecticut, believed that "you can't get people to sit over an explosion." As he moved his company out of bicycle manufacturing and into the automobile business, he determined to concentrate not on noisy, smelly gasoline-powered cars, but instead, on clean, quiet electric vehicles. By 1897, the Pope Manufacturing Company had produced some five hundred electric cars.[1]

While Pope pursued this entrepreneurial strategy, thousands of Americans proved him a bad prophet and purchased gasoline motorcars. In response to demand, Pope began to produce some gasoline cars, but the company remained committed to the idea that there was a natural market for slower, cleaner electrics. As Pope suggested in a 1903 advertisement for the Pope-Waverly electric model, "electrics . . . will appeal to any one interested in an absolutely noiseless, odorless, clean and stylish rig that is always ready and that, mile for mile, can be operated at less cost than any other type of motor car." Lest this message escape those it was intended to attract, the text accompanied a picture of a delighted woman driver piloting a smiling female passenger.[2]

Pitching electric cars to women represented a strategy that was at once expansive and limiting, both for automakers' opportunities, and for women who wanted to be motorists. After all, in the infancy of the automobile industry, men like Pope had to unravel mysteries of design and production—what kinds of devices might make a carriage move without benefit of a horse? Would gasoline, steam, or electricity prove to be the most practical source of power? Might not all three have their disparate uses? How should such devices be manufactured? What materials should they be made of? How might they be distributed? Neither omniscient nor omnipotent, auto manufacturers generally produced individual vehicles on order and groped only haltingly toward perceiving a wider market.

The French and German automakers who pioneered the business in the late nineteenth century had produced luxury motorcars for the sporting rich, and at first, American manufacturers followed the European example in catering to the domestic carriage trade. As early as 1900, American socialites, male and female, vied with one another in devising ways of using the auto for entertainment. Wealthy men held races and rallies at various posh watering holes; women attended, and sometimes participated.[3] Prominent women also developed their own automotive spectacles. They besieged Newport in flower-decked car convoys, held drive-in dinner parties where they demanded curb service at fashionable Boston restaurants, or simply stepped from their elegant conveyances at the opera house door, dripping diamonds and pearls. In keeping with the tastes of their owners, expensive motorcars featured such "refinements" as cut-glass bud vases and built-in vanity cases.[4]

These male and female motoring larks differed more in terms of style than substance; wealthy men and women shared a taste for luxury and leisure, as well as bracing adventure, in their motoring. Nevertheless, manufacturers tended to associate the qualities of comfort, convenience, and aesthetic appeal with women, while linking power, range, economy, and thrift with men. Women were presumed to be too weak, timid, and fastidious to want to drive noisy, smelly gasoline-powered cars. Thus at first, manufacturers, influenced by Victorian notions of masculinity and femininity, devised a kind of "separate spheres" ideology about automobiles: gas cars were for men, electric cars were for women.

The electric automobile had been around since the birth of the motor age, and its identification with women took hold early and tenaciously. Genevera Delphine Mudge of New York City, identified by one source as the first woman motorist in the United States, drove an electric in 1898, and one Miss Daisy Post also drove an electric vehicle as early as 1898.[5] In 1900, the City Engineer of Chicago complained that many women drivers were not bothering to get licenses, and *Horseless Age* magazine, conflating all women drivers with those who drove electrics, noted that "so far only eight women have secured permits to operate electric vehicles, but . . . there are twenty-five to fifty women regularly running the machines through the city."[6]

Certainly some women who wanted the increased mobility that came with driving a car believed that gasoline vehicles, being powerful, complicated, fast, dirty, and capable of long-distance runs, belonged to men, while electric cars, being simple, comfortable, clean, and quiet, though somewhat short on power and restricted in range, better suited women. Electrics tended to be smaller and slower than gasoline-powered cars, and often were designed as enclosed vehicles.[7] If electrics offered less automobility than gas cars, they offered greater mobility than horses, and more independence and flexibility than trolleys. Understandably, some women—most of them well-to-do—thus chose to drive electrics. In April of 1904, *Motor* magazine's society columnist noted:

> Mrs. James G. Blaine has been spending the last few weeks with her parents at Washington, and has been seen almost daily riding about in an electric runabout. The latter appears to be the most popular form of automobile for women, at any rate in the National Capital. . . . Indeed, judging from the number of motors that one sees driven by women on a fine afternoon, one would imagine that nearly every belle in Washington owned a machine.[8]

Like Pope, other electric car manufacturers were quick to see women as a potential gold mine. In the years before World War I, articles on electric vehicles, or on women drivers, and advertisements for electrics in such publications as *Motor* and *Country Life in America* featured photographs of women driving, charging, and otherwise maintaining electrics, reflecting both a specific marketing strategy and a more diffuse cultural tendency to divide the world between masculine and feminine.[9] Electric vehicle manufacturers including the Anderson, Woods, Baker, Borland, and Milburn companies featured women in their advertisements. Touting such virtues as luxury, beauty, ease of operation, and economy, manufacturers attempted to appeal to an affluent female clientele without alienating men who might wish to purchase an electric for their wives or daughters, or even for themselves. The Argo company advertised its 1912 model, a sporty low-slung electric vehicle, as "a woman's car that any man is proud to drive."[10] The Anderson Electric Car Company invited men to purchase its Detroit model "for your bride-to-be—or your bride of many Junes ago. . . . No other bridal present means so much—expresses so perfectly all that you want to say. . . . the most *considerate choice* for her permanent happiness, comfort, luxury, safety."[11] The Detroit electric was said to be not only "the last word in luxury and beauty, as well as efficiency," but also a boon to feminine comeliness:

> To the well-bred woman—the Detroit Electric has a particular appeal. In it she can preserve her toilet immaculate, her coiffure intact.
> She can drive it with all desired privacy, yet safely—in constant touch with traffic conditions all about her.[12]

However much manufacturers trumpeted the appealing qualities of electrics, automobiles powered by electric batteries had serious disadvantages compared to gas-powered vehicles. They were generally more expensive to manufacture, had limited range (averaging twenty to fifty miles per charge), and were too heavy to climb hills or run at high speeds.[13] Inventor Thomas Edison promised that he would develop a long-distance electric storage battery, but his efforts in this regard proved fruitless.[14] By 1908, even some of those who applauded the use of electrics admitted their limitations. Writer Herbert H. Rice noted that despite improvements in charging technology and vehicle design, "there are not apparent any great opportunities for extraordinary changes unless in the battery."[15] Rice advised the motoring public to give up hoping for a battery that would go one hundred miles on a single charge (a hope which, he admitted, had caused electric sales to suffer) since "not one in one hundred users requires a service extending beyond thirty-five miles, while in the majority of cases the odometer would record less than fifteen miles for the day's errands."[16]

This acknowledgment of the electric auto's problems suggests that its association with women was at once a symptom of, and an attempted cure for, its competitive disadvantages. The electric's circumscribed mobility seemed adequate to those who assumed that "the electric is the vehicle of the home," adequate, that is, for homemakers who did not expect to take long trips, or frequent trips, or to get stuck in traffic jams.[17] Playing on the domestic theme, the General Electric Company asserted, "any woman can charge her own electric with a G-E Rectifier," advertising with a photograph of a woman charging her car, using a machine that occupied most of one wall of the family garage. Declaring that "there are no tiresome trips to a public garage, no waiting—the car is always at home, ready when you are," General Electric implied that using the rectifier would relieve the woman motorist of such inconveniences as often accompanied having to leave home.[18]

At times the electric car and its purportedly female clientele seemed entwined, as the electric's advocates used a Victorian language of gender to talk about cars. *Country Life in America* writer Phil M. Riley combated the criticism that "electric power is weak," by asserting, "It is important with an electric not to waste power needlessly, that is all." Riley assured his readers that "the proper sphere of the electric vehicle is not in competition with the gasolene [sic] touring car."[19] Just as conservative commentators admonished women to forego high-powered business and political activity and conserve their energy for domestic tasks, so, Riley said, the electric vehicle might fulfill its mission as "an ever-ready runabout for daily use," leaving extended travel and fast driving to men in gas-powered cars. Moreover, both Rice and Riley chose to refer to the electric vehicle's venue of operation as a "sphere." Victorian Americans commonly represented women's and men's respective social roles as "separate spheres." This simple visual image often served as a shorthand description of complex relations not only between individuals of different biological sexes, but between feminine and masculine attributes (including passivity and activity), private and public life, household and workplace, homemaking and paid work, culture and politics.[20] The automobile might be novel, but it could not escape entanglement in a web of meaning spun with the threads of masculinity and femininity.

That many people subsumed a variety of ideological, economic, familial, political, and spatial relations under the heading of "separate spheres" testified to Americans' tenacity in using gender to order experience. But however powerfully evocative, this image vastly oversimplified both human relations and social forces.[21] Sometimes people act in accordance with gender prescriptions; sometimes they do not. Men, supposedly rugged, seek shelter from the rain. Women, supposedly soft-spoken, yell at their children. Men and women continually revised both their actions and their expectations, more often by the minute adjustments of private negotiation than by legal fiat or national proclamation. Through the small changes of personal life, leading to larger transformations on a social scale, activities and entities assigned to one sphere or the other, considered appropriate for either women or men, sometimes lost or recast their gendered meanings. When women refused to conform to expectations, when new technologies unsettled traditional assumptions, when entrepreneurs defied common wisdom in search of profits, change accelerated.[22]

All three forces—female nonconformity, technological innovation, and economic competition—were very much in play in the first third of the century, and the future of the car culture was far from clear. Consumers, engineers, and businessmen would interact in ways no one could predict precisely. In the years before 1920, Americans used all kinds of transportation: their own legs, mules and horses, trains and trolleys, and electric, gas, and steam automobiles. Each method had benefits and drawbacks. Supporters of electric motorcars were at least as inclined to point out the electric's advantages over the horse and buggy as they were to compare electric and gas vehicles. C. H. Claudy, an early and staunch advocate of electric vehicles (he would later become the automotive columnist for the *Woman's Home Companion*), had written in 1907 that the electric car "now does more work, in certain lines, than horses ever did."[23] Claudy claimed the electric would be a boon to all women, asking whether there had "ever been an invention of more solid comfort to the feminine half of humanity than the electric carriage?" He observed that the woman who drove an electric "finds it very convenient to call up the garage, have her runabout sent around instantly and not have to wait for a complicated hitching or a currying and combing of horses."[24]

Although Claudy staunchly supported women's driving, he was slow to recommend gasoline cars for women. Describing the electric as "the car which has a circumscribed radius," he joined the ranks of those who envisioned the electric in terms of woman's special, yet limited, sphere. Women, he believed, might use electrics to accomplish the social and domestic tasks that were part of the middle-class homemaker's vocation, without overstepping the bounds of feminine propriety. "What a delight it is," he wrote, "to have a machine which she can run herself, with no loss of dignity, for making calls, for shopping, for a pleasurable ride, for the paying back of some small social debt."[25] The electric might even be just the thing to reconcile motoring and motherhood. Pointing out that "in no way can a child get so much air in so little time as by the use of the automobile" Claudy declared that "it would not be amiss to call the electric the modern baby carriage. . . . It is the light electric runabout which deserves the title of scientific perambulator."[26] Thus he painted a rather odd, infantile picture of the woman driver, tucked in alongside her baby in a "scientific perambulator."

While promoters of electrics tried to forge a positive link between the woman driver and the battery-powered motorcar, an occasional critic suggested that women's purported deficiencies in driving ought to disqualify them from operating anything more powerful than rather tame electrics. In an article on reckless drivers published in *The Outlook*, writer Montgomery Rollins drew on the notion that femaleness unfitted some people for the adult responsibility of driving a powerful gasoline automobile. Rollins argued, "It's no child's play to run a motor car. No license should be granted to anyone under eighteen . . . and never to a woman, unless, possibly, for a car driven by electric power."[27]

Against such disparagement of both electrics and women, electric vehicle manufacturers and their supporters worked to protect whatever claim they might have to women motorists, while also struggling to get a foothold in the male market so clearly dominated by gasoline cars. C. H. Claudy believed that electrics would be useful to an elite group of men who might value comfort, cleanliness, and everyday utility over extended range and sportiness. Like others, Claudy assumed that a few fastidious men, such as doctors and some businessmen, would be willing to forego speed and range for the advantages of simple mechanical construction, reliability on short errands, quietness, cleanliness, and simplicity of operation.[28] The implicit corollary of such assumptions was that most men had little desire for the kinds of comforts and conveniences electrics offered, preferring a more rugged and vigorous, less restrictive form of motoring. The Detroit company tried in 1910 to counteract the electric's fussy feminine image by introducing one of its electric models as a "new car for 'him' . . . a brand-new extra-low and rakish Detroit Electric model for *men* is our Gentlemen's Underslung Roadster."[29] Yet men continued to spurn the electric, quite simply because it did not go far enough or fast enough.[30]

As men registered their indifference to the electric, women were demonstrating their own unwillingness to leave long-distance touring and high-speed driving to men. As a consequence, the application of separate spheres ideology to motive power in automobiles had lost force by 1912, when C. H. Claudy announced that "the time has gone by when motor cars had sex—when the gasolene [sic] car was preeminently for the man, and the electric, because of its simplicity, for the women." Beliefs, however, die hard, and even this exponent of technological progress remained unable to abandon completely the idea that "motor cars had sex." Once again invoking a female disposition toward convenience, Claudy predicted that "of all the types of self propelled vehicles, the electric is now, and seems likely to remain, the simplest to handle on the road and to care for at home, whereby it still is, and seems likely to continue to be, the ladies' favorite."[31]

Like Colonel Pope before him, Claudy very quickly proved a poor prognosticator. Relating the story of a bride who told her young husband, "I don't want an electric. I want a car that can go a long distance. I want a car that can go fast, and an electric can't go either far or fast," Claudy commented incredulously, "The lady was right in one thing—she did not want an electric. What she wanted was a six-cylinder touring car!"[32] Instead of acknowledging women's similarity to men in this matter of automotive taste, he set about trying to reconcile female drivers to the more womanly form of motoring. Rather than demanding the speed, range, and hill-climbing power of gasoline vehicles, he advised female motorists to accept the electric's limitations. Claudy admitted, "A practical electric vehicle cannot be built so that it can go fast *and* far *and* climb hills. *Speed* you can have, or great *radius* you can have—but not both at once and still keep down weight and cost."[33] Women, he maintained, had no need for speed:

> It can be roundly stated without fear of contradiction that the times a woman wants to run an electric 30 miles an hour, are few and far between. . . . It is an unnecessarily fast speed for pleasure driving. . . . If the car you select has a maximum speed of 25 miles on the level, it goes quite fast enough.[34]

In much the same manner that he had dismissed women's claim to velocity, he would also disparage women's desire to cover distance. Claudy explained that "a radius of 60 to 80 miles is ample for any electric car," stretching the capabilities of the average electric vehicle, and suggesting that women had no need to go further. For women to accept such circumscribed mobility ruled out cross-country travel, or even extended day trips, in an era when gas stations were beginning to dot the countryside, but electric charging stations had not spread beyond major cities. In addition, electric batteries needed servicing so often that they would have forced cross-country travelers to stop more frequently, and for much longer periods of time, than most Americans cared to do, particularly in an era when poor road quality forced more than enough stops for the average traveler.[35] Ignoring such restrictions, Claudy reminded readers of the electric's advantages for women, given their bulky clothing, innate preference for luxury, and inability to learn to shift gears:

> Practically all the modern electric cars are arranged with special reference to their ease of control by women—that is, the controlling and reverse levers are (or should be) simple in operation and few in number, they work easily, and are so placed and arranged as not to catch and tear the dress. Besides these points, women naturally choose those cars the interior appointments of which please them the most.[36]

Despite their narrow view of women's talents and desires, we need not blame the electric's advocates too much for finding virtue in electric automobiles. After all, motorists of any era and either sex might find the qualities of simplicity, convenience, and aesthetic appeal worth having in a motor vehicle. However, when automotive designers and promoters, acting in part under the influence of cultural imperatives regarding gender, coupled these desirable attributes with the electric's limited power and circumscribed range, they misread their audience. No law of nature dictated that automobiles could not be designed to be comfortable, reliable, handsome, and powerful, qualities that might appeal to men and women alike. And even if automakers continued to insist that males and females had different automotive preferences, a sex-specific promotional strategy made very little business sense in an economy where consumers, male or female, had some choice, and where families buying only one vehicle were likely to have to accommodate male drivers who were presumed to want to go farther and faster than their female counterparts.

Perhaps most damaging, the electric was too cumbersome to manage bad roads. At the turn of the century, few localities in the United States could claim many miles of improved highways. Thus the electric car had limited appeal for motorists of either sex in places where distances were great and paved roads were few. In Tucson, Arizona, for example, twenty-three women owned autos in 1914. Twenty-one of those owned gasoline-powered vehicles, and none of the 402 male car-owners listed in the *Tucson Automobile Directory* owned electrics. Only one vehicle listed could be definitely identified as an electric, and one other may have been an electric.[37] The Houston, Texas automobile directory of 1915 revealed that only 30 out of 425 women auto owners had electrics, and most of those appeared to have registered their vehicles in the very earliest years of the car culture. Thus in Houston, by 1915, only one woman car owner in fourteen, or seven percent of the total, had an electric. Even during the electric's pre-Model T heyday, four out of five women auto owners in Houston had gasoline cars.[38] The economic folly of Claudy's advice was compounded by the fact that, particularly after Henry Ford's introduction of the Model T in 1908, numerous gasoline cars were available for prices under $1,500, while electric autos appear to have remained more expensive than gas cars.[39] (See Table 1.)

The rapidly growing number of women driving gasoline cars did as much to disrupt the link between women and electrics as any force of nature or engineering. By 1913, C. H. Claudy, who had put so much effort into promoting electric vehicles to female drivers, had changed his mind. He had come to believe that many women had both the ability and the determination to drive gas-powered automobiles. Moreover, he recognized that male prejudice, more than female preference, stood in the way of women who wished to drive gas cars. In a piece on "The Woman and Her Car," Claudy imagined the feelings of a young woman who aspired to the driver's seat: "Oh, I'd love to have a car, but father doesn't think I could drive it. He wants me to have an electric, and they don't go either fast or far enough."[40] The columnist noted: "Father frequently does think his daughter hasn't the strength, skill, or natural ability to acquire it, necessary

TABLE 1   SOME PRICES OF ELECTRIC AUTOMOBILES, 1903–1919

Manufacturer	Price Range (Dollars)	Year
Pope-Waverly	850– 900	1903
Woods	2100–2700	1909
Bailey	2400–2600	1910
Hupp-Yeats	1750	1910
Waverly	2250	1912
Standard	1850	1912
Argo	2500–3100	1913
Detroit	2550–3000	1913
Milburn*	1285–1685	1916
Milburn*	1885	1917
Milburn*	1885	1918
Milburn*	2385	1919

Source: *Motor* magazine, advertisements for electric vehicles including price information, 1903–1920.

*Prices given are for the "Milburn Light Electric," a model that apparently became more expensive between 1916 and 1919.

to drive a gasolene car successfully. Many husbands think the same about their wives." By this time, however, he no longer shared such views, and argued that "there is no reason at all why . . . you [women] cannot drive with pleasure to your friends, as skilfully [sic], as gracefully, and with as obedient a car as anyone, even father, can wish."[41] Thereafter, in articles for the *Woman's Home Companion*, Claudy encouraged women to drive gasoline vehicles, providing sensible advice on motoring and introducing women to the intricacies of auto maintenance.[42] Having placed the gas-powered motorcar within the compass of woman's sphere, Claudy had also stretched his definition of the feminine. By 1920, he would assert, "The number of women who drive motor cars with skill and enjoyment is sufficient proof that there is nothing in the modern Pegasus which femininity cannot master."[43] In an effort to keep up with consumers' changing demands, producers would at once modify their notions of gender and the machines they made.

A few gasoline auto manufacturers had long since recognized that there was a female market for their products. They realized that the automobile was unlikely to supersede the horse as a popular mode of transportation until it became a family vehicle, offering power as well as simplicity, range as well as convenience. The Winton Company, promoting its Model C in 1905, declared that "Women Praise the Winton," a vehicle "ideal for women's use because it was "as easily controlled as the best mannered horse," but "safer, because it cannot scare." The company also noted that the Model C went "as far, and as fast or as slow, as the lady at the wheel desires."[44] To prove its point, Winton included testimonials from two women drivers. One had written, "I much prefer my new WINTON to the electric I formerly owned, and its control is fully as perfect. It is a comfort to know that one has the power to go fast or slow as desired."[45] Another satisfied female motorist belied the image of women drivers as too feminine to tackle gear-shifting, cranking, and simple mechanical work. The ad quoted her to the effect that

> every day since [the Winton] came into our possession it has had no small mileage, and at no time has the engine "missed" an explosion. Neither has there been occasion to make a single adjustment, beyond once retightening the clutch. I have not the slightest difficulty in handling the car—motor has not yet failed to start with a single throw of the crank. I like the magneto. The WINTON system of individual clutch is pleasingly effective, and the control is so delightfully simple that to drive the car—even through congested city thoroughfares, is the easiest thing imaginable.[46]

In 1909, the Maxwell-Briscoe company also made an effort to market gas-powered cars to families that included women drivers, sending Alice Huyler Ramsey and three women passengers on a highly publicized cross-country drive and mounting an advertising campaign based on the notion of the inexpensive family car.[47] In praise of its Model AA, a "reliable business runabout" priced at $600 to compete with the Ford Model T, the company asserted: "Everyone should own this car, because it fills the universal need. As easy to drive as an electric. Your wife, daughter, or son can run this MAXWELL and care for it— a chauffeur is unnecessary."[48] The Maxwell, advertising copywriters insisted, was much more than a pleasure car for buffs or thrill-seekers. "For errands, shopping, calls, meeting trains, taking the children to school, for business or pleasure, this automobile is the gateway to outdoors and health. Picture yourself in it—how would you use it?"[49]

By 1910, the White Motor Company had joined Winton and Maxwell-Briscoe in the effort to attract women drivers to gasoline cars. The company promoted its White coupe as "a woman's town car," explaining that "most women have felt compelled to drive electric cars—especially in the Winter—because no gasoline car was designed for a woman to drive." White, however, claimed to have solved this design problem with the "inside drive coupe," a closed car very much resembling the boxy electric coupes of the day, featuring doors on both sides wide enough to accommodate cumbersome skirts and a driver's seat that folded up "to make entrance easy from either side."[50] Calling attention to the car's "upholstery, electric lights, and the little accessories . . . all of the finest imported materials," the company insisted that "nothing has been overlooked that could contribute to a woman's satisfaction in a car which is so particularly designed for her personal use."[51] While upholding most of the sex-stereotyped ideas about women's automotive abilities and preferences, such advertisements undermined the exclusive identification of gasoline power with male drivers, thus gently challenging the consignment of women to the realm of the electric-powered vehicle.

As these pre-World War I reworkings of the notion of separate automotive spheres indicate, many observers recognized that women were driving in increasing numbers, and were not confining themselves to electrics. The most ambitious automotive capitalist might imagine a potential female market numbering into the millions; if such consumers could not be manipulated, they had to be heeded. In 1913, the high-toned *Vanity Fair* ran a "Casual Cutouts" column on "motoring for the very rich," highlighting technical information on various vehicles and illustrated with photographs of women drivers.[52] In 1915, a writer for the *Illustrated World* announced: "Starting a few years go with a little timid venturing on the boulevards in their electrics, women have gradually conquered the motorcar. . . . Their fear of gasoline and monkey wrenches has vanished."[53] Moreover, middle-class women's magazines like the *Ladies' Home Journal*, sensitive to women's consumer power in both the magazine and automotive marketplaces, began to include features on driving and maintaining cars.[54] Such publications had also begun to attract auto advertisements.

Notions about femininity and women's growing demand for automobility had collided in the automotive marketplace, and the chief casualty was the electric car. The surprising thing, however, is not that electrics faded so early, but that they lasted so long, given their manifestly lower power, frequently higher prices, and smaller range than gas cars. Even in their heyday, electrics never comprised more than a tiny share of the market for cars. As early as 1908, according to a survey of fourteen major cities in which electrics were relatively widely used, in no city were more than 900 electrics in operation, and there were fewer than 4,300 electric vehicles in use all together. (See Table 2.) Furthermore, these figures do not reflect purely private use of electric vehicles, since the Electric Vehicle Company (popularly known as the "Lead Cab Trust") had operated a fleet of some two thousand electric cabs in a number of these cities between 1899 and 1907.[55] While this survey did not include figures from a number of major cities (New York, Boston, and Philadelphia are among those omitted), the cities included represented centers of electric vehicle manufacturing, where electrics were likely to have been in proportionally more widespread use than anywhere else. That same year, a total of 194,400 automobiles were registered in the United States.[56] In 1915, *Motor* magazine estimated that there were some 50,000 electric motor vehicles in service in the United States, representing approximately two percent of the total of 2,490,900 motor vehicles of all types registered in the country that year.[57] Electric models continued to be produced on order until 1938, but passenger cars powered by electric batteries had largely disappeared by the mid-twenties.[58]

The electric car, marketed primarily as a woman's vehicle, provides a striking example of the influence of gender ideology

TABLE 2   THE NUMBER OF ELECTRICS IN USE, 1908
(Selected Cities)

City	Approximate Number
Toledo, Ohio	400
Cleveland, Ohio	650
Atlanta, Georgia	175
Columbus, Ohio	140
Denver, Colorado	450
Detroit, Michigan	250
Washington, D.C.	300
Chicago, Illinois	900
Buffalo, New York	300
Rochester, New York	350
Indianapolis, Indiana	125
Hartford, Connecticut	100
Rockford, Illinois	75
Binghamton, New York	75
TOTAL	4290

Source: Wilhelm Nassau, *Motor* magazine, July 1908

on automotive production. Paradoxically, the electric's failure also illustrates the impossibility of maintaining rigid gender distinctions in motorcar technology at a time when a declining proportion of customers could afford the luxury of his-and-hers automobiles, and where in any case consumers shared certain preferences regardless of sex. Still, we should be wary of declaring a victory for technology over culture, for the power of the automobile over the stubbornness of gender ideology. The electric vehicle would slip off the automotive stage, reappearing occassionally at the behest of environmental visionaries and (more often) golfers. Culture, however, continued to influence technology. Since people, regardless of sex, insisted on sitting over an explosion, contested notions about masculinity and femininity entered the domain of the gasoline car. As the century moved into its second decade, the auto industry's towering figures engraved differing ideas about gender into the early car culture's epic machines.

4

Power and Comfort

A<small>MERICAN</small> women embraced, early and with glee, the adventure of motoring in speedy gasoline-powered cars.[1] In May of 1905, the *Los Angeles Times* breathlessly recounted the "Cross-Country Dash" of a young woman who, with two female friends, drove from Los Angeles to Santa Barbara in less than ten hours. The driver, "a Miss Reedal of this city," had made "a sensational cross-country run. . . . Once in a while she just touched a high place along the road." Sounding like a caption for a silent movie melodrama, the newspaper continued: "Part of the distance the roads are very bad, over the mountains. She must have hit a perilous pace over these, or else travelled on the breath of a hurricane over the flat places."[2]

Like their female contemporaries who marched for better wages and working conditions, agitated for the vote, and pushed their way into library and laboratory, Miss Reedal and her friends took part in a new and variegated effort to widen women's claims in male domains. Yet such spirited, unseemly figures remained anomalies to those who reassured themselves that this drive for public authority meant little. Women, traditionalists reasoned, were by nature retiring domestic creatures, devoted to husband and hearth. Spoiled debutantes, headstrong girls, and dessicated spinsters might seek to conquer new worlds, but real women understood that there was no place like home.

The men who were shortly to revolutionize the automobile business shared this view of womanhood, Henry Ford foremost among them. Ford envisioned the motoring public not as a select group of privileged, pleasure-loving individuals like the daring Miss Reedal, but instead as a nation of well-ordered, hard-working families. Nature ordained, Ford believed, that such families would be headed by ruggedly assertive fathers, nurtured by deferential yet strong-charactered mothers, and reproduced by children who learned from an early age how to balance obedience to their parents with the independent temperament befitting free Americans.

This companionable, hierarchical family, once set on wheels, would arrange itself without conflict or even conscious effort into what would become an archetypal configuration: a man behind the wheel, a woman in the passenger's seat, children enjoying the ride in the back. Since the husband-driver, also the car's owner, would be expected to take material and physical responsibility for his riders, automakers ought, by logic, to exert themselves to please him. Ford and other auto manufacturers thus saw themselves as facing one major challenge—developing the means to mass-produce cheap cars to suit the desires and resources of vigorous, middling men like themselves.

Henry Ford was by no means the first American car maker to endeavor to produce a car for the low-priced market, or to try to make use of the economies of mass production. Ransom Olds's curved dash Oldsmobile represented a first attempt at an economy car; the Brush Runabout, advertised as "Everyman's Car at Last," sold for only $485 in 1909.[3] However, Ford's Model T, introduced in 1908, represented automobile manufacturers' great breakthrough in reaching less affluent consumers. Almost instantly, the Model T lived up to its maker's ideal as a sturdy, cheap car for the masses, becoming a familiar figure in American life and lore under the names of "flivver" and "Tin Lizzie." Ford sold 5,986 Model Ts in 1908; by 1916, Americans would purchase 577,036 of the vehicles. At the end of World War I, fully half of American automobile sales belonged to Ford. By May 26, 1927, when Ford Motor Company discontinued production, more than fifteen million "Tin Lizzies" had rolled off the assembly line. American life would never be the same.[4]

Millions of Americans, male and female, used, abused, and praised the Model T. In its time, it was both the emblem and the primary vessel of the car culture. But Everyman's car went to market accompanied by the customs of the country, including the notion that Everywoman would not use the automobile in the same way that her husband, father, or son did. The Miss Reedals notwithstanding, automakers in general and Henry Ford in particular continued to see women as homebodies, neither quite equal to the challenges and inconveniences of the gas-powered car nor particularly interested in the power and range it offered. Ford's own family proved to him the point. The same year that he introduced the Model T, Henry Ford bought an electric car for his wife Clara to use for social calls and short trips around town. "For visits to Dearborn or more distant points," explained Ford's biographer, Allan Nevins, "she would go with Henry or [their son] Edsel."[5]

While Clara Ford fulfilled her husband's expectations and restricted her personal motoring to an electric car, more and more women drove gasoline cars including Henry's flivvers, cussed and unadorned as they were. No national figures on female automobile ownership are available, but local statistics tell fragments of a story. In Tucson, Arizona, in 1914, twenty-three women owned automobiles, with seven, or almost one third, owning Fords. In Houston, Texas, in 1915, ninety-seven women, or about twenty-three percent of all women auto owners listed in the city automobile directory, owned Fords.[6] The growing population of female Ford owners and operators could not escape the manufacturer's attention, and ultimately the company would come to terms with its female clientele, even producing a publicity pamphlet, "The Woman and the Ford." The company's booklet explicitly linked the Model T to woman's social emancipation. "No longer a shut-in," the pamphlet said, the new woman

reaches for an ever wider sphere of action. . . . And in this happy
change the automobile is playing no small part. . . . It has broad-
ened her horizon—increased her pleasures—given new vigor to
her body—made neighbors of faraway friends—and multiplied
tremendously her range of activity. It is a real weapon in the
changing order.

More than any other—the Ford is a woman's car.[7]

This progressive advertising message notwithstanding,
Henry Ford believed the common man to be superior to both
the Wall Street banker and the common woman. Though he
supported the cause of woman suffrage, men, Ford thought, belonged in the driver's seat, in the family and in the workforce.
Men ought to be breadwinners and women ought to keep house;
the family car and the family wage went hand in hand.[8] "I will
build a car," he said, "for the great multitude. It will be large
enough for the family, but small enough for the individual to
run and care for. . . . It will be so low in price that no man
making a good salary will be unable to own one—and enjoy
with his family the blessing of hours of pleasure in God's great
open spaces." In such a view, ordinary families grasped new
opportunities, but women remained passengers rather than pilots, content to support their husbands' achievements, just like
Clara Ford, whom he proudly dubbed "The Believer."[9]

Patient, uncomplaining, and self-effacing, Ford's sentimen-
tal ideal of femininity lived to serve her husband and children,
not to steer them. When he introduced the celebrated Five Dollar
Day in 1913, Ford explained that he was doing so because "there
are thousands of men out there in the shop who are not living
as they should. . . . Wives are going out to work because their
husbands are unable to earn enough to support the family. . . .
It's especially bad for the children . . ." Ford at first exempted
his female employees from the profit-sharing scheme because
"we expect the young ladies to get married." He finally extended
the new wage plan to women, explaining that "I consider women
only a temporary factor in industry. "Their real job in life is to
get married, have a home and raise a family. I pay our women
well so they can dress attractively and get married."[10]

Robert Lacey has aptly described the Model T as "the most truly creative expression of self that Henry Ford ever achieved."[11] Ford designed the car to be, literally, Everyman's Car: sturdy, thrifty, and powerful. Though millions of women found such characteristics appealing, he and others associated these attributes with masculinity. But if the Model T reflected Ford's lack of concern for convenience, beauty, and comfort, qualities associated with femininity, men and women alike were willing to put up with the car's shortcomings to take advantage of what it offered them. Growing cheaper by the year, the Model T opened new vistas for ordinary people and coped brilliantly with the wretched roads of the American countryside. It brought mobility within the reach of men and women in out-of-the-way places. As auto prices dropped, working-class families, both urban and rural, bought cars. Wealthy women in electric vehicles may have tried to avoid the more taxing aspects of motoring, but certainly women in working-class families regularly performed physical labor at least as arduous as the job of driving, especially in rural areas.[12] If the Model T's shock absorbers were, as wags observed, the passengers, farm wives were more than accustomed to jolting over rutted dirt roads in wooden-wheeled wagons. When Ford owners, male or female, referred affectionately to the car as the Mechanical Cockroach, the Galloping Snail, Leaping Lena, the Spirit of St. Vitus, or (as Gertrude Stein did) Auntie, they displayed a perverse pride in the car's quirky ungainliness, which seemed to attest to the individual's sense of adventure and mechanical mastery. They also reconstituted the Model T's allegedly masculine virtues as androgynous. The driver, like the car, knew how to do a day's work, and made no excuses on account of sex. Like the farm wife herself, or the Tennessee working girl who blasted the horn of her Ford roadster to protest working conditions in the textile mills, Lizzie was no fainting lady.[13]

Yet as much as they liked to boast about their victories over the Model T, it is by no means clear that ordinary male motorists disdained comfort, or that they always enjoyed demonstrating masculine prowess by deliberately choosing a spartan automobile. Most Ford owners, like most people who held title to other makes of cars, were men. Americans bought Model Ts not because they were difficult to handle, but because they were cheap and widely available. By 1916, through Ford's famous innovations in mass production, and through James Gould Couzens's development of a system of mass distribution, the company had brought the price of the Model T touring car down from the 1908 figure of $850 to $360; by 1926, customers from coast to coast could purchase a Model T for only $290.[14] Ford owners valued the car for its economy and sturdiness, but they also spent money on a host of devices and accessories to make the Tin Lizzie more cozy and stylish, from weatherproof tops and automatic windshield wipers to chrome-trimmed radiators. In the early 1920s, the Sears-Roebuck catalogue listed no less than five thousand accessories for Model Ts. By the mid-1920s, Ford dealers carried an extensive line of accessories and counted on selling them to fill out their profit statements.[15]

Thus drivers were unpredictable, embellishing their vehicles in highly personal ways, just as machines were malleable assemblages of interacting, changeable parts. No legislative or divine authority required that an automobile had to be either cheap, manly, and difficult to operate, or costly, womanish, and easy to run. At the turn of the century, when both manufacturers and consumers had assumed that professional chauffeurs would do the driving, they had worried very little about whether the car was easy to operate. Chauffeurs were, after all, servants hired to perform work, not to please themselves. Paradoxically, Ford's own successful attempts to put a robust Everyman behind the wheel, his pride in the Model T's rough, tough, and economical ride, catalyzed a new demand for driver comfort. To be sure, those who made very expensive cars had long advertised their products as both vessels of passenger luxury and masters of speed and range. And some owners of lower-priced cars simply assumed that for those without the benefit of inherited fortunes, the fun and utility of motoring meant putting up with hard starting, stiff steering, and tumultuous rides. However, as an increasing proportion of owners took the wheel, motorists began to hope that driving might be made as pleasant as riding in the car. A subtle yet growing popular interest in convenience and comfort would galvanize a second enduring revolution in automotive design and marketing. As Henry Ford's factories cranked out Lizzies for the multitudes, other manufacturers of gas-powered vehicles, competing for car buyers' dollars, began to try to reconcile power and convenience, to work to make motoring less arduous for middle- and working-class automobile users.

Some industry insiders assumed that women's presence in the driver's seat had catalyzed the new effort to make operating the car easier. "In the past," wrote Charles Duryea in the *New York Times*, "it has simply been assumed that women would not drive, and so long as the tonneau was roomy, comfortable, and well inclosed her needs were supposed to be well met." More recently, he allowed, "the growing competition of the past few years, as well as the needs of the feminine buyers themselves, has conspired to make a considerable change in this position."[16] Duryea acknowledged that a desire for comfort in motor vehicles was not an exclusively female characteristic, commenting that "any vehicle which may be ridden in for hours at speed should be built as comfortably as possible."[17] Nevertheless, he saw women as particular advocates of labor-saving contraptions, including a new innovation in some cars, "the seat-starting device." Duryea described this invention as "a further item of ease and convenience for the lady," particularly in that era of sweeping skirts and prolific horse traffic, since such an option would obviate "getting out of the vehicle, an annoyance which the ladies do not forget lightly, and often saves a very disagreeable trip around to the front of the engine in a street which more often than not is far from clean."[18]

Duryea's interest in the seat-starter reflected the industry's new thinking. Whether in response to a general demand for comfort, or in an effort to cater to a growing corps of female motorists, gasoline car manufacturers began incorporating into their designs more and more features deemed appropriate for women drivers, options and systems often inspired by electric vehicle design. Electric cars, which one historian dismissed as "the most conservative form of the automobile," had led the way in two important areas of automobile technology, electric starting and closed vehicle design.[19] To start electric cars, the driver had only to flick a switch which started current flowing. Early gasoline cars, how-

ever, required complicated multistep procedures to accommodate start-up and warm-up of "cold" engines. For one thing,
gas-powered vehicles generally needed to be cranked to start, a
job aptly described as "backbreaking, frustrating, and risky."[20]
"The trick," said *New Yorker* writer E. B. White,

> was to leave the ignition switch off, proceed to the animal's head,
> pull the choke (which was a little wire protruding through the
> radiator) and give the crank two or three nonchalant upward lifts.
> Then, whistling as though thinking about something else, you
> would saunter back to the driver's cabin, turn the ignition on,
> return to the crank, and this time, catching it on the down stroke,
> give it a quick spin with plenty of That.[21]

Women surely were not alone in wishing to avoid such a
ritual. Men who cranked automobiles had reason to hope for
some innovation that would take the physical hardship out of
the act of starting a car, particularly when drivers wished to be
neat, clean, composed, and punctual upon arrival at their destina-
tions. Even as cranking was seen as a kind of masculine rite
offering proof of a man's fitness to motor, a growing number of
fastidious white-collar employees found that the crank inhibited
the auto's usefulness as a way of getting to work.[22] If competing
automakers wanted to capture Everyman's dollar, they would
have to see him in a new light, to revise their thinking about
what suited his needs. In the interaction between changing public
tastes and manufacturers' overtures to potential customers, the
crank would come to seem a greater commercial liability than
it ever had been.

The self-starter, the device that would replace the crank,
offered advantages to all motorists, but nonetheless began its
automotive career marketed as a supposedly feminine accessory
akin to doors designed to accommodate long skirts, custom-
crafted vanity cases, and luxurious upholstery. In 1906, the Harrison Wagon Company of Boston advertised its "car without a
crank" with the pitch that "A LADY AT THE WHEEL of the
HARRISON MOTOR CAR can start and operate it—the motor
is started from the seat by the HARRISON SELF-STARTING

DEVICE, a crank is not necessary."[23] A 1907 ad for Mors cars, expensive French imports appealing to an elite clientele (models were priced from $2,500 to $15,000), insisted that "owning a MORS car is just as much a stamp of position as one's rating in Dun and Bradstreet or one's ownership of a place at Newport." The Mors automatic starting device, copywriters pointed out, was as much a concession to style as a mechanical innovation: "A girl can work it. . . . Without this device you are very, very far from good form in motoring." Two photographs illustrated the advertisement, the first of a pretty young woman driver starting the car from her seat, captioned "The Mors Way," the second of a man dressed in chauffeur's livery kneeling in the street to crank, captioned "The Old Way." This ad also featured a specific pitch for the Mors town car, "a very beautiful little car designed for city use, to take the place of electrics . . . [equipped with] a low, wide side entrance into which a lady may step with ease, no matter how long and full her skirts may be."[24]

While those catering to the carriage trade emphasized their sensitivity to fashion, industry opinion in general had begun to shift toward an enhanced regard for motorists' ease. Automotive engineers had launched a variety of efforts to develop automatic starters, and by 1911, *Motor* magazine columnist Harry Wilkin Perry declared the day of cranking—"the most humiliating requirement that still remains for the driver of a machine"— nearly over. Noting that many auto manufacturers were experimenting with self-starters, and that some 1912 models would be equipped with such devices, Perry discussed five different proposed designs for self-starters: pneumatic, electric, explosive gas, spring, and lever or mechanical movement. Each type of starter required more or less physical effort on the part of the driver, but the devices saved labor in all cases, a development the writer saw as a boon to all motorists, male and female alike. "Probably there is no driver who will not welcome the coming abolition or retirement of the starting crank," he declared, noting that "the movement is already in swing and it is evident that 1912 promises to mark the beginning of the end of that long-tolerated but needless producer of perspiration, profanity, and pernicious contusions."[25]

Manufacturers who adopted the self-starter made driving easier for all motorists. They also redefined the boundary between men's and women's automotive spheres, no longer identified as the distinction between gas and electric motorcars. Coinciding with the recognition that women were not confining themselves to the electric's circumscribed venue, electric starting mechanisms for gasoline vehicles were treated, early and late, not as innovations furthering all drivers' efficiency, but instead as concessions to feminine convenience. Historian John B. Rae has called the electric starter "a major factor in promoting the widespread use of the automobile, particularly because it made the operation of gasoline cars more attractive to women."[26] Surely the electric starter also made gas cars more attractive to men. Nonetheless, some promoters and manufacturers of automobiles preserved popular assumptions about masculinity and femininity, and enabled male drivers to save face, by perpetuating the idea that women, not men, favored such labor-saving innovations. Instead of acknowledging that men might desire increased comfort in motoring, many agreed that gas cars had begun to adapt to "feminine" standards.

If, in these years, the self-starter was often depicted as a gallant automotive bow to the ladies, it could also be seen as the chivalrous male motorist's defense against the dangers posed by female weakness. Henry F. Leland of Cadillac Motor Company, who would commission the first successful electric starter, liked to tell a tale that achieved the status of folklore in the history of the automobile in the United States. According to Leland, Byron Carter, designer of the Cartercar and a friend of Leland's, "went to the assistance of a lady whose car had stalled; he suffered a broken jaw when the crank handle kicked back, and gangrene subsequently caused his death."[27]

This story is interesting in several regards. First, it offers us a picture of a woman already at the wheel of a gasoline car, driving despite the lack of an automatic starter.[28] Second, it demonstrates that cranking was a risky business even for the most seasoned male motorist; Carter, after all, was an auto manufacturer. In another version of this story, historian Frank Donovan noted that Carter's fatal accident had happened because he was holding the crank properly, with his thumb tucked against his index finger, not wrapped around the crank: "One never put the thumb around the crank, because when it kicked back, as it often did when the spark was not properly adjusted, the result might be a broken thumb or wrist. With the thumb in the proper position the crank usually flew out of the hand without mishap—but not in Carter's case."[29] Third, this anecdote reveals assumptions about gender associated with the act of starting a car. Carter might just as easily have been killed cranking his own car; somehow, though, the helpless and anonymous woman driver in this story is implicitly to blame. A third variation of this anecdote, recounted by Theodore F. MacManus and Norman Beasley, clearly found the woman driver at fault. According to these authors, the crank kicked back and struck Carter in the jaw because "unthinkingly, the strange woman had not retarded the spark."[30]

The necessity of cranking balky stalled automobiles, particularly in bad weather or heavy traffic, surely encumbered men driving their own cars. Doubtless men also sometimes forgot to retard the spark, and did themselves some damage as the price of their absentmindedness. In this story, however, the development of the self-starter appears not as an innovation based on convenience and safety for all drivers, male or female, but rather as a response to the perils presented by a woman's weakness and flightiness. The story thus conveys the impression that left to themselves, men would not have bothered with such mechanical fripperies as the automatic starter, but that they did so out of loyalty to gallant brother motorists who endangered themselves through chivalrous concern for less hardy (and potentially lethal) women in traffic.

Whatever Henry Leland was feeling, and however much auto industry folklore preserved the image of male mastery and female weakness, the man who actually designed the pathbreaking electric starter, Charles Kettering, was less wedded to the industry's conventional gender paradigm than interested in saving labor for everyone. Like Ford and the Dodge brothers, Kettering was a tinkerer who distrusted "experts" and distinguished himself as a man's man (his language was notoriously salty, and even after he had grown wealthy he still liked to spit on the floor while he worked).[31] He differed from many of his fellows, however, in believing in the value of comfort and convenience for men as well as women. As early as 1904, when he was head of the Inventions Department at the National Cash Register Company, Kettering had been convinced that "the demand for electrical operation of labor-saving devices is becoming greater every day."[32] In 1906, he explained the success of his electric cash register, saying that "a man will use the electric machine for the same reason that he will use . . . any other conveniences, because it reduces the actual work, saves time, and makes the apparatus readily accessible."[33]

Leaving NCR in 1909 to join with others in founding the Dayton Engineering Laboratories Company (more familiarly known as Delco), Kettering went straight to work on an electrical ignition system for autos. When Leland recruited him for Cadillac the following year, Kettering had already begun to envision the electrical starter as part of an integrated system of starting, lighting, and ignition. Electricity had always been a factor in gasoline auto design (Henry Ford's first car, the 1896 Quadricycle, used a battery), but Cadillac engineers scoffed at Kettering's idea of using an electric storage battery to start a gasoline engine, predicting that an electric battery would be too weak and would cause the engine to knock.[34] Kettering, ignoring such reasoning, persisted, and by 1911, he met with his lawyer to discuss a patent for Delco's electric starter. Such devices were subsequently installed on Cadillac cars.[35] Within a year, electric self-starters had replaced cranks on one third of the models in the Madison Square Garden auto show.[36]

Delco and Cadillac initially ignored gender in promoting the electric starter, and many of those who celebrated the abolition of the crank did so without reference to sex-specific advantages. In 1916, *Motor* magazine's voluminous "Ford Supplement," a special section featuring advertising and articles about items of interest to drivers of Ford cars, sponsored an essay contest on "The Question of a Starter." Two of the three winning essayists noted the benefits of the electric starter without referring to women drivers. The third, an opponent of the electric starter and an advocate of hand-operated mechanical devices, complained that he believed electric starters to be less durable, more complicated, and more expensive than other kinds of starting equipment. Nevertheless, he said, "if the Ford is to be operated by a lady, either an electric or air starter is the proper equipment, although there will be more care and expense in keeping the starter in working order."[37]

Though the benefits of the electric starter were not restricted to one sex, promoters more often than not advertised the device as a feminine convenience. In particular, those who manufactured starters for Model Ts marketed their products as ladies' aids. In keeping with Henry Ford's image of the rugged American driver, the automatic starter did not appear as a standard feature of the Model T until the 1920s. Ford drivers could, however, do away with the crank if they so chose. By 1915, *Motor's* "Ford Supplement" included ads for companies manufacturing self-starters for the Model T priced from ten dollars to sixty-five dollars. Advertisers appealed to potential customers on their own gender-laden terms. They also sought to attract the attention of female Ford drivers, who, like their male counterparts, were becoming more numerous.[38] The Hunter Auto Supply Company proclaimed that its starter was so easy to operate that "a woman or child can do it," emphasizing the point with a picture of a smiling woman at the wheel of a Model T.[39] The Splitdorf Electric Company insisted that "Women Can Drive Ford cars with perfect freedom and comfort if they will be sure to see that the car is equipped with a Splitdorf-Apelco electric starting and Lighting System."[40] The Stewart-Warner Speedometer Corporation informed readers that "Ford owners, particularly their wives and daughters, see in this Stewart Starter complete emancipation from all the trouble of driving a car."[41] And Westinghouse Electric encouraged owners to "Let *Her* Drive Your Ford—Of course she can't do it so long as the engine has to be turned over by hand at every start. But she can drive it easily and comfortably if it is provided with *Westinghouse Electric Starting and Lighting Equipment.*"[42]

∞

The instant and widespread acceptance of the electric starter prompted manufacturers of automotive goods to broaden their efforts to enhance drivers' comfort and convenience, while often attributing demand for such innovations to women. The Cutler-Hammer Manufacturing Company, a Milwaukee producer of electrical equipment, moved quickly to develop and market the Vulcan Electric Gear Shifter, an electromagnetic push-button device installed on or near the steering wheel. Advertising for the Vulcan gear shift, not surprisingly, focused on the woman driver. Declaring manual gear shifts "often dangerous in the hands of a novice," the company's ads pictured women drivers and played up the idea that without the electric shift, fear and weakness would keep women from driving gas cars. "It is a well known fact that the average woman prefers an electric, because she knows she can control it, no matter how powerful it may be, by the simple pressing of a button or the movement of a light hand controller," a June, 1914 ad in *Motor* declared. The Vulcan Electric Gear Shift, said the ad, "eliminates the need for muscular effort, making it possible for a *woman* to enjoy those things which her lack of muscular strength and general aversion to mechanical things has prevented her from using."

While invoking female weakness enabled male drivers to maintain a rugged self-image, this advertising strategy had its perils. By 1917, the Cutler-Hammer company had begun revising its sales pitch to suit a changing market. The manufacturer modified and renamed the device the C-H Magnetic Gear Shift, possibly downplaying the electrical dimension of the technology because the association of women with electric autos was breaking down, and electric vehicles were generally losing favor. Cutler-Hammer nonetheless continued to focus on women drivers, insisting that "for women especially, the C-H Magnetic Gear Shift simplifies driving—making it more comfortable and convenient."[43] In changing its appeal from a bald and absolute statement about women drivers to a relativistic emphasis on greater ease, especially for women, the company acknowledged the fact that manual gear shifts apparently were less problematic for women (and men) than crank-starting had been. An April, 1917 ad retained the symbol of the female driver, but left out all reference to women drivers' presumed handicaps and concentrated instead on projecting a gender-neutral message of up-to-dateness. This ad featured "the dainty Prima Donna" Claire Rochester, a woman who had driven from New York to San Francisco in eleven days in a Premier automobile equipped with the C-H Magnetic Gear Shift. According to the caption below her photo (which revealed a woman not precisely "dainty"), one notable stop on that cross-country journey had included a drive up the steps of the San Antonio, Texas courthouse! Rochester asserted: "For years I've shifted gears by hand. Now I simply press a button on my Premier and electricity does the shifting for me. Today I wouldn't be bothered with the difficulty of shifting gears by hand. No other up-to-date motorist should, and wouldn't if they saw the C-H Magnetic Gear Shift of the Premier."[44]

The application of electromagnetism to gear-shifting proved an innovation less revolutionary than the development of the electric starter. Yet the identification of electrical technology with women, whose right and ability to drive gas cars remained an open question, meant that gender ideology continued to affect automotive devices including the electric starter and the electric gear shift, the former an immensely important labor saver, the latter of limited appeal. The assumption that only women required comfortable, convenient motor vehicles may have helped men to save face, to preserve the fiction that masculine drivers, ever in pursuit of the strenuous life, scorned feminine accessories. But it also handicapped male drivers in practical ways, preserving the crank and for a time curbing the automobile's possibilities as a time- and labor-saving tool for busy Americans.

While Kettering and the other engineers who worked to develop a self-starter deserve credit for their imagination and their hard work, technological know-how was not the only reason that manufacturers took so long in doing away with the crank. The application of electricity to the problem of starting an automobile was a relatively simple engineering problem, particularly when compared to the complexity of the internal combustion engine and the amount of creative energy that went into its design and modification in the years before 1910. Partly because of popular assumptions about proper masculinity and femininity, the self-starter and the American car culture took rather longer in coming than they might have done. In other words, some of the very items that gasoline car manufacturers, dealers, and consumers had considered feminine frills were at length incorporated as standard automotive equipment, transforming the automobile from a quirky novelty useful only to those with enough leisure to enjoy a physically taxing hobby, to a tool of middle-class workers, both those employed in the household and those who worked for pay.

Ironically, the trend toward "feminine" comfort and convenience in gasoline automobile design only came about once women drivers challenged gender norms, proving their ability to operate relatively comfortless, cumbersome gas-powered vehicles. In the process, many women discovered how much driving could do for them. Women like Claire Rochester drove in races and on cross-country tours. The woman suffrage movement made ever more effective use of the auto. And women served as auto mechanics and drivers in various relief groups during World War I. As these bold female drivers helped to popularize the auto, they also pursued their own interests, claimed new cultural territory, and remapped the geography of American women's lives.

CHAPTER **5**

Spectacle and Emancipation

AUTOMOBILE manufacturers who pondered ways to make motor vehicles meet the distinctive needs of purportedly weak, timid female drivers were right in step with the prevailing wisdom of their times. Many Progressive Era reformers believed that women's biological differences from men required special measures, particularly in the industrializing workplace.[1] But while social commentators and auto industry spokesmen sought to delineate men's and women's differences, including those connected with the motorcar, individuals struck out on their own. Some American women sought to prove that protective measures were unnecessary, and a number of the more privileged among them used the automobile to prove their point.

Some hoped the motorcar would simply make their lives easier, more fun, and more interesting. Whether venturing out in cars on mundane errands, competing in organized racing events, or undertaking ambitious cross-country journeys, they challenged the social limits of femininity. Others took to the road in search of political emancipation, seeking converts to the cause of woman suffrage. A few hoped the burgeoning automotive field would provide new chances for financial independence. But if their goals ranged from seeking explicitly political or economic ends to looking for a good time, women motorists made a conspicuous cultural statement about female assertiveness. Donning goggles and dusters, wielding tire irons and tool kits, taking the wheel, they announced their intention to move beyond the bounds of woman's place. As suburban housewife Christine Frederick exulted, "Spark, throttle, cylinders, gear, magneto and steering wheel have yielded their secrets to me . . . learning to handle the car has wrought my emancipation, my freedom."[2]

When Frederick and her contemporaries seized the wheel, they challenged prevailing notions of the feminine. A drive in the cantankerous, usually open vehicles of the early motor age meant dust, wind, public display, and the probability of frustrating mechanical problem-solving, none of which appeared compatible with seemly bourgeois femininity. Driving was, quite baldly, men's domain, in part because many of the car culture's first wealthy motorists hired male chauffeurs. Even among those who did their motoring from the back seat, male auto owners were generally regarded as "motorists," while female owners were depicted as "passengers." When the elite Automobile Club of America (ACA), an organization of auto owners founded in New York in 1899, barred women from membership, the group institutionalized the common identification of masculinity with motoring.[3]

However many men worked as chauffeurs, and however strong the propensity to equate control over automobiles with maleness, this notion often proved false in practice. For one thing, driving and holding title to a car were different matters; women who owned cars and hired chauffeurs expected obedience from their drivers. Moreover, even at a time when automobiles were still curiosities on most American streets, women were doing their own driving. The New York Times reported in November, 1903 that the "number of licenses taken out by fair operators of motor cars is increasing daily." Not surprisingly, given the high prices of most early automobiles (often in excess of $1,000), the Times focused on the affluence and leisure of female motorists, noting that a group of women, many of whom were members of the "fashionable set" and wives of ACA members, planned to found their own auto club. The club's "social side will be the most prominent," the account continued, describing the potential participants as "those who go back and forth between their country homes on Long Island, at Tuxedo, and in Westchester County, and wish to have a place to put up their cars and have a bit of luncheon while in the city."[4]

Wealthy women, accustomed to deferring to men of their own social standing, might have had mixed feelings about asserting control in a masculine arena. Yet the first female motorists also expected to exercise certain class privileges. The automobile was not only a symbol and a source of independent mobility, but also a badge of status, a tool of leisure, and a very expensive material possession. Each of these automotive attributes held some appeal for affluent women. Thus the driver's seat tempted many who started out in the tonneau. Motorist Luellen Cass Teters wrote in 1904 that "many women, believing that discretion is the better part of valor, prefer to accompany their husbands and rely on the masculine ability instead of their own." Yet, Teters said, the lure of motoring, "this Atalanta form of traveling," provided a strong challenge to the notion that woman's place was, if not in the home, in the passenger seat. "There is a charm of independence about the automobile that strongly appeals to one," she affirmed.[5]

When she mentioned the mythical Atalanta, Teters wrote a modern ending to an ancient story. That speedy Greek girl, declaring that she would only marry a man who could beat her in a footrace, had been bested by a suitor who distracted her by throwing three golden apples her way. Becoming a wife, her racing days were over. Teters, however, invoked Atalanta in the name of female velocity and suggested that there was hope that husbands might acquiesce to their wives' desire to drive. The auto, that most visible emblem of twentieth-century technological advance, might thus bring real progress in women's lives; marriage and mobility might mix. Driving a car, an act combining the use of a means of transportation and the exhibition of a luxury purchase, could mean claiming speed and getting the golden apples too.

The Atalanta story also reflected some women motorists' preoccupation with speed. In this earliest phase of the car culture, when the term "pleasure car" was a synonym for the private automobile, auto racing served as a potent way of publicizing the sporty, yet socially approved, delights of motoring. Later in 1903, a French woman driver, the happily named Mme. Camille Du Gast, expressed her determination to take part in a transcontinental race from New York to San Francisco. Prohibited from racing by the Automobile Club of France, Du Gast, described as a "wealthy Parisian widow and beauty," perhaps unwittingly captured the class character of motoring at the time. Asserting that "no such unchivalrous act has been committed since the French cut off the head of Marie Antoinette," she said that she had "no fear that broad-minded, generous, large-hearted America will discriminate against a woman. In the United States woman is treated as the equal of man and is respected by him." Du Gast was apparently unaware of the ACA's all-male membership:

> No other woman has ever taken part in motor races. Nevertheless, it is a gross injustice to deprive them of the right. . . . Suppose foreign clubs were to follow the example of the French club, women would be excluded all the world over. Our men are simply putting back the hands of the clock. There is no fear that America, where flourishes the emancipated woman, will follow their example.[6]

There is no record of what happened to Du Gast upon arrival in the United States, but the ACA did not admit women to membership until 1914 (even then it would deny women members voting privileges and a share of equity in club property).[7] By that time, other auto clubs, including the more democratic American Automobile Association (founded in 1902) included female members, and in California, Chicago, and Philadelphia, women had formed independent clubs.[8] Even if many club members employed male chauffeurs to do their driving for them, American women drivers had obviously begun to appropriate the personal speed, range, and flexibility that made the automobile such a revolutionary transportation innovation. The much vaunted discomforts of motoring would, in time, be ameliorated; if automobiling was a dirty pastime, there were plenty of Americans only too eager to solve the problem by selling women motorists soap.[9]

While entrepreneurs explored the potential of the female market, adventuresome and highly visible young women of the social elite challenged the male claim to the driver's seat. The "first young lady of the land," Theodore Roosevelt's daughter Alice, chose to defy conservative opinion and her father's wishes in this as in other matters, and learned to drive a powerful gasoline car.[10] The President, famous for his horsemanship, his passion for physical fitness, and his general advocacy of "the strenuous life" thought automobiles were playthings of the degenerate smart set. But Alice Roosevelt liked to steer her own course in society. Flamboyant in dress, caustic in speech, often impertinent in manners, she gained further notoriety in Washington riding in a bright red touring car with Countess Marguerite Cassini, the Russian ambassador's daughter, a friendship Theodore Roosevelt saw as tantamount to embracing czarist decadence. The father reached the end of his patience when he discovered that Alice and a friend had traveled, unchaperoned, from Newport, Rhode Island to Boston in a Panhard racer, sometimes going as fast as twenty-five miles per hour. The incorrigible Alice pushed the matter further, driving from Newport to Washington entirely alone. The former Rough Rider, himself at first unwilling to try the new contraptions, finally relented, concluding that in this matter as in others, he could run the country or he could control Alice, but he could not do both. The President's acquiescence signaled to traditional mothers and fathers across the nation that if willful daughters would insist on driving, wise parents might simply have to give in. Erstwhile driving daughters, and for that matter, wives, might take Theodore Roosevelt's permission as a sign of popular acceptance. *Motor*'s Teters concluded optimistically, "it needed only this edict from the White House to completely establish [women's driving] among those whose puritanical scruples had kept them reluctant lest in some occult manner this highly masculine pleasure should reflect against them."[11]

Alice Roosevelt was no suffragist, but neither was she a

model of fragile femininity. She eschewed feminist political advocacy, but she, like many American women in the years before World War I, embraced the cause of female social emancipation.[12] She was her father's most intimate critic, and many years later, as she reflected on her rebellion in this matter, she saw it as part of her more general rejection of Theodore Roosevelt's deep belief in silent and subordinate womanhood. The President, for example, opposed efforts to disseminate birth control information because he believed that the trend toward lower fertility rates among women of "the old native American stock, especially in the northeast," sapped American power. He felt that women who reduced their maternal responsibilities in this way were fomenting what he termed "race suicide," using the phrase in presidential messages and highly publicized letters to friends.[13] For Theodore Roosevelt, a drop in the birth rate of native-born Americans, and Alice's fondness for the modern pleasures of fast cars and cigarettes, were signals of the decline of civilization at the hands of irresponsible women. Alice Roosevelt Longworth told interviewer Michael Teague:

> It was my father's attitude to Large Families, the Purity of Womanhood, and the Sanctity of Marriage which humiliated, shamed, and embarrassed me. I mean, have you ever read what was called his Race Suicide letter? . . . Its sentiments are absolutely outrageous and it was to protest what I called the *indecent* behavior of my father that I founded something called the Race Suicide Club. . . . We were making the rudest game of my father, who would not have been at all amused if he had known.
> Thank God the Race Suicide Club was not unmasked. Coming on top of my other eccentricities, it might have proved the final straw. Driving a car alone and smoking in public were bad enough. . . . Protesting a bit, I suppose, but I was pretty much alone in doing so. The Lonely Libber.[14]

For Alice Roosevelt, driving a car thus represented a mild, if ostentatious, protest against her father's (and many people's) notion of deferential femininity. Opposing him from behind the wheel, she engaged in a form of public protest, but was surely on safer ground than she would have been had she chosen to mock his views on the family and on female purity from a speaker's platform.

Women did not have to be as famous as Alice Roosevelt for their automotive exploits to amaze the public. Any exhibition of skill or daring caused a stir, particularly as women began to make forays into organized racing, competing against men. A Mrs. Clarence Cecil Fitler, driving a twenty-eight horsepower Packard touring car, won two races at Cape May, New Jersey in August of 1905. The *New York Times* noted that "Mrs. Fitler was loudly cheered by the thousands of spectators who crowded the boardwalk. She deserved her honors, for she drove with skill and judgment, and won merited approval from the racing sharps."[15]

The 1905 season also marked the racing debut of the best-known woman speedster of the era, Joan Newton Cuneo of Richmond Hill, Long Island. Like most other nonprofessional drivers of her day, Cuneo possessed wealth and social status. At first driving a White steam vehicle, later piloting gasoline-powered touring cars, Cuneo won numerous track races in the years between 1905 and 1909, and in 1905 had the distinction of being the only woman driver to compete in the first Glidden Cup tour, a one-thousand-mile event that year.[16] She was indeed one of the star attractions on the Glidden tours, held annually as part of a campaign to publicize the motorcar's reliability. In 1907 she completed a fifteen-hundred-mile round-trip trek, limping back into New York with a broken spring and a cracked axle, receiving a silver cup "for her skillful driving and pluck."[17] She would demonstrate both qualities again in 1908, in an incident reminiscent of a scene from a silent film. According to the *New York Times*, she barely avoided a run-in with a train:

> In approaching a railroad crossing she was motioned to proceed by the flagman, and then he must suddenly have seen a train coming, for he dropped the bars, and the only woman driver in the tour had to do some quick steering to avoid running into the closed gates. She did hit them, but only slightly, and no damage was done. An express train flashed by at the same time, but Mrs. Cuneo did not seem to be worked up over the occurrence.[18]

By 1909, she had become such a celebrity that when the tour passed through Albany, New York, spectators greeted her with a song:

> O Mrs. Cuneo, O Mrs. Cuneo,
>   The greatest woman driver that we know;
> She keeps a-going, she makes a showing,
>   Does Mrs. Cuney-uney-uney-O![19]

A dozen other women drivers joined Cuneo in making a two-hundred-mile round-trip run between New York and Philadelphia in that same year. They agreed not to carry any male passengers. However, in keeping with the upper-class practice of delegating dirty work to servants (as well as observing the evolving rules of automotive competition that recognized specialized pit crews as a standard feature), they were permitted to have male mechanics accompany them in other cars, "to do such work as cranking the motor . . . and generally doing the unpleasant mechanical work."[20] Gasoline, steam, and electric-powered vehicles were eligible, but despite the contemporary assumption that women preferred clean, quiet electric vehicles, no entrant drove one, for the obvious reasons that electrics were much slower than gas or steam cars, and no electric could go the distance without recharging. The competitors set out from New York, all in open touring cars and bundled up in bulky dusters, impressive hats and heavy veils, in fine, sunny weather on January 11. Alice Huyler Ramsey, who later that year would become the first woman to drive across the United States, led the pack into Trenton in a cloud of dust, shouting "Where can I wash my face?" After an overnight stop in Philadelphia, they headed back to New York under overcast skies which, before long, produced a downpour that lasted all the way to the finish line. Since the contest was intended not only to measure the drivers' endurance, skill, and speed, but also to advertise the safety and dependability of motor vehicles, corporate sponsors awarded manufacturers' trophies to five entrants, including Cuneo and Ramsey. In the end, the winners paradoxically not only proved their motoring prowess, but also demonstrated that the sponsors' automotive products were simple and safe enough for even women to drive.[21]

Among early women racing and touring enthusiasts, Cuneo walked a particularly fine line between womanly deference and automotive eminence. February of 1909 would find her in New Orleans, breaking speed records in the Mardi Gras races and holding her own against Ralph De Palma, the most prominent male racing driver of the time.[22] Whether she might have gone on to establish a record comparable to De Palma's or to that of the celebrated Barney Oldfield is impossible to say, since for reasons unknown, the AAA decided later that year to ban women drivers, and even women passengers, from events under its sponsorship.[23] One might expect that Cuneo, whom writer M. M. Musselman described as a "feminist" because of her willingness to challenge feminine stereotypes in pursuit of speed, would have protested such blatant discrimination. However, despite her daredevil driving and her obvious enthusiasm for the sport of racing, she accepted this limitation meekly. Instead, she presented herself as a feminine creature, ruled more by emotion and delicacy than indignation or ambition. "Would that I could cultivate some suffragette tendencies and fight for my rights," she said. "But I can't, having instead always tried to keep the woman's end in automobiling sweet, clean, and refined. I drive and race just for the love of it."[24]

Generally successful in masking her claim to automotive power with a stance of ladylike deference to male prerogatives, Cuneo continued to purchase new cars annually and have them stripped down for racing, taking part in competition wherever possible. Still, being deemed ineligible to participate in a favorite activity "because, unfortunately, I am a woman" sometimes rankled. A note of defiance crept into her assertion in 1910 that "I would very much like to challenge any man driver to-day to show a better record in *all-around* driving."[25]

When she brought up the topic of "all-around driving," Cuneo reminded the public that there was much more to motoring than speed and power. Track racing publicized the auto's role as a thrilling toy for those with enough money to support the hobby, and female participation in the sport challenged beliefs that women were too timid to drive fast and too weak to handle large vehicles. Long-distance touring, on the other hand, served the purpose of convincing a wary public that motorcars would provide both a reliable form of transportation and a vast expansion of personal mobility. From the first, women took part in cross-country motoring events. While the auto promoters and manufacturers who backed the tours hoped women's participation would persuade potential car-buyers that auto travel would not be too rough on them, female motorists could view their touring adventures as tests of courage and proficiency.[26]

For cars to become the nation's dominant form of transportation, over long and short distances, manufacturers had to convince the public that extended auto trips were not only possible, but easy. Automobile enthusiasts regarded the transcontinental automobile trip, first successfully accomplished by male drivers in 1903, as a testament to the motorcar's permanent utility.[27] Finding a way across the North American continent has ever been a theme of American history, symbolizing the intent of the United States and its citizens to take possession of all the land, from coast to coast. Since the middle of the nineteenth century, Americans have undertaken the transcontinental journey, often as not, in families.[28] Yet well into the twentieth century, most people continued to see such journeys as tests of masculine strength and endurance at the wheel. Paradoxically, automotive concerns relied on the expertise and bravery of exceptional women to convince the public that anyone could drive anywhere. The Maxwell-Briscoe company, eager for publicity, determined to put this message across in 1909, by sponsoring Alice Huyler Ramsey, the first woman to drive across the United States. Ramsey, a twenty-one-year-old Vassar graduate from Hackensack, New Jersey, claimed that she "was born mechanical, an inheritance from my father. My husband wasn't mechanical at all." Though he never did learn to drive, John Rathbone Ramsey was willing and able to buy his wife "new automobiles in frequent succession," and he endorsed her cross-country venture. She left New York, smartly garbed in a sensible duster and high-crowned, billed motoring cap, with three women passengers (none of whom knew how to drive) in June, 1909, bound for San Francisco.[29] The trip took forty-one days at a time when roads were often no more than dirt tracks, and fear of highway robbery colored travelers' accounts. Maxwell-Briscoe, alert to every advertising opportunity, coordinated advance publicity in towns along the way, and pilot cars often announced Ramsey's arrival. Doing all the driving and making all but the most major repairs, Ramsey obviously possessed plenty of stamina. She declared that her transcontinental "journey demanded a sturdy crew and no invalids were invited." Yet even though her achievement won her a commendation from the Automobile Manufacturers' Association, and the AAA's recognition as "Woman Motorist of the Century" in 1960, she would be commended not for skill and endurance, but for her part in proving that "automobiles are here to stay—rugged and dependable enough to commend any man's respect, gentle enough for the daintiest lady." Accepting the AAA award, Ramsey diffidently included herself among "the great women drivers who were convinced we could drive as well as most men."[30]

Despite her remarkable achievement, we can appreciate Ramsey's self-effacement, recalling that her trip was a corporate publicity stunt aimed at proving that automobiles were safe, reliable, and simple enough for even well-heeled ladies to drive. Women who undertook extended automobile tours in the years following Ramsey's pioneering journey were aware of their contradictory position. They strove to demonstrate that there was no need to treat them as freaks or second-class drivers, even as splashy promotion enabled them to prove that women's competence at the wheel deserved no more or less attention than did men's driving ability. Paramount Studios billed actress Anita King's 1915 trip from Los Angeles to New York in a six-cylinder, sixty-horsepower Kisselkar as a daring solo venture, though the company sent along an army of publicists.[31]

For all the paradoxes of their journeys, female cross-country drivers, literally revealing themselves to the public eye in their open vehicles, challenged the notion that women ought to remain sequestered in the home. Some assuredly believed that they might claim the freedom of the road only by presenting their trips as unremarkable. Blanche Stuart Scott, "a young society woman" from Rochester, New York, announced her plan to drive to San Francisco in the summer of 1910, accompanied by a female friend, insisting that "there will be nothing spectacular, strenuous, or notorious in the performance." She delighted in "the pure enjoyment of the sport [of motoring] with its wide range of possibilities in the quest of pleasure, travel, and experience." Scott dismissed arguments that nature had fitted women no better for motoring than for other public endeavors:

> It is my belief that touring, especially some distance, has never been indulged in by the different lady motorists largely on account of their extreme modesty, of self-deprecation rather than on account of physical unfitness or inability on their part.[32]

For her own part, Scott welcomed "new and novel experiences with very keen anticipation." She expressed confidence in her skill as a mechanic, maintaining that she "really enjoy[ed] the little work which the operation of the modern automobile involves." Rejecting masculine protection, she insisted that she had "often experienced more embarrassment through the proffered assistance of men who happen along when making some tire repair on the road than the mere execution of the repair has involved." Once again asking to be treated like the run of male motorists, she declared her willingness, in the event of a major breakdown, to seek out a garage mechanic "like any tourist." She was not, however, just another tourist—she was a prominent, wealthy woman driving across the continent. When she set out from Manhattan's Hotel Cumberland on May 16, she was accompanied by an escort of forty cars.[33]

American women drivers would tour not only the country, but the world. Emily Post, later celebrated as an arbiter of polite manners, related her experiences on a tour to San Francisco; businesswoman Harriet White Fisher in 1910 reported on her adventure as the first woman to cross India in a motorcar, capturing in one sentence the class privileges accorded many early women motorists: "I was salaamed from Bombay to Calcutta."[34] Many such women drivers hoped to appropriate the social and spatial possibilities of motoring without taking the risks of doing so on feminist grounds.[35] Others, however, saw more radical political potential in women's driving. Some woman suffrage activists, aware that the motorcar provided both a symbolic vehicle of women's autonomy and an important means of transportation for the women's rights crusade, attempted to make an explicit connection between female automobility and feminist politics.[36]

New York activists had set a precedent for such a development in 1908, when speakers toured that state by trolley, holding open air meetings.[37] For larger states, or states in which interurban trolley systems were less developed than in New York, the motorcar provided a technological solution to the problem of cross-country campaigning. In 1910, marking a new departure in suffragist tactics, the Illinois Equal Suffrage Association sponsored the first major effort to use the automobile on behalf of woman suffrage, a series of automobile tours of the state. From this time forward, the movement would use the auto not only as a convenient form of transportation, but as public platform, object for ritual decoration, and emblem of the cause of women's emancipation. Illinois organizer Catherine Waugh McCulloch, an Evanston attorney, recalled that the 1910 auto tour was intended to bring the cause of woman suffrage to a new and broader constituency than ever before:

> We decided that the adherence of the educators and religious people and even the hard working trades union folks was not enough. We began to plan for open air meetings in autos. Our first idea was that with one of our experienced suffragists heading a tour covering six or seven counties in a week, we might reach most of the State in the summer of 1910, beginning in June.[38]

That summer, despite problems in securing reliable autos and slip-ups in local arrangements, fifteen suffrage auto parties toured Illinois. Each expedition was ideally to consist of a movement veteran, "some other professional woman, some woman to represent the workers, and if possible, a singer to open the outdoor meetings."[39] Chicago lawyer Mary E. Miller, who led one party, had to borrow cars and beg rides in order to complete her assigned circuit. She nevertheless concluded that all the trouble had been worthwhile, having found "very enthusiastic listeners . . . [and] many places where, not only did no suffrage organization exist, but also no suffrage lecture had ever been given in the town previous to ours."[40]

Illinois women gained presidential suffrage in 1913, and Catherine McCulloch wrote that "many of us felt that these auto tours, which met *the people,* was [sic] one of the great causes of our final victory in 1913. . . . This was the largest measure of suffrage secured by the women of any state east of the Mississippi River at that time."[41] She would go on to assist in organizing a similar tour in California in 1911, and to participate in a suffrage auto tour of Wisconsin in 1912. With each tour, featuring open air meetings, the suffragists advertised themselves more brashly. Charlotte Anita Whitney of the College Equal Suffrage League of California recalled that near the end of that state's suffrage auto tour, they adopted the practice of speaking from automobiles and moved from using a bugler, who attracted a crowd by playing "America," to announcing their presence by sending around a wagon carrying a brass band.[42]

Such blatant self-promotion aroused concern among more traditional women within the suffrage movement. In Wisconsin, some suffragists were no more eager than Joan Cuneo had been to connect challenges to the feminine social role with equal political rights for women. Catherine McCulloch assured co-workers that suffrage auto campaigning "is perfectly safe. No timid woman need hesitate." She insisted at the same time that "we must have conservative, refined, well-educated women" in order to overcome resistance to the motor tour idea. Some of her colleagues in the movement feared that such "spectacular and sensational" public appearances would overstep the bounds of feminine propriety. In Wisconsin, some participants even worried that suffragist women who found the auto tours unseemly might stage a public protest. Ada James, president of the Political Equality League of Wisconsin, supported the auto tour idea on the grounds that "we *must* go to the people." James told McCulloch that she had to contend with League members who had "opposed the auto work bitterly last summer, and if they send out some kind of a protest against the outdoor speaking and urge parlor meetings, your splendid ability won't be much of a factor as far as the result of the election is concerned. For these indoor affairs reach the converted, not the indifferent or opposed."[43]

Echoing Harriot Stanton Blatch's pronouncement that "we must seek on the highways the unconverted," McCulloch believed that in the auto tours, suffragists had found "the best possible means of reaching the man in the street."[44] Within a few years, the automobile would become an important feature of suffrage work in New York state, though in that venue, particularly in New York City, the identification of cars with class privilege would engender a particular set of difficulties. Many wealthy New York suffragists had long since adopted the motorcar as a mode of daily transportation, and thus were used to attracting public attention. Moreover, the New York City tradition of parading, along with population density in Manhattan, made the suffrage motorcade an effective tool of publicity. In 1912, one such spectacle included six automobiles, carrying activists including historian Mary Beard and actress Veda Sutton. That night, standing in the open touring cars, the women stopped to address crowds at street corners. They knew that despite the participation of working-class women in the movement, the New York public tended to associate both private automobiles and the suffrage movement with upper class figures like the enormously wealthy militant suffragist Alva Belmont, who was among the earliest motoring enthusiasts in the United States, and may have been the first American to import an automobile from France.[45] One speaker attempted to minimize such connections by telling the crowd that "we did not eat our little lunches in lobster palaces, but out in the street in front of lobster palaces. We stand for plain living and high thinking. That's it." Unfortunately for the suffragists, the press was all too quick to report the fact that at that point, the speaker's chauffeur approached reporters to tell them that he had not had any lunch at all, and asked them if they would be willing to take up a collection to buy him a bite to eat.[46]

Whatever the political disadvantages of using a means of

transportation still associated, in New York at least, with the elite, the favorable publicity associated with auto tours and the practical advantages of automobility were evident to New York suffragists. Further, Ford's Model T was bringing car ownership within reach of an ever-wider segment of the population, and more and more women were learning to drive. In 1913, after taking part in the previous summer's round-trip tour between New York City and Albany, one Olive Schultz established a taxi service for the convenience of suffragists and other women, operating from a spot in front of the Women's Political Union on Forty-second Street. Sponsored by Harriot Stanton Blatch, Schultz agreed to split her profits with the cause. The *New York Times* depicted Schultz in terms starkly contrasting the language then current in arguments for protective labor laws for women, as not only an advocate of women's political equality, but also as the embodiment of emancipated New Womanhood. Where those who worked for protective legislation hoped to limit women's working hours and tailor job requirements to purportedly frail female physiology, Schultz was said to be "not afraid of night work" and "able to climb down from the wheel and fix her car no matter what has happened to it. She can do more to improve a peevish carburetor with a hairpin than most mechanicians can with a hydraulic drill and an assortment of monkey wrenches. What she knows about hill climbing will fill a book."[47]

While Olive Schultz exemplified womanly strength and competence, her five-passenger suffrage taxi combined "all the comforts of home" for women passengers with the goal of attracting public attention to the fight for votes for women. Equipped for winter driving with "a warming device that will do everything but fry an egg" and "a wardrobe of fur coats and woolen mittens" for women passengers' convenience, the car sported a suffrage banner. Driver Schultz, "the newest recruit to the army of night riders," promised to wear a cap decorated with the purple, white, and green colors of the state suffrage campaign.[48] At once domestic and theatrical, the suffrage taxi represented the merging of female and male spheres, and announced women's arrival on the public stage.

The suffrage taxi was also, for Schultz, a business venture.

That point did not escape those New York suffragists whose political agenda extended beyond the vote, hoping that the movement would not only bring new legal rights but would also create new social and economic options for women. To those whose goals included opening new careers to female talent, and equal pay for equal work, the auto was not only a political vehicle but also a potential tool of financial independence. Movement activists including Crystal Eastman, Mary Beard, Mary Garrett Hay, and Inez Millholland noted the growing importance of the auto industry to the American economy and the new career opportunities opening up in automotive fields. In 1914, they inaugurated a program to promote women's entry into automobile sales.[49]

The suffragist effort to get women to sell cars meant confronting deep-rooted cultural assumptions. Persuading people, mostly male, to spend a lot of money on a complicated machine was, then as now, regarded as a task suitable only for those with particularly aggressive personalities, a category from which women were encouraged to exempt themselves. As familiar a cultural figure as the American car salesman has become, the notion and the very sound of the term "car saleswoman" continue to jar. The story of an early woman auto broker in England, described as a "well-known peeress whose resources are not commensurate with her passion for cards," amply illustrated the peculiarity of proposing that women be hired to sell cars. Like a character out of an Edith Wharton novel, this noblewoman's class and gender combined to discourage her from admitting financial embarrassment and openly seeking to make money. Prevented from identifying herself as a professional purveyor of motorcars, her place of business and entrepreneurial strategy could not have been farther from the archetypal car salesman's showroom hard sell. She had persuaded an auto manufacturer to furnish several cars, complete with chauffeurs, for the convenience of guests at her country estate. Making sure that her parties always included several nonmotorists, she also took care to demonstrate the automobile's virtues by having chauffeurs pick up and deliver guests at the train station and by organizing motoring entertainments. Her guests, unaware of their hostess' financial interest in their new enthusiasm for automobiles, often went home to order cars "just like that of My Lady, mentioning her name in order to secure special attention." In this demure and devious manner, the woman was said to have scored nineteen healthy commissions in six months in 1903.[50]

By 1914, feminists like Crystal Eastman believed that women had come far enough to cast off their customary deference and join the contentious world of car sales.[51] The Maxwell Motor Company, which had sponsored Alice Ramsey's transcontinental voyage, again garnered some good publicity by cooperating with Eastman and her cohorts, announcing a plan to hire automobile saleswomen on an equal basis with men. The company held a reception at a Manhattan dealership to inaugurate its new policy, featuring speeches by Beard, Hay, Millholland, and Eastman (identified by the *New York Times* as "manager of the enterprise"). During the reception, Barnard graduate Jean Earl Moehle, dressed in a leather apron and blue jeans, stood in the showroom window assembling and disassembling a motor. According to the *Times*, many activists in the women's movement attended, and the speakers praised "the opportunity which this new occupation gave to women to prove the contention that women were not only equal to the task of sharing occupations with men, but when engaged in them, were worthy of equal pay for equal service."[52]

In the long run, the audacious Maxwell-feminist experiment with car saleswomen made little headway in the male world of automobile sales, and other saleswomen reported varying experiences. Mrs. Flora B. Barber, described as "the only automobile saleswoman on the Pacific coast," managed sixteen auto agencies in the West, with headquarters in Reno and Los Angeles and "several hundred men in her employ." She believed that "women can sell automobiles just as well as men. In fact, I believe that they can in some instances sell them better," although she did not elaborate on such instances.[53] Another woman auto broker, Mrs. Florence P. Reesing, took a dim view of car saleswomen's prospects. After seven years of selling cars, she asserted that "it is no business for a woman. . . . You must be prepared to be out in all kinds of weather and at all times of day. You must come in contact with men who are not always as polite as you might wish, and yet you must not antagonize them." Barber also took note of working-class males' opposition to competition from women drivers, saying that she had given up demonstrating cars, since "I find that hack drivers and chauffeurs do not like to see a woman driving a car. 'Butting in' on their business, they consider it, and they will take every opportunity to bump into one."[54]

Whatever their attitudes or professional qualifications, women who sought to enter jobs in auto-related fields were considered oddities. Wilma Russey, who in 1915 became the first woman to try to make a living driving a taxi in New York City, was an expert garage mechanic who was reported to have "invaded" Broadway dressed for work in a leopard skin hat and stole, a brown skirt, high tan boots, and long black gloves.[55] The following year, the *New York Times* carried a story about a New York City stenographer who was looking for a job as a chauffeur. Claiming extensive experience as a driver and mechanic, the typist complained, "It is hard to know the automobile from the head to the tail lights and yet . . . to be compelled to spend days in the cramped indoors, bending over a typewriter. . . . Unless I have a position as chauffeur offered me I will be condemned to sit before my typewriter and watch the automobiles go past."[56]

Attempts by such nonconformists and by feminists to use the auto as a vehicle of women's occupational mobility were largely ineffective; American women's economic subordination proved a more tenacious and complex problem by far than their political disfranchisement. Meanwhile, suffragists, taking advantage of a clearly delimited goal and an organized movement, grew ever more creative in using motorcars to publicize the crusade for votes for women. They held parades, auto tours, and "open-air revivals" in various parts of New York state in the following months, attracting new supporters in sometimes unexpected ways. En route to Rochester from New York City on one such excursion in 1914, Jane Olcott found herself volunteering to transport firemen to a burning house in Cortland, New York. Once the fire had been extinguished, she held a suffrage meeting and was made an honorary member of the Cortland Fire Department.[57]

Motoring also facilitated colorful forms of pageantry. A "Suffrage Treasure Parade" in the spring of 1915 featured women in automobiles carrying gold and silver jewelry and artifacts to a "melting pot," to be melted down and sold to finance the state campaign. That summer, Harriot Stanton Blatch barnstormed the state by automobile, carrying a "Torch of Truth" on one trip to Buffalo.[58]

On a more ambitious scale, the Congressional Union (CU), the militant offshoot of the National American Woman Suffrage Association, determined to capitalize on the publicity that still attended women's transcontinental motor treks. The CU sponsored a cross-country trip by Oregon suffragist Sarah Bard Field and two Swedish women from San Francisco to Washington, D.C. at the close of its national convention in August, 1915. When the travelers arrived in Washington, the CU put on a pageant (reportedly organized by writer Mary Austin) featuring forty mounted women and numerous flag-bearers in long purple capes with gold and white stoles, hundreds of women waving purple, gold, and white banners, and a band playing "Dixie" and the "Marseillaise." The petition, some one hundred feet long, was ceremoniously unrolled by twenty bearers. President Wilson attended, though he refused to commit himself to the cause.[59]

In April, 1916, the National American Woman Suffrage Association (NAWSA) sent Illinois activist Alice Burke and Virginia suffragist Nell Richardson on a propaganda tour of the United States. They began their trip in the vehicle they called the "Golden Flier" leading a thirty-car parade in Manhattan. Carrie Chapman Catt christened the car by breaking a bottle of gasoline over the hood. They planned to drive down the eastern seaboard, then west via New Orleans and Galveston through Texas, New Mexico, and Arizona, proceeding up the West Coast through California, Oregon, and Washington, then heading back to New York through South Dakota, Iowa, and Illinois. Burke and Richardson carried banners and literature and used their car as a speaking platform. When they reached New York City in October, having traveled some 10,700 miles, they pronounced the tour a great success, having made speeches "in cities and in the byways where suffrage orators are seldom heard." The only trouble along the way had come when "they were lost four nights in the desert and feared trouble on the Mexican border, where they were when the troops [for General Pershing's "punitive expedition" into Mexico] were called out."[60]

In making such excursions, suffragists not only carried their message to new listeners, they also demonstrated women's equality at the wheel. Racing drivers like Joan Cuneo had claimed the auto in the name of fun. Tourists like Alice Ramsey served corporate ends as well as their own preferences in promoting the safety of motor transportation. Suffrage auto campaigners seized the practical advantages of automobility with regard to both travel and spectacle in the name of personal and political emancipation. A 1919 story in *Motor*, relating "how the motor vehicle has aided in the long fight for suffrage now happily ending," featured a photo of the aging but still robust Anna Howard Shaw, former president of NAWSA, cranking her car.[61] No picture could more graphically have conveyed the message that women were strong enough, and fearless enough, to have a hand in guiding the state. Such an image was a far cry from the earlier vision of women as pampered passengers.

Women racing drivers and tourists often pursued personal pleasure more than anything else, but their achievements helped to promote the notion that motorcars were a safe and reliable form of transportation, thus aiding the growth of automobile use in the population in general.[62] Racing and touring also focused attention on the auto as both a symbol and vehicle of female emancipation. The woman suffrage movement quickly seized upon this doubly sharp tool in its crusades at both the state and national levels. Not only could the auto help suffragists reach new and dispersed constituents, but their use of it furnished a sensational means of announcing the arrival of the emancipated woman. Although they adopted different strategies and embraced diverse visions of women's independence, women drivers pursuing thrills, new experiences, and political rights successfully promoted the idea that the auto would serve as a key to greater female freedom. If their attitudes illustrate the difference between

new "freedoms in manners and morals," and political empowerment, forms of female emancipation not necessarily linked to
one another, their activities embodied a new female sense of
self, more mobile, more active, more public.

These women drivers did not operate in a political vaccuum.
On a worldwide scale, public events would propel ever more
women into the driver's seat in the years before 1920. While
NAWSA's auto tourists were encountering American militarism
on the Mexican border, the European war had already begun
to call upon the services of women drivers. As women joined
motor corps in service to high ideals, home, and nation, they
would explore new terrain, master new skills, and lend new
legitimacy to their presence at the wheel.

CHAPTER **6**

Women Drivers in
World War I

As American women took the wheel in search
of personal and political freedom, Europe braced for a war that
would shake fundamental beliefs even as it destroyed land and
life. Many Americans opposed entry into the battle, and the
United States government tried to remain aloof. But by 1917
the nation entered the war vowing, in President Wilson's words,
to "make the world safe for democracy." The war effort enlisted
the services of citizens of both sexes in a variety of endeavors,
from compulsory combat duty to voluntary service behind the
lines and on the home front. As the hostilities wore on, women
and men would be called upon to set aside conventions of femininity and masculinity, uniting their efforts toward victory, while
coping with social and political disruptions that cut to the very
core of their gendered identities.[1]

For thousands of women in the United States and Europe,
the coming of war meant putting their driving skills at the service
of their nations. Most offered to work without pay, making a
sacrifice that could be construed as both patriotic and womanly.
Yet driving was not simply another demonstration of feminine
philanthropy. Women's wartime motor work occupied a middle

ground between traditionally female voluntary enterprises, such as nursing, knitting, and food conservation, and nontraditional wage work such as operating streetcars and making munitions.[2] Women who drove in the war effort, particularly those stationed on the European continent, found themselves in a critical occupation which was, for once, not fully segregated by sex. Wartime discipline and battlefield conditions pushed drivers of both sexes beyond gender conventions, forcing women to abandon feminine delicacy and demonstrate strength, resourcefulness, mechanical skill (and what ambulance driver Ernest Hemingway would doubtless have identified as masculine grace under pressure), while compelling men to cultivate supposedly feminine traits like compassion, carefulness, and nurturance.

Often daughters of well-to-do families, American motor corps women also presented a challenge to assumptions about the fatuousness and parasitism of rich women. Heading off to France to do automotive work, they first appeared as debutantes and charitable matrons hungering after thrills. Coping with the hungry, the homeless, and the wounded, not to mention ambulances, trucks, and flivvers, forced them to prove that even heiresses and great ladies could do hard work. In the United States, women offered their vehicles and their labor to maintain medical services, social conventions, and political order in a nation mobilized for war. Homefront motor volunteers not only delivered goods and services, but also patrolled the borders of class and gender. In doing their part to make the world safe for democracy, these diverse female motorists also demonstrated that they were less threatening than useful behind the wheel.

∞

An international group of female drivers, beginning with British and French women but including American women even before the United States officially entered the war, volunteered for service to the Allied cause. Their efforts underwrote a broad array of activities, including support services for soldiers, medical operations, refugee relief organizations, and economic reconstruction projects. The British anticipated the need to organize women drivers as early as 1907, when their secretary of state, Richard Haldane, set up the Territorial and Reserves Force, a civilian corps established to defend the country against invasion. That same year, Mabel St. Clair Stobart founded the Women's Convoy Corps in an effort to demonstrate women's ability to contribute to national defense. When in 1910 Haldane established Voluntary Aid Detachments (VADs) to assist with medical services in case of invasion, the Women's Convoy Corps would become an official part of the preparation for the outbreak of war in 1914.[3]

The British Women's Convoy Corps and its successor organizations (particularly the VADs) paved the way for women's entry into motor service on an international scale. Women who joined those efforts accepted military discipline and rigorous training in transport duties, cooking, laundry, first aid, and nursing. Still, they had difficulty being taken seriously. The VADs, for example, were acutely sensitive to charges of dilettantism. Helen Fraser, chronicler of British women's wartime service, wrote that "the V.A.D.'s suffered a little at first from confusion with the ladies who insisted on rushing off to France after taking a ten day's course in first aid. We had suffered a great deal from that kind of thing in the South African War and were determined to have no repetition of it."[4]

Soon enough, under the aegis of the British Red Cross, VAD ambulance units would be proving the worth of women's work, both in Britain and at the front. In London, the Women's Reserve Ambulance Corps was first on the scene after the city's first serious zeppelin raid in September of 1915.[5] As the desperate need for drivers, mechanics, and other volunteers contended with public resistance to women's motor work, such organizations as the Munro Corps and the Scottish Women's Hospital Unit would ship off to the war theater. Celebrated for their sacrifices on behalf of the nation, these women were also taken for granted as part of a campaign to free skilled men for more important work.[6]

In a more homely vein, British women had begun to drive tractors and taxis, "as patriotism demands that every man possible should be free to give his services to the needs of the country."[7] Their contribution to the war was not, however, enough to protect them from "jibes and jeers and active antagonism from men."[8] Class differences may have fueled such friction, since the first British women to enter motor service in any numbers came from the upper classes. Because high social status did not guarantee financial security, some women from prominent families may have entered automotive occupations out of economic necessity. Those who took jobs as paid chauffeurs in wealthy families, drove delivery vans, and carried mail were not purely engaged in acts of patriotic sacrifice, and they were replacing working-class men. Trade unions tried to block the government's program to license women to drive taxis and buses in London. British women nevertheless worked as auto mechanics, drove ambulances and tractors, and filled a variety of jobs in military and civilian transportation.[9] Their supporters hastened to assure doubters that well-heeled women drivers would neither imperil wage standards nor compete with returning veterans for jobs.[10]

Women drivers met further opposition in France, where they began driving for the French and British branches of the Red Cross as early as 1914. One account of a controversy over Frenchwomen's participation in the war effort indicated that a struggle over the meaning of gender was "another battlefront" in the war.[11] Mme. Jeanne Pallier, aviator and founder of Paris's Club Feminin Automobile, told American journalist Blanche McManus that the club had offered to provide both ambulances and women to drive them, but the French government had at first refused. Forced to relent, the government issued a national call for 250 female ambulance drivers. Those drivers, to be recruited by the Club Feminin Automobile, would enroll in the French Army Sanitary Corps, signing up for three-month enlistments. They would be expected to conform to military codes of discipline and obedience.[12] In 1917, McManus reported that "in fifteen years of motoring from one end of France to the other, in season and out, I had never met a single Frenchwoman driving a motor car upon the open country road up to that August which ushered in the war." She recalled that on a recent trip to the railway station, she and a French male companion had seen a woman driving a touring car. McManus's friend greeted this unlikely spectacle with the remark, *"Ma foi! C'est la guerre!"*[13]

Surely McManus underestimated Frenchwomen's prewar presence in the driver's seat. But however partial her view, the war brought into the streets of Paris and other European towns and cities a host of unfamiliar people doing unexpected things. "I hope," Mme. Pallier had said, that "our large-hearted American cousins will show their interest and collaborate with us in [the Club Feminin's ambulance] enterprise." Pallier had every reason to assume that such help would be forthcoming, since numerous American women expatriates living in Paris already belonged to the Club Feminin Automobile.[14] Despite the neutral stance of the United States government, Americans were already engaged in war relief work. In November, 1914, prominent Americans in London established the French Wounded Emergency Fund, an organization devoted to raising money and recruiting volunteers for the war effort. The next year, the organization was renamed the American Fund for French Wounded (AFFW), and by the summer of 1916, the AFFW had begun to recruit drivers of both sexes to deliver supplies to hospitals in France.[15] Although numerous organizations administered American relief efforts in France, the AFFW was probably the best-known, in part because of the wealth and social position of its supporters. Facetiously referred to as the "heiress corps," its members included Anne Morgan, daughter of J. P. Morgan, who served as treasurer, and her sister Jane, who drove her own Mercedes (most AFFW cars were more modest Buicks or Overlands, or, most mundane and numerous of all, Fords).[16]

Wartime women drivers in organizations like the AFFW felt "exhilaration" at being emancipated from feminine immobility. "These post-Victorian girls," wrote feminist critic Sandra Gilbert, "raced motorcars along foreign roads like adventurers exploring new lands, while their brothers dug deeper into the mud of France."[17] It would be a vast understatement to say that they spurned the trappings of frail femininity. They cut dashing figures, often favoring the cropped hair worn by many women working in the war theater, and wearing black beaver hats, military-cut leather coats, and high rubber boots. According to Blanche McManus, "When on furlough in Paris they carry canes or swagger sticks and sometimes they have a dog-on-leash attachment. Invariably they hand out a military salute to a superior with infinite grace."[18] The wealthy young women of the AFFW were visible targets for resentment directed against both their class and their sex. Such flamboyant female self-assertion may indeed have infuriated men who felt that while they suffered and died, the war had become a "festival of female misrule."[19]

Yet life at war was not all Paris cafes, graceful salutes, and sporting adventure for AFFW volunteers, who had, after all, put themselves and their resources at the service of a bloody international crusade. Members not only paid their own expenses, including the cost of shipping their automobiles overseas; they drove and usually maintained their vehicles themselves, a sometimes difficult task given the fact that emergency conditions might call them out on a moment's notice. Despite the widespread assumption that volunteer work offered a chance for untrained females to make themselves useful, these young women of the leisure class possessed precisely those skills and habits that made them ideal for automotive work in wartime France. They could speak French and drive cars, and they did not expect or need to be paid for participating in philanthropic enterprises. Their duties included acting as translators, transporting supplies to canteens in the dangerous areas near the trenches, and undertaking rehabilitation work in devastated French towns that were sometimes still under fire. AFFW drivers served throughout France, often living in the ruins of the villages they had been sent to aid. The driving itself was no simple matter, since roads might be blocked by shell holes or wreckage or, in the Alps, snowdrifts. At night, to avoid detection by enemy troops, they often drove without lights, so that, as Radclyffe Hall wrote of the English women drivers in the fictional Breakspeare Unit, "they must just stare and stare into the darkness."[20] After long and difficult journeys, the volunteers could not count on having time to sleep, if indeed they could find a dry place to lie down.

Women who had always had servants found themselves doing menial and arduous tasks when they joined the AFFW. In July, 1917, ten AFFW volunteers set up headquarters at Blerancourt in the Aisne district, using pieces of broken glass to scrape mud off the walls of the ruined chateau that was to house them, cleaning out the stable that was to be their storeroom and garage, and whitewashing the entire operation. For the first three days they went without beds. In the succeeding weeks, working with the French army, they helped to plow and seed four thousand acres of land, planted three thousand fruit trees, and opened a dairy. Within three months they had also renovated forty-seven houses, and in an effort to restore the local civilian economy had distributed livestock and farm tools to local residents.[21]

For those who took the job seriously, joining the "heiress corps" meant dirt, sweat, and an unfamiliar lack of privilege. Some AFFW workers also discovered pride in mastering new tasks under difficult circumstances. Elizabeth Ayer, a New York volunteer attached to the Paris staff of the AFFW, described some of the ways she spent her time:

> Every morning you crawl under your car to see if the oil runs out of the top spigot and then you put in the essence [gasoline] for the day. That is a very lengthy process, because essence is not only very hard to get but very bad when you do get it, and every drop has to be strained through chamois. Then everyone turns to and cranks. Then you get your orders for the day.
>
> There is an order to go to a hospital on a street that you never heard of. . . . You take a map in one hand and all your French in the other, and try to run your car at the same time. At the hospital . . . the infirmière major will insist on your coming in and inspecting the wards. By this time it is twelve o'clock and you leave your car . . . and walk home to lunch. Essence is far too costly an article to be expended on feeding motor drivers. . . .
>
> Saturdays are spent in cleaning spark plugs, oiling the cars for the week and seeing that everything is as it should be. The length of time you work on Saturday depends on the state of health of your car and it generally needs a good deal of tinkering.[22]

AFFW volunteers may have drawn the scorn of those who considered them to be spoiled rich girls on a holiday, but the war theater hardly afforded them an untroubled vacation, and to more admiring eyes they were living recruiting posters for their organization. "One day we were walking down the rue des Pyramides and there was a ford car being backed up the street by an american girl and on the car it said, American Fund for French Wounded," wrote Gertrude Stein in The Autobiography of Alice B. Toklas. "There, said I [Toklas], that is what we are going to do. At least, said I to Gertrude Stein, you will drive the car and I will do the rest."[23] This impulsive decision to volunteer was an interesting response given the fact that at that time, they did not own a car and neither Stein nor Toklas knew how to drive. Since all AFFW drivers had to furnish their own vehicles, Stein wrote to a cousin in New York, who managed to raise enough money to buy and ship a Ford, which would be fitted out for carrying supplies. The car (variously called "Auntie" and "Aunt Pauline" after Stein's aunt of that name, a person "who always behaved admirably in emergencies and behaved fairly well most of the time if she was properly flattered") did not arrive until the following February, giving her plenty of time to learn to drive.[24]

If many things about Gertrude Stein were eccentric, her driving was no exception. She apparently never mastered the reverse gear, and was often so intent on conversation with her passengers that riding with her could be hair-raising. She nevertheless proved a dedicated and useful volunteer for the AFFW. A photograph of Stein, Toklas, and the Ford was made into a postcard and sold in the United States to raise money for the organization. Despite Stein's erratic driving and her propensity to rely more on instinct than on maps for navigation, she and Toklas mastered their job, bringing supplies to hospitals in Perpignan, distributing "comfort kits" to soldiers, opening a depot and evacuating the wounded at Nimes, traveling through No Man's Land to set up a supply station at Mulhouse in Alsace. Stein had a tendency to bring mechanical mishaps on herself, but she could perform such tasks as changing spark plugs, and "anyone, anywhere, would help her fix a flat, crank the car, or assist in any necessary repairs." Willing to accept male help whenever it was offered, Stein told other AFFW drivers that no one offered to help them because they "looked so efficient, of course nobody would do anything for them." She attributed her own ability to attract such aid to good humor and a democratic temperament. "You must have deep down as the deepest thing in you a sense of equality," she said. "Then anybody will do anything for you."[25]

Although they sometimes found themselves in mortally dangerous situations, AFFW volunteers generally worked well away from the lines, as did women who joined groups like the Duryea War Relief, the American Women's Over-Seas Hospital, the America Girls' Aid, the Society Le Bien-Être du Blessé, and the Smith Girls' Unit. They did not face death daily, but these workers subsidized the war effort with their money, their time, and their labor, committing themselves to fixed terms of enlistment and living under military discipline.[26] They put up with unaccustomed hardships and rigorous training, often keeping their gas masks at the ready. A young Boston woman attached to a British relief organization wrote a friend:

> My dear, I wish you could see me now. The mud is ten inches deep here in _____ and after four hours under my car making repairs, I am literally unrecognizable. . . . We live in a hut, or "baraque" of wood with wood floors of planks. . . . We have a cot, but no sheets, or chairs, fireless for days and no hot or often no cold water either for washing. In severe weather like now, due to the cold, we don't undress for a week. . . . I have been three weeks qualifying as a skilled mechanic and getting hardened before being entrusted to go into active service.[27]

As some relief groups employed women in procuring and delivering supplies, other organizations, such as the Red Cross, the YMCA, and the Scottish Women's Hospital recruited American women to drive ambulances at the front. In April of 1916, a year before the United States formally entered the war, Frances Randolph Peaslee of New York responded to an American Red Cross call for women drivers. Peaslee offered to buy, maintain, and drive an ambulance in the European theater, and the *New York Times* erroneously stated that she had become the "first woman to take up what has been considered a man's part in hospital work." The daughter of a prominent surgeon, Peaslee belonged to the social and economic elite. The *Times* reported that a "search of newspaper files fails to show that Miss Peaslee has ever publicly appeared in any activity except to hold a place in society. She is not listed as either a suffragist or an anti." Peaslee claimed to be "a good natural mechanic," fit for rugged automotive work, though seemingly the model of retiring femininity in other regards. Obliquely acknowledging that women who sought to help out in this way would have to be wealthy enough to furnish their own vehicles, as well as competent and brave enough to keep them running under the worst circumstances, Peaslee declared, "It is going to be hard for American women to leave their pleasures and think of serious things, but I am not afraid for them, because of their adaptability."[28]

Peaslee represented a growing group of women ready to recast or dispense with feminine propriety and take on wartime motor work. Frequent evacuations and the flood of new wounded from battles kept these women busy not only driving motor vehicles but carrying stretchers, loading and unloading supplies, digging mired trucks out of the mud, and commandeering such auxiliary forms of transportation as ox carts. On the eastern front, Scottish Women's Hospital ambulance drivers repaired bridges and moved wounded soldiers on muleback.[29]

Physical hardship and danger were not the only thing about American women's presence overseas that provided cause for worry. Those who occupied themselves with questions of morals wondered what might befall young and innocent American women recruits in their off-duty hours in the bohemian bistros of the Latin Quarter. Blanche McManus sought to assuage such concerns, saying that whatever the benefits of protecting American girls from the temptations of wartime romance, American women's presence might serve as the best way to protect doughboys from French prostitutes. According to McManus, "The idea of enlisting nice, wholesome American girls to shed a home atmosphere to counteract the wiles and wilds that beset and surround the 'Champs d'Honneur' is altogether worthy."[30]

The assumption that American girls might elevate the moral tone of a nation at arms, combined with the practical exigencies of national transportation needs, catalyzed campaigns to recruit women and their automobiles for service at home as well as abroad. Organizers believed women could contribute to the war effort not only by providing goods and services, but by helping to keep soldiers physically healthy, morally straight, and happy. The National League for Women's Service, a multipurpose organization working in conjunction with the Red Cross, had formed a domestic Women's Motor Corps in January, 1917. The League's slogan, "For God, for Country, for Home," provided a powerful, conventional justification for training women in tasks ranging from nursing and home economics to signaling, map reading, telegraphy, camping, and motor driving.[31] Since the organization drew on philanthropy as well as female automobility, women drivers were expected to come from the comfortable classes. By June of the same year, the *New York Times* reported that "society women are mobilizing for automobile war service in all the important cities," to deliver packages, take milk to "babies' dispensaries," deliver seeds, plants, and tools for war gardens, transport passengers, and run errands for the Red Cross. The motor corps workers engaged in such missions of mercy would be identified by their khaki uniforms with Norfolk jackets. According to the *Times*, socialites in their own electric vehicles were expected to participate in great numbers.[32]

If the motor corps enterprise began with expectations that women drivers would limit themselves to ladylike duties, volunteers were quick to seize opportunities to expand the scope of their activities. When volunteers from the Atlanta, Detroit, and New York motor corps drove nine three-quarter-ton trucks from the Reo factory in Detroit to Atlanta, the *New York Times* declared that their journey marked "the first time in the history of American motoring that an overland drive of auto trucks has ever been attempted by women drivers."[33] The return of gravely wounded soldiers to the United States, the pressure for martial regimentation, and the rising tide of war hysteria soon transformed the Women's Motor Corps into a paramilitary organization. By the summer of 1918, the motor corps was no longer formally a part of the National League for Women's Service, but a separate volunteer body directly subject to the United States government. The corps had branches all over the country, with two thousand female volunteers in the New York State Ambu-

lance Corps alone.[34] In New York City, the Women's Motor Corps
unit had ties to the New York City Police Reserve and the Federal
Justice Department's Secret Service. Their duties included meeting hospital trains and troop ships to transport the wounded
and sick and taking convalescents for outings. But they also
conducted searches of women entering and leaving the Port of
New York, and reportedly took on secret espionage projects for
the Justice Department.[35]

The work motor corps women performed, the style they
adopted, and the role of the state in supervising their efforts
propelled them further and further from the private precincts
of feminine delicacy and modesty. Every woman who sought
to enlist in the corps in New York had to have a state chauffeur's
license and a mechanic's license (as granted by one of the three
top auto mechanics schools in New York, with an examination
grade of eighty percent), had to have passed a physical examination administered by a U.S. Army medical officer, had to have
been inoculated for typhoid and paratyphoid, and had to take
an oath of allegiance before a federal officer. Once enrolled as
privates in the Women's Motor Corps, trainees practiced ambulance driving, took a hospital-administered emergency first aid
course, drilled with stretchers, performed infantry drills, and
learned the fine art of army cooking. Most New York motor corps
women drove their own cars, although the number of ambulances
available to them grew from four in April, 1918 to sixteen by
November of that year, with vehicles serviced by "an expert
mechanical department of twenty-five women."[36]

Still, observers attempted to mute breaches of gender. After
motor corps workers had taken on a week of twenty-four-hour
duty in September, 1918, a *New York Times* writer remarked
that "if our soldiers are to be praised for their manly qualities,
the young women also ought to be praised for their spirit of
service. . . . The conditions of service impose no special sacrifice
of feminine qualities. Who can doubt that their uniforms make
them even more attractive?"[37] A photograph of the group showed
an assemblage of grim-faced volunteers in severely cut khaki
uniforms calculated to minimize both individuality and femininity, and to maximize discipline and efficiency.[38]

For some wealthy volunteer drivers, automotive work provided a chance to shrug off the constraints of Victorian femininity. For less privileged women, working with cars presented a vocational opportunity previously out of reach. Motor corps volunteers were by no means the only American women to attempt to learn auto mechanics during World War I. Automotive schools for women had existed in the prewar years, and wartime manpower shortages fostered a boom in such enterprises, catering both to those who hoped to get paying jobs working on cars and those who wished to know more about their own vehicles. From the first, promoters of auto mechanics for women had denied that learning about cars conflicted with femininity. Magazine writer Hamblin Rossiter argued that "a woman does not spoil her hands or even roughen them slightly handling machinery if she takes care of them," comparing the job of fixing ailing engines with nursing sick family members, each being "an accomplishment that is essentially feminine."[39] By 1916, one auto mechanics instructor affirmed that "there is no reason to believe that men are essentially better mechanics than women," although methods of teaching sometimes reflected instructors' assumptions about their students' purposes and goals. In one case, the teacher prefaced an exercise in diagnostic and repair work for women students with the introductory remark, "You will kindly imagine yourself twenty miles from home and the dinner getting cold."[40]

The scarcity of skilled mechanics soon fostered the belief that women ought to learn to fix automobiles in order to serve not dinner, but the nation. Stories about women mechanics in the popular presses drove home the message that whether running civilian garages or learning to fix military vehicles, females in overalls were rising to the national emergency. In a 1918 article titled "Women Motor Mechanics for War-time Work," a photograph of a woman working on a truck engine bore the caption, "Not Exactly a Woman's Job, Perhaps, but These Patriotic Sisters Stop at Nothing When They Have Once Entered the Work."[41]

As the ability to drive and the willingness to take on a host of automotive tasks carried some women into activities that would previously have been considered far from feminine, their forays redefined the parameters of femininity and the image of ideal American womanhood. The same *Times* writer who had found khaki-clad women attractive noted that "only a few years ago the uniform could not have done that for them. Then the feminine ideal was somewhat lackadaisical. Now they reflect another feminine ideal. They are robust young women of the athletic type, and the product of outdoor exercise."[42] The new ideal called not only for competence and courage, but for camaraderie with men. In a *Motor* magazine feature on the Brooklyn branch of the motor corps, a photograph of women repairing ambulances bore the caption, "This is surely woman's natural sphere." Yet the story also called attention to how women volunteers' training at Fort Totten, "when they lived exactly as soldiers do," created "a veritable transformation of society buds into military 'buddies.' "[43]

At home as overseas, women's motor service in the war effort did much to promote fraternization between women volunteers and men in the armed forces. An organization called War Camp Community Service, designed to foster hospitality toward servicemen, encouraged drivers to pick up hitchhikers in uniform. Community Service recruited female as well as male drivers to take soldiers on outings and transport them between camps and the nearest civilian communities. In Louisville, Kentucky, citizens provided transportation so that soldiers could attend dances with local girls. In Montgomery, Alabama, the YMCA and Community Service hired thirty women to teach reading to illiterate draftees from the Tennessee mountains. The local branch of the Women's Motor Corps enlisted fifty-two "women and girls owning automobiles" to provide transportation between Camp Sheridan and Montgomery. "Those in Community Service," explained *Motor* writer Arthur L. Drew, "are always willing to furnish motor transportation to the soldiers and sailors," illustrating the point with a picture of a young woman driving a sailor passenger, with a sign on her car windshield declaring, "Soldiers, Sailors, Marines, Have a Lift."[44]

Community Service clearly assumed that unknown servicemen posed no threat to women motorists, and that regulating soldiers' access to transportation was a means of protecting local girls who turned out to entertain men from the camps. In general, where service organizations promoted fraternization, they seem to have assumed that preserving class distinctions would safeguard both the women who drove (a predominately middle- and upper-class group) and the soldiers who rode (often officer trainees, referred to as "college men").[45] If "good" girls and women from respectable families could be enlisted in collective schemes to take soldiers on drives, transport them to civilian-sponsored dinners and dances, and generally take up servicemen's leisure time, military men would have fewer opportunities to patronize speakeasies, meet working-class women (often treated as prostitutes), or hitch rides with bootleggers.

Servicemen would also be closely supervised in their contacts with affluent women. Community Service carried on its work in the spirit of prewar Progressivism, mingling the desire to serve with the impulse to control. A considerable uneasiness marked these efforts to provide, thus manage, transportation for men in military camps. Private autos and taxis had been and would continue to be favorite settings for sexual experimentation, and the years of the Great War, after all, saw the emergence of the flapper, whose erotic adventurousness challenged attempts to control middle-class women's sexuality. As Zelda Fitzgerald would write in *Save Me the Waltz,* "The war brought men to town like swarms of benevolent locusts eating away the blight of unmarried women. . . . Girls swung from one to another of the many men in the intimate flush of a modern Virginia reel."[46] Secretary of War Newton D. Baker, addressing a group of women volunteers in September of 1917, encouraged their efforts, reminding them, "Because we are a moral people, we have determined to surround our army, not with a system of prohibitions and restraints, but with a system of wholesome environments and stimulating inducements to self-improvement and high conduct." The Women's Committee of the Council of National Defense, working to ensure "rational recreation facilities within and without the camps," asked volunteers to invite "the boys" into their homes, take them on motor drives, and furnish them "healthful amusements and wholesome company." To ensure that volunteers lived up to their shining image, the Women's Committee established subcommittees on Protective Work for Girls and Proper Chaperonage of Girls.[47]

Intent on upholding proper social distinctions, the National League for Women's Service and other homefront organizations segregated their activities not only by class, but also by race. While motor driving divisions attracted affluent recruits, the league also sponsored a Bureau of Registration and Information which not only attempted to compile a national list of women able to volunteer for a variety of services, but also tried to coordinate the mobilization of wage-earning women to do war work in factories, mills, and government offices.[48] State organizations honored local laws and customs; where the Georgia Federation of Women's Clubs (white) provided services for white soldiers in camp, the Georgia Federation of Colored Women's Clubs worked with black soldiers at Camp Gordon in Atlanta.[49]

Community Service's program thus relied not only on observance and reinforcement of class and race hierarchies, but also on women's proper behavior and the good intentions and protective chivalry of potential male passengers. Though the camps existed to train soldiers to kill, though combat veterans experienced firsthand the violence that obliterated social convention, and though American newspapers were full of atrocity stories of rape and pillage at the front, women volunteers clung to the notion of servicemen's essential gallantry. "We always stopped and gave a lift to any soldier, and never had we any but the most pleasant experiences with the soldiers. And some of them were as we sometimes found out pretty hard characters," wrote Gertrude Stein, speaking for Alice Toklas. Stein, with exquisite irony, pointed out the naivete of this genteel social bargain; when she had complimented a helpful French soldier on being so nice and kind, he had replied, "Madame, all soldiers are nice and kind."[50] But while voluntary transportation programs were meant to conserve and fortify standards of proper conduct, wartime conditions had also led many Americans to redefine their views of women's ability to cope with men. Writer Mary Roberts Rinehart described the New Woman the war had brought into being: "The pampered woman of last year is gone. The luxury-loving woman of the pre-war period is gone. The weak-mouthed, pouting woman of 'the days before we were in it' is gone. In her stead we have the self-respecting, quiet, tight-lipped woman of today, in whom there is gradually and surely developing a keen distaste for ostentation and frivolity."[51] Obviously, this picture of womanhood ignored the growing number of pleasure-loving flappers. But if some danced through the war, others drove into the heart of it. Rinehart's description seems particularly apt for those wealthy young women whose pleasure in driving expensive automobiles may have led them into motor work as a lark, but who would find themselves suddenly transported into a world of militarized Model Ts, mud, pain, and death.

The question remained as to whether the changes the war had wrought would persist after the armistice. In some cases, women motor workers remained in the field after the soldiers had gone home. The Red Cross continued to work in the United States and in Europe well into the 1920s. With some three hundred branches and twelve thousand members, the domestic Red Cross Motor Corps spent the days after the armistice still transporting wounded soldiers, and also providing relief to victims of forest fires in Minnesota, explosions at a New Jersey munitions plant, and outbreaks of influenza across the nation.[52]

Some of those who remained in motor service after the war had made a decisive break with bourgeois femininity. AFFW treasurer Anne Morgan had since childhood insisted that she planned not to marry and wanted to be "something better than a rich fool, anyway." A longtime expatriate who lived with the decorator Elsie de Wolfe in a villa near Versailles, Morgan, working with a Mrs. Norman Dike, organized the American Committee for Devastated France, a group that had established seven centers for relief work after the armistice. In February of 1921, the Committee sent out a call "to any girl who can drive a Ford car" to work in the Aisne. Volunteers traveling to two hundred villages and hamlets would transport wounded and sick people to hospitals and carry supplies of food, clothing, medicine, tools, seeds, and even livestock. They were required to speak French and to pass driving and mechanical tests, to pay their own expenses, and were expected to maintain their cars and make minor repairs.

While their lodgings in town were considerably more comfortable than had been the case during the war, they otherwise faced many of the same difficulties wartime motor workers had encountered.[53]

Back in the United States, demobilized veterans of the Women's Motor Corps sought to perpetuate their connection with automobiles and moved to found the Woman's National Automobile Club of America. The WNACA identified itself more with emerging peacetime concerns, including the growing movement for an improved highway system and the urban dilemma over how to regulate automobile traffic, than with the discipline and military bearing of the wartime motor corps. While they pledged to continue with philanthropic activities such as taking wounded veterans and residents of convalescent homes for outings, members seem to have been more interested in using the WNACA as a social and political vehicle. They sponsored entertainments, advocated good roads and observance of traffic laws, and lobbied for "legislation that will benefit the motoring world."[54]

Most of the "society buds" who had flocked to wartime motor work put aside their wrenches along with their khakis. Still, some women stayed interested in auto mechanics after the termination of hostilities. When the Knights of Columbus founded a vocational school for women in Washington, D.C. in 1920, hundreds of women took auto mechanics training. Described as ex-servicewomen and workers in various federal departments, these women evidently hoped "to step forth into the world capable of earning their living in some of the various subsidiary branches of the automobile industry."[55]

Many women had learned to handle the dirtiest automotive jobs in the name of patriotism, and some clearly aspired to improve their financial status and occupational position through postwar automotive training. Nevertheless, men rapidly reasserted dominance in the expanding auto mechanics profession after the war. In part because those women who burst the bubble of feminine frailty to take on wartime motor work were often from wealthy families and thus were those who least needed to capitalize on their new skills, neither technical competence for some women nor a new definition of acceptable feminine

behavior translated into greater economic or occupational opportunity for women in general.[56]

Still, motor corps service had transformed some women's
lives. They resisted conforming to the new, heterosexually erot-
icized feminine ideal of the flapper, choosing instead to retain
the androgynous or masculine style of their wartime days. In
some cases, as Radclyffe Hall would write in *The Well of Loneliness*, friendships formed in war work had led them to discover
or affirm lesbian identities which put them far outside the pale
of social acceptance.[57] Those who persisted in defying gender
conventions in the absence of international crisis would be deni-
grated and ridiculed as unnatural. In Anita Loos' enormously
popular 1925 portrait of the flapper, *Gentlemen Prefer Blondes*,
protagonist Lorelei Lee describes her wealthy but strange future
sister-in-law. "It seems that Henry's sister has never been the
same since the war," Lorelei writes,

> because she never had on a man's collar and a necktie until she
> drove an ambulants in the war, and now they cannot get her to
> take them off. Because ever since the armistice Henry's sister
> seems to have the idea that womens clothes are effiminate. So
> Henry's sister seems to think of nothing but either horses or auto-
> mobiles and when she is not in a garage the only other place
> she is happy in is a stable. . . . Henry says that what the war
> did to a girl like his sister is really worse than the war itself.[58]

For many other volunteer drivers, who viewed their wartime
activity as consistent with women's duty to sacrifice and serve,
motor transport work had shifted but not obliterated the bounds
of femininity. The short-term transition from society "buds" to
training camp "buddies" facilitated a longer-lasting trend toward
the emerging companionate ideal of relations between women
and men. As the war emergency subsided, the heroic image of
the female ambulance driver would recede, and cultural commentators of the twenties would turn to reflect on the automobile's
role as vehicle of fun, sex, and sin. At the same time, women
drivers' wartime service had publicized and legitimized driving
for women in general. Because women in motor service had

generally driven their own or their family's private cars and had worked without pay, returning veterans had no material reason to push them out of the driver's seat. Moreover, because they had rationalized sometimes unconventional behavior at the wheel in terms of women's service to "God, Country, and Home," they could join the "return to normalcy" by simply shifting the emphasis in motor service from country to home.

In December of 1918, the Lexington Motor Company had run an advertisement-within-an-advertisement headlined, "The Advertisement We Did Not Use—and Why." The one the company had chosen not to run featured a plain and motherly looking woman at the wheel, and the caption, "For Hands That Rocked The Cradles." In a campaign to reach civilian women drivers, the copy read:

> Mothers of the boys at the fighting front are giving more than their sons—they are giving *themselves*, their time, ability, and labor to the at-home-work necessary to win the war. For their Red Cross and numerous other activities a time-saving, energy-conserving car, such as Lexington, is of inestimable value to their personal efficiency, and in the aggregate, to their country.[59]

In the remaining copy, the company explained that the government had "asked us to get upon a 100% war basis," a plan that did not include producing cars for civilian use.

Now the emergency was over, but the potential market remained. The first two decades of the century had witnessed a transformation of woman's place in the car culture, from perennial passenger to potential driver. Because some American women had been bold enough to challenge conventions mandating female passivity toward autos, those who came of age during World War I would grasp the wheel with greater confidence than had most of their mothers. By 1921, the Girl Scouts offered a driving badge, The Order of the Winged Wheel. The "motor scouts" who earned the badge had not only to prove driving ability but also to demonstrate knowledge of auto mechanics and first aid. Noting that "the activities of the Red Cross and Y.M.C.A. ambulance drivers, and the motor training of the National League for Women's Service during the war undoubtedly stimulated enthusiasm in the rising generation," an article in *Motor* depicted the Girl Scout driver training program as "an inducement for every girl to become a driver."[60]

The enormously varied, sometimes contradictory outpouring of activity that comprised women's wartime driving, encouraged by private and public institutions in the name of crisis, both illustrated and legitimated the place of the woman motorist in the American car culture. Formerly portrayed in popular discourse as creatures dedicated to pleasure and personal advancement, women who used cars would, of course, join men in the fun of motoring in the 1920s. But they would also emerge from the war as volunteers in service to workaday life in modern metropolitan America. If the prewar woman driver had seemed to present something of a peril to the status quo, her wartime successor had proven that she could be trusted to defend the nation and its mores.

Women in World War I motor services nevertheless unhinged conventional understandings of masculinity and femininity. They would return, in Gertrude Stein's words, to "a confused world . . . a restless and disturbed world."[61] Americans would tackle postwar reconstruction on the field of gender as elsewhere, and women drivers of the 1920s would take to the road in the midst of a stunning transformation in the place of the motorcar in American social and economic life. How they would be regarded by the booming postwar automotive industry, and what American women would do with their newfound automobility in the 1920s, revealed as much about postwar attempts to deal with wartime destabilization of masculinity and femininity as about the gendered future of the car culture.

CHAPTER 7

Corporate Masculinity and the "Feminine" Market

THE Great War had diverted Progressive energies, forced American men and women out of their accustomed places, and redrawn the boundaries of gender to meet the national emergency. After the armistice, what President Harding called "returning to normalcy" required repatriating people from a cultural No Man's Land. If young Americans of the 1920s were, as Gertrude Stein put it, a "lost generation," their sense of disorientation included confusion about the nature of masculinity and femininity. The war had been won, and so, for that matter, had woman suffrage, but what did such victories mean?[1] So subtly and profoundly had the wartime crisis shaken convention that virtually every person and institution in postwar America shared in the struggle to reconstruct a way of making sense of the world; notions about gender would be central to that process of readjustment.

While at the personal level Americans grappled with the war's dislocation of deeply held ideas, at the social level they found the nation's economy vastly stimulated and transformed. By 1920, the United States was the richest country on earth, its industries augmented and consolidated with the help of a friendly U.S. government. In organizing to meet wartime conditions, businessmen and bureaucrats forged an alliance that would dominate American politics and culture for the decade to come, channeling the multifaceted spirit of twentieth-century reform into a drive for productivity, for efficiency, for management.[2] American manufacturers were ready to turn from producing tools of destruction to meeting and fostering demand for new consumer goods. And no single industry played a greater role in the postwar consumer economy than the auto business. In 1919, there were 6,771,000 passenger cars registered in the nation. By 1929, 23,122,000 passenger cars were registered in the United States, a nearly fourfold increase in a ten-year period, and a number representing approximately one car for every five people in the country.[3]

As the car-buying public moved to replace old vehicles and demanded more from new car purchases, the corporate giants that would rule the industry for decades competed fiercely with one another.[4] Those who made and promoted automobiles captured the public's imagination and its dollars, but they did not command a passive populace from a place outside social mores. Disciples of economic rationality that they were, they still shared the prejudices, desires, interests, and insecurities of their gender, class, and culture.[5]

And so, as the automobile industry revolutionized the nation's geographical, economic, and cultural landscape in the 1920s, it also played no small part in reinscribing assumptions about masculinity and femininity. Still very much dominated by white middle-class males, the industry had changed since prewar days, adopting novel tactics and a different social identity in the new decade. The army of publicists, promoters, and salesmen who flocked to Detroit in the twenties represented a new phase in the history of the auto business. To be sure, automobiles and automotive goods, in all their diversity, had been advertised from the earliest days of the car culture. But before 1920, auto makers had concerned themselves primarily with production and finance. Henry Ford had gained his fame by working out a way to produce as many identical cars as possible, as cheaply as possible. After World War I, led by General Motors' Alfred P. Sloan, car manufacturers would focus on marketing and management.[6] No longer interested simply in offering the middle-class consumer a car, they now wanted to offer the average car buyer something more: a choice. Midpriced and inexpensive automobiles of the twenties would be notable not so much for their standardization, as the Tin Lizzie had been, but for their variety—assorted colors, various models, different options, epitomized by General Motors' "car for every person and purpose."[7]

What some observers of the 1920s saw as a retreat from spartan utilitarianism and a drive toward the decorative in automotive design, others interpreted as the emasculation of both industry men and the cars they made. Prewar auto manufacturers like Ford, William C. Durant, the Dodge Brothers, and Walter Flanders had seemed to their admirers to embody Frederick Jackson Turner's manly American archetype.[8] Theodore F. MacManus and Norman Beasley, introducing their story of *Men, Money, and Motors*, affirmed that "there was a rugged picturesqueness to those pursuers of fortunes. . . . The stuff from which men are made heroic was not altogether lacking in them. . . . Business has become the last great heroism . . . a conflict of the hard-muscled and strong-willed, for only they will survive."[9] Alfred P. Sloan described his predecessors in the auto business as "hard-muscled machinists who had become manufacturers . . . diamonds in the rough."[10]

Henry Ford, who epitomized the prewar auto producer, had a well-known scorn for "knickknacks" (as well as a resistance to the "economic waste" of advertising), lending his own authority to the idea that catering to a feminine desire for ornamentation corrupted automotive virtue.[11] Women, extravagant by nature, were said to scorn the Model T's homely utility. Jokes about the Ford, legion from the time the Model T first appeared, illustrated the popular view opposing female frivolity to male practicality. "In a Denver divorce case," said the *Los Angeles Times*, "the suffering wife testified that her brutal husband forced her to ride in a Ford car. In the face of this fiendish disclosure the sympathetic judge promptly granted a decree."[12]

Portraying the Model T as the embodiment of automotive masculinity implied that male auto owners had chosen the Tin Lizzie over a range of competing cars because they valued its uncompromising asceticism. If so, one wonders who bought the extraordinary variety of independently produced accessories for Fords advertised in *Motor*'s voluminous monthly "Ford Supplement."[13] The Model T's strongest selling point had always been its price. By the mid-1920s, budget-conscious car buyers could purchase a used car more cheaply than a new Ford. Owners might look back fondly on the flivver's quirks, but when they moved to replace their first cars, they found available to them more low-priced cars with a greater variety of options. General Motors, offering consumer innovations including installment buying, used car trade-ins, and the closed body, profited enormously from the public's tendency to opt for more comfort at a slightly higher price. Alfred Sloan would write: "There is a legend cultivated by sentimentalists that Mr. Ford left behind a great car expressive of the pure concept of cheap, basic transportation. The fact is that he left behind a car that no longer offered the best buy, even as raw, basic transportation."[14]

As those who contested for dominance in the auto industry battled over market shares, they struggled also over definitions of masculinity. By the mid-1920s, the successful auto manufacturer, epitomized by Sloan (and reviled by Ford), had traded overalls, monkey wrenches, and autocratic control for a white collar, an organization chart, and delegated authority.[15] As an individual, the new car maker did not, strictly speaking, make anything; instead, he gained his livelihood according to his ability to orchestrate, calculate, and persuade. If the industry had been "built up by and around people of mechanical and technical characteristics rather than commercial," Sloan wrote, "I think we are just beginning to realize the great importance of the commercial side of the business."[16] Sloan insisted that managerial and marketing jobs required "men—aggressive men—of experience and ability."[17] But in the bureaucratic twenties, the bluff, brawny, unbridled manliness of the prewar industry had taken on a grey flannel tinge of special pleading. To some observers, the shift in business strategy seemed to have unmanned both the industry and the market. Manufacturers faced a consuming public that had begun to demand increased comfort and convenience for its car-buying dollar, displaying conspicuously unmasculine preferences. *Motor* magazine editor Ray W. Sherman would write in 1927 that "the automotive business has almost over night become a feminine business with a feminine market."[18]

Reconciling producers' masculinity with consumers' purportedly feminine demands was a problem not exclusive to the auto industry. As auto makers turned to the question of marketing, industry people worked closely with executives in the growing advertising business.[19] An elite, male-dominated, anxious subculture of entrepreneurial advertising agencies developed to serve corporate clients during the interwar period. Advertising trade publications commonly attributed eighty-five percent of consumer spending to women, so ad men of the period worked hard to convince their employers of the importance of female consumers. At the same time, knowing *who* purchased goods carried no guarantee of knowing *what* the public wanted. Advertising agencies and the clients they represented could never be quite certain that a given campaign would succeed. Small wonder that ad men regarded the unpredictable woman customer with a mixture of affection, awe, fear, and aversion. Neither is it puzzling that many in the advertising industry saw the buying public as female, fickle, emotional, and powerful, while also hoping that consumers were essentially malleable, passive, conservative, and conformist.[20]

Hard to calculate as the public was, the changing social profile of the auto business, from domination by burly grease monkeys to manipulation by pencil-pushing desk jockeys, contributed to tension and uncertainty about the role of gender in the marketplace. Even as copywriters like Theodore MacManus, "the genius of Cadillac advertising," celebrated the heroic manliness of early automakers, they complained of feeling themselves "emasculated by revisions" of their work and degraded by the necessity of deferring to corporate managers (a phenomenon referred to as "client prostitution"), and found business in general "dreary and cheapening."[21] Like Sinclair Lewis's George Babbitt, they felt constrained by the white-collar world and suspected that corporate life had expropriated their manhood. Insisting on vast, immutable, reassuring differences between men and women was one way to retain a sense of control. They could, in short, manage uncertainty by preserving such sex distinctions within their profession. The very few women who worked in the advertising business were expected to represent a monolithic "woman's viewpoint" and to "work on the premise that the masculine is the superior sex."[22] Ad men and their employers nevertheless faced a paradox. Auto industry decision makers, virtually all male, wanted to believe in the continued dominance and desirability of men's privileged position in society and in economic matters. Yet now they felt that they had to reckon with complicated consumers, upon whom they depended for their livelihood. The lingering image of the wartime woman driver, independent, fearless, militant, challenged both traditional feminine ideals and entrepreneurs' imaginations.

Consequently, auto industry promoters developed a dual strategy designed at once to preserve their own masculine identities and to serve their economic interests, tied to selling more cars. As commentators in trade publications like *Motor* magazine attempted to explain to each other the public's changing taste in cars, they often invoked men's and women's unchanging biological natures. At the same time, since profits depended on putting more people (including women) in the driver's seat, convincing more people (chiefly men) to buy their cars, and predicting what automotive features would attract customers of both sexes, manufacturers hedged their bets in their advertising appeals to the public. Offering themselves a reassuring Victorian vision of rugged manliness and soft and retiring womanhood, they presented the public with a more varied, ambiguous, and modern automotive palette.

∞

In trying to read the mind of the American public, the auto business of the 1920s lacked the tools of precise modern market research. Instead, most of the men who made their living gauging public taste relied on guesswork, based on both traditional values and thumbnail observation. *Motor* magazine had started out in 1904 claiming to be "The National Magazine of Motoring," aiming both at consumers and at auto industry insiders. By 1924 the magazine would recognize its narrowing audience by declaring itself "The Automotive Trade Paper." *Motor* editor Ray W. Sherman, a man attuned to business trends, expressed both a sense of the auto's enormous potential for changing male-female relations and the industry's nervous attitude toward women in 1927 when he noted that "there are millions of women drivers where there were only hundreds a few years ago," and "every time a woman learns to drive—and thousands do every year—it is a threat at yesterday's order of things."[23]

The vast increase in women's driving claimed by Sherman is difficult to pin down precisely. The war had made women drivers both more visible and less astonishing, and more and more women were driving, but it is hard to know how many, since state licensing practices varied widely and not all women who drove owned cars. By December, 1920, according to one estimate, there were 15,000 women motorists in New Jersey, accounting for five percent of all that state's drivers.[24] Earlier in the year, *The Los Angeles Times* boasted that "California has taken the lead of all States in the number of women drivers. In Los Angeles, San Francisco, and Oakland, 20 percent of all the motorists are women, the new 1920 registration indicate[s], while the country sisters constitute 15 percent of the motoring population."[25] The National Automobile Chamber of Commerce (NACC) reported in 1923 that a sample of 100,000 registration cards taken in random blocks from ten states revealed an average of five percent of car ownership by women.[26]

Driving, in the 1920s, must thus be seen as a male-dominated activity, just as access to motorcars and ability to drive them appear to have been the privileges of a minority of women.[27] To gear design and marketing strategies to such a small group of buyers would hardly have been wise, but including them in a multifaceted publicity campaign, and urging more women to join them, seemed sensible. Threatened or not, Sherman and others in the industry encouraged female driving and tried to figure out how to approach a female clientele. They did so, in part, hoping that families would buy more than one car, but manufacturers also assumed that even among one-car families, women generally played a role in automobile purchases.[28]

What kind of women did car manufacturers hope to reach?

In the main, they focused on Anglo women of the upper and middle class, the same constituency that had dominated reports of women's wartime motor work, with one difference. The wartime motor corps, both at home and abroad, had included a noticeable proportion of single women. Postwar auto trade journals sought to evaluate and expand the market for the family car, so they commonly represented the woman driver as a married homemaker, rather than as either single or employed. Broadbased demographic data, as well as the widespread assumption that most women would eventually marry, supported such an image. According to the United States census of 1920, sixty-six percent of American women described themselves as "home housekeepers not gainfully occupied," a group that included one third of the nation's workforce, even at a time when women's participation in the paid labor force was rising.[29] And if women learned to drive while they were single and employed, most American women, especially those of the white middle class, left the workforce upon marriage, and female motorists would do the bulk of their driving as housewives.[30]

While homemakers might not hold title to their own vehicles, industry wisdom in the twenties, as articulated by auto salesmen, engineers, copywriters, and manufacturers, held that wives "influenced" their husbands' choices, particularly as buying patterns reflected an increased desire for comfort and aesthetic appeal in low- and medium-priced cars.[31] Bob Evans, a salesman for the Los Angeles Paige distributorship, allowed that "most of the cars nowadays are sold or rather purchased through the influence of a woman."[32] Manufacturer Edward S. Jordan put the matter more baldly. "Men buy automobiles," he said, "but it is the women who choose them."[33] In a 1922 piece on auto advertising strategy, copywriter Elizabeth Hallam Bohn surveyed one hundred New York auto sales managers and found that they believed that women influenced seventy-five percent of auto purchases. "Today the American Woman is the Power behind the man-car-hunting, and the Power that makes the sale," Bohn concluded.[34] Humor writer O. O. McIntyre poked fun at the very idea that women's preferences might not affect men's car buying. "Fancy any husband greeting his wife in the evening when he goes home with: 'I saw a car I liked today and bought it. They'll send it around in the morning. I hope you like it.' "[35]

Assuming, then, that women's opinions were a factor in car purchases, industry strategists discussed what *kind* of influence women were likely to exert. Important as it was to know where people planned to go in their automobiles, ideas about female influence rested less on the question of how people wanted to use cars than on the common, longstanding assumption that men and women, quite naturally, would have different expectations and desires. Commentators of the twenties continued the industry practice of identifying women with automotive features associated with affluence and leisure and considered cosmetic or superfluous. They described men's preferences as practical and mechanical, linking male automobility with thrift and work, ignoring the car-buying habits of luxury-minded upper-class men and the emerging importance of the auto for working-class women.[36]

These gendered notions also tended to reinforce a questionable distinction between automotive function (identified with masculinity and with such qualities as power, endurance, economy, price, and service) and form (identified with femininity and with such attributes as luxury, comfort, style, and even safety). Women had for years been accused of letting vanity goad them into ordering overpriced vehicles painted and upholstered to match their hair, skin, evening gowns, and even the shrubbery around their country houses.[37] As writer Margaret Burlingame had commented in 1913, "To a man, it would make little difference if his car were finished in black, blue, or red, just so the required number of horsepower was there." Women, on the other hand, supposedly demanded "refinements": "those things about an automobile which are not absolute necessities, except in the sense that a refined taste demands them," including glossy paint jobs, tapestried upholstery, cut-glass perfume bottles and vases, and electric signals.[38] Wheeler Earl, an actor-turned-salesman for Hupmobile in New York, declared that women "are the biggest factors in deciding sales. They must be perfectly satisfied about the appearance and comfort of the car. A man, on the contrary, will study the points and operations of the motor."[39]

Edward S. Jordan declared that men were "ready to be sold on anything that will add to the joy and harmony of the home." To preserve domestic tranquility, he said, husbands would give in to their wives' desire for "good lines," pretty colors, comfortable seats, "artistic hardware," and "an atmosphere of refinement." Jordan explained that women were particularly concerned with public display, with how they would look riding in the car.[40]

Motor magazine showed retailers how to cater to women's presumed predilection for the cosmetic by carrying features on "feminine" motoring accessories like silk cushions, dressing cases, compacts for face powder and rouge, and enameled flower vases.[41] This emphasis on love of luxury led some to see women's influence as inimical to wise purchasing (and thus a force to be curbed by the more prudent man). In 1924, a *Motor* writer deplored car buyers' tendency to judge vehicles on looks, a habit the writer attributed to female shallowness and blamed for men's willingness to buy cars they could not afford. The writer argued that auto manufacturers wanted to educate the public to buy well-made motorcars, and held that male buyers might learn to judge vehicles on performance, price, and other practical grounds. Women were portrayed as obsessed with "superficial charms," lacking the sense to spend money wisely. When the male narrator exclaimed, at the end of the article, that "car service goes a longer way with me than just car beauty—*any* day," a scornful manufacturer responded, "How about the Mrs.?"[42]

Despite their position as representatives of a presumably uniform "woman's point of view," the few women who took part in this industry discussion offered varied analyses of female influence on car sales and design. Margaret Burlingame had supported the dominant view, as did copywriter Elizabeth Bohm. But Mrs. R. S. Hollander, Metropolitan Secretary of the American Automobile Association, believed that "the time has gone when the motor is explained to the husband, and the powder-puff holder is shown to Friend Wife. . . . Women want to *drive* the cars as well as sit in them and be taken along." Mrs. Hollander observed that as drivers, women "are much more interested in the springs than in the upholstery," thus identifying a desire for comfort as a functional, rather than frivolous choice.[43]

As many embraced the notion that women sought style and ease above all else, some lamented the costs and implications of feminine influence on automotive design. Forgetting that there had always been a market for high-priced, luxurious motorcars, and lacking conclusive evidence of sex differences in car preferences, these writers seemed nostalgic for a simple, bygone golden age of the automobile when women knew their place, men were men, driving was a part of the strenuous life, and cars were rugged black Model Ts.[44] Wives were often depicted as nagging their husbands into making unnecessary and extravagant new car purchases. As a writer in the *Los Angeles Record* quipped in 1920, " 'My wife drove me to drink' is an alibi which is now being supplanted by 'My wife nagged me to auto.' "[45]

While manufacturers hoped to appeal to both men and women by *combining* masculine and feminine automotive characteristics, in designing cars not for individuals but for whole families, some male consumers assumed that any concession to women came directly at men's expense. One male motorist asked, "Why don't some manufacturer put out an honest-to-God he-man car?" and asserted, "My first interest as a prospective buyer of a new car is whether I can drive it comfortably. If not, all of the other factors are nil." This correspondent held that cars built to suit women drivers were far too small for the average man.[46] *Motor* reader Roscoe Peacock protested that "as a direct result of all this woman stuff," there had been "an undue neglect of mechanical and operating excellence and an over-emphasis of beauty, color, chic, style leadership and other fashion patter." He complained that there was no place to put his tools in his new car, and that cloth upholstery was harder to clean and less durable than leather: "I like to hunt and fish . . . and I thought nothing of piling dogs, guns, tackle, and the fruits of the chase into my leather-upholstered cars." But Peacock's use of the car for hunting trips, and his complaint that "I didn't feel comfortable in it at first unless I was in my Sunday best" supports the notion that male consumers valued their own leisure and comfort as much as women did.[47] For these men, woman's convenience was man's burden.

Clearly, those who hoped to sell cars to American families had to contend with male customers who wanted both an assurance that their own masculine preferences were above question and a comfortable, useful family car. Auto industry strategists and publicists of the 1920s preserved male customers' masculine self-image as well as their own by holding the American woman responsible for the much-mentioned feminization of automotive tastes.

The tendency to divide car buyers' preferences by gender grew particularly acute in discussion of the most significant automotive design innovation of the 1920s, the closed car. In 1919, less than ten percent of all cars produced in the United States were enclosed models. By 1929, closed cars comprised eighty-seven percent of all passenger automobiles produced in the United States and Canada.[48] Even the Model T, which Alfred Sloan described as "pre-eminently an open car design" because its light chassis was ill adapted to the heavy closed body, would sprout a roof; nearly forty percent of 1924 Model Ts were closed cars.[49]

The industry-wide decision to manufacture cars with fixed roofs was frequently depicted as a concession to female vanity and frailty. Women were said to prefer sedans and coupes because they wanted to ride in opulent comfort without messing up their hair and clothing.[50] Advertisements and trade features on various makes of closed autos employed a vocabulary reflecting the industry's common assumptions about feminine preferences, noting the model's "refinements," "conservative lines," "comfort," "smartness," "ease," "grace," and "beauty."[51]

Whatever its decorative advantages, the sedan or coupe had numerous practical advantages over the open touring car or roadster for motorists regardless of sex. Those who rode with a roof over their heads stayed dry in wet weather, cooler on hot sunny days, and warmer during the cold weather. The closed car was a year-round means of transportation, while the open cars that dominated the market before World War I had to be stored during the winter and overhauled in the spring.[52] As early as 1920, the Anchor Auto Top manufacturer pointed out such benefits in an advertisement rare for its message that "the whole family wants the open car made a closed car for winter." The ad featured samples of testimony from a typical family, the father noting the advantages of driving "to and from the office in snug warmth no matter how hard it snows or blows," the children citing transportation for grandparents and trips to and from school, the mother declaring the closed car superior for visiting, theatergoing, comfort, and style.[53] By 1929, even the stridently masculine Roscoe Peacock defied gender stereotype by announcing that he preferred closed to open cars, citing warmth, comfort, and adaptability to business trips as reasons for his opinion.[54]

Had manufacturers recognized the benefits of providing mobile shelter from the beginning of the automotive era, the private auto might have made a more rapid transition from "pleasure car" to practical means of daily transportation for middle-class workers, both those employed outside the home and those who pursued a domestic vocation. Why, then, was the closed model an automotive afterthought? And if woman's influence was responsible for the innovation, as so many assumed, "why didn't she make her voice felt in the matter much sooner?"[55]

Price was certainly an important factor in delaying the coming of the closed car. Closed models before 1920 cost hundreds of dollars more than open versions of the same vehicles; a 1922 editorial claimed that "the sedan of any given make costs at retail anywhere from $500 to $1,500 more than the touring model of the same make."[56] Price differences, however, did not completely explain the belated trend toward closed vehicles, since a number of manufacturers offered inexpensive tops for low-priced cars. As early as 1916, the Anchor Buggy Company had advertised a sedan top for the Ford touring car selling for $77.50, and a coupe top for the Ford roadster at $62.50.[57] Moreover, the price of automobiles was not simply a function of the amount of metal or cloth or labor required for the machine itself, since wages were set in the context of ideological considerations and conflict over the labor process, and automobile manufacturers' costs included substantial fixed investment in assembly lines, tools, skills, and materials geared to existing designs.[58]

Once manufacturers realized that there was a market for closed vehicles they quickly narrowed the price gap. Roy D. Chapin of the Hudson Motor Company pioneered in the effort to bring down closed car costs. In 1920, Hudson offered an Essex sedan priced at $2,450, with a comparable touring model at a cost of $1,595. The following year, the Essex coach sold for $1,495, only $300 more than the touring model. By 1925, the Essex coach, priced at $895, cost $5 *less* than the touring car.[59] Scientists and engineers had to work out technological problems concerning metallurgy, steel processing, machine tools, and spot welding before the closed all-steel body that Dodge introduced in 1924 could be made at a reasonable cost.[60] Still, these material and intellectual barriers were rapidly surmounted in the wake of the success of the Essex closed model. Closed cars rapidly came to dominate the low-priced market. In 1922, manufacturers in the United States and Canada produced 1,338,000 open vehicles and 436,000 closed cars in the "under $1,000" price category. By 1929, in the same price category, 592,000 open cars and 3,328,000 closed cars were produced.[61]

"For some reason or other," wrote Alfred Sloan, "it took us a long time to realize that the way to keep dry in a motorcar was to keep the weather out of the car."[62] Car makers' assumptions about gender blinded them to the potential market for enclosed vehicles, thus delaying the industry's effort to meet the technological challenges of producing closed cars, and contributing to their tardiness in bringing America's motoring families in out of the rain. Given a tendency to identify women's activities and perceived preferences as at best supplementary, and at worst harmful, to men's interests, manufacturers' identification of enclosed automobiles with women and with home may have done as much to perpetuate price differences between open and closed cars (with the concomitant early market predominance of touring cars and runabouts) as more material factors.

When American family men bought closed cars, they defied expectations that rugged masculinity governed their automotive taste. They, and the industry that hoped to sell ever more automobiles, asserted manhood by attributing the change to "feminine influence." A Colorado man said that his next car would be a closed model, but explained: "The reason for this preference (for the closed body) is my wife. I personally prefer an open model, as I drive a lot in the mountains." A Californian insisted that he would buy an open model "because it is a *man's* car, not a society car."[63]

As the sedan and coupe gained popularity, definitions of male and female automotive taste shifted, though many remained inclined to contrast simple masculine practicality with complicated feminine subjectivity. "To father," *Motor* columnist John C. Long wrote, "the automobile means transportation. It will take him around on his business trips and it will get him out in the open air in the evenings. Similarly, he regards his house as a place for keeping the heat in and the rain out." If men dispassionately regarded cars and houses as tools, women, Long believed, expected both the auto and the home to serve as vehicles for domestic cultural missions: "Mother sees the car, like the home, as a means for holding the family together, for raising the standard of living, for providing recreation and social advantages for the children."[64]

Throughout the decade, commentators would describe roofed vehicles in domestic terms, calling the closed car a "delightful living room on wheels," "a drawing room on wheels," or "a boudoir on wheels," or suggesting that cars could be accessorized to provide "all the comforts of home."[65] Couched in such terms, the car roof appeared as a prelude to interior decoration rather than a utility feature. But there was no necessary contradiction between men's and women's interests when it came to choosing a family car; the closed car offered advantages to both. It makes sense to see the adoption of this consumer good as the product of familial agreement, rather than as the result of male-female conflict resolved by the triumph of women's vanity or physical timidity over men's better judgment, particularly given the husband's power as titleholder and the practical advantages the closed car offered to individuals regardless of sex.

The tendency to confuse preferences believed to be masculine or feminine with men and women led many to see woman's influence at work where there was no evidence to support such a conclusion. Those on the supply side of the auto sales equation assembled relatively little data on what women consumers of automobiles *said* they wanted. The powerful assumption that women would invariably act feminine seemed to need no proof, and it offered a reassuring explanation for men's changing consumption patterns. According to trade logic, male buyers' taste had not altered; husbands had simply decided to start humoring their wives, and manufacturers ought gallantly to follow suit. When a survey of 20,000 auto owners revealed that sixty percent planned to purchase a closed car, John C. Long deduced, with circular logic, that "the reasons given for the preference, such as appearance, cleanliness, and comfort, indicate the influence of the woman in the home, directly or indirectly." Despite the reported preference of some women for open cars and the endorsement of closed cars by many men, Long and others continued to insist that sex governed the preference for open or closed cars.[66]

Fragments of personal testimony suggest that industry strategists and publicists oversimplified and distorted women's (and men's) wishes. To be sure, in some instances women consumers confirmed stereotypes. Lucile Lady Duff-Gordon, owner of several cars, claimed that color, graceful lines, and "little accessories which . . . make all the difference in the world" were women's paramount considerations. Comparing autos to sedan chairs, Lady Duff-Gordon insisted that the auto ought to be a work of art, a romantic setting, and a symbol of luxury. She believed that "if one could afford to have an automobile decorated for each mood or occasion, it would be ideal." Although such views were clearly in harmony with assumptions about female extravagance, Lady Duff-Gordon insisted that her ideas did not "apply to women alone. A man ought to have at least two or three cars decorated according to his needs."[67]

While this fashion expert urged both sexes toward the ornamental, car buyer Edith M. Garfield described her experience visiting several automobile dealers, suggesting that manufacturers, advertising agents, and sales personnel were acting according to conventional beliefs about feminine frivolity rather than paying attention to women consumers' stated preferences. Her ideas about what she wanted in a car spanned conventional notions of the businesslike masculine and the hedonistic feminine. She explained that she had narrowed her search to "eight or ten automobiles, all in the same price and performance class." After making this pragmatic judgment, she "wanted to be convinced that the car I finally signed on the dotted line for was absolutely the smartest, most comfortable, smoothest and hill-climbiest one of the lot." Some salesmen ignored her and some bowled her over with hard-sell tactics, but none treated her as a serious and informed consumer. One dealer "greeted me with an amused smile much like the one I use on my collie when he's trying to pick up a stick several sizes too big for him. Somehow that smile made me feel that I should be home playing with paper dolls, leaving such matters as buying an automobile to a *man.*" When the dealer persisted in disregarding her questions about power, while rhapsodizing about "delicate little touches that *make* a car," she fumed that "he had me down as a dumbbell! But dumbbell is a compliment compared with what I thought of him." She concluded that the salesman "should not harp on the cute design of the door handles to a woman who is interested in knowing how the Lanchester Dampener works out."[68]

Had women motorists acted in the fatuous manner so many industry commentators alleged, we might well see them as too stupid to decide how to spend their money. The woman who could be satisfied entirely by plush upholstery and the aptly named vanity case, paying no attention to the question of whether the car would get her where she wanted to go, would not pose a profound threat to yesterday's order of things. Neither would she need to get into an automobile; she might as well stay at home and buy new slipcovers. To imagine so passive and narcissistic a person pursuing her own interests—even knowing what she wanted or needed—is difficult to say the least. At the same time, attributing all demand for automotive amenities to women reassured men that when they chose a car that offered comfort and aesthetic appeal, they were doing something nice for the little lady, not getting soft themselves.

∞

Questions of comfort, for the driver and the passengers, lay at the heart of the automobile business debate about woman's influence. Whenever industry men and male consumers invoked customary notions about feminine behavior, they used the terms "comfort" and "convenience" to cover a spectrum of meanings, from sober concern for safety to lavish luxury. Magazine articles and advertisements had long touted everything from thermos bottles and pneumatic seat cushions to shock absorbers, windshields, heaters, long-handle jacks, and detachable-rim tires as boons to women's comfort, though many such items enhanced men's motoring experiences as well.[69] Imprecise ideas about comfort led to observations that ranged from the idiotic to the sensible. One self-proclaimed expert declared that "while a man's pleasure in his motor trip depends on a smooth running engine and punctureless tires, a woman places her faith in her cold cream pot and powder puff."[70] Another advised female motorists to wear simple clothing and keep the windshield clean.[71]

Despite the identification of women with extravagance, not all comfort or convenience accessories were frivolous, even those likely to be most useful to women drivers. Consider the child's car seat. From the beginning of the automotive era, those who have combined the tasks of motoring and motherhood have faced the problem of how to transport children easily and safely.[72] Some early commentators had little sympathy for the dilemma posed by trying to drive while taking care of even one helpless infant or energetic toddler, let alone manage a car full of excited children. In 1912, a *Motor* writer had sympathized with an auto maker who "balked at designing a hammock for a baby, to swing below the roof of a costly limousine."[73] Others, however, recognized the profit potential in auto cribs, baby hammocks, and child car seats. The "Rock-a-Bye-Baby Seat," one of two collapsible canvas infant-carriers featured in *Motor*'s accessory column in July, 1918, fastened to the back of the front seat. It was described as "a comfortable and safe place for carrying the baby," doubling as a parcel carrier. Such devices were said to be desirable because "small children are uncomfortable in the car unless provided with suitable accommodations."[74] The child's contentment and safety were not the only reasons to buy such an accessory. A picture of a similar carrier in the August, 1920 edition of the magazine featured the caption, "When baby goes motoring, he annoys the passengers less when he occupies a very definite place."[75] Even with father at the wheel, having the baby firmly secured was in the driver's interest as well.

If auto business analysts were often reluctant to acknowledge convergence between men's and women's automotive preferences and interests when they spoke among themselves, the "feminization" of the market forced them to address the public in different terms. They would come to admit that men and women might be fundamentally different and still agree, sometimes, on what they wanted. *Motor* writer J. L. Wilson noted that "most of the comforts and conveniences which we have in this world are due to feminine influence, and motoring does not provide an exception." Still, women's influence might have utilitarian advantages, even for men: "A great many of the things which have been installed on the car for the convenience of lady drivers have been found indispensable by men since their introduction."[76]

Motor editor Ray Sherman, as always promoting the marketing potential represented by women drivers, suggested that women were themselves becoming more practical. He declared in 1925 that the time had passed "when the man prospect was presumed to be interested in speed and power—the woman in paint and doodads. . . . Has any sales psychologist ever eavesdropped among the thoughts of a woman driver who tries to make a beautiful car with an anemic engine run up hill? Try to sell her on paint and doodads alone."[77]

Some in the automotive community shared Sherman's view, and advertised accordingly. As a way of satisfying customers of all kinds, manufacturers both invoked gender stereotypes and hoped to get around them. The Lexington Minute Man Six was introduced to readers of *Sunset* as "a man's car in power and speed—and a woman's car because of its luxury, ease of handling, and simplicity of control." A 1924 Hupmobile ad asked *New York Times* readers "WHO MADE IT THE MODE?" and answered, "HE DID . . . and SHE DID, but for different reasons . . ." Men, the ad explained, liked the Hupmobile because it was "good looking, yes. But its specialty was mileage . . . tireless and endless motor car efficiency." Pointing out the car's power, speed, and endurance, qualities making it "A MAN'S car," the ad proclaimed the *new* Hupmobile models featured "Stamina . . . clothed with style. The Viking became a fashion plate . . . and his car became HER car too."[78]

Meanwhile, women's magazines were attracting more and more auto ads, employing similar attempts to combine masculine and feminine appeals. A Chevrolet advertisement in the May 1924 issue of *Good Housekeeping* explained that "although designed with special consideration for our women friends, we find this model is also favored by many men for business and family use."[79] The Willys-Overland company claimed that women were bound to appreciate the Overland Six's beauty, comfort, power, and endurance, not to mention the "wonderfully balanced crankshaft . . . ingeniously drilled to received perfect lubrication at all speeds," because "women are by nature the great students of quality, the close judge of value, the shrewdest of buyers."[80] Even Ford would approach the female market in 1926, with ads depicting stylishly dressed women approving the Ford for being good looking, easy to drive and park, reliable, and inexpensive to buy and maintain.[81] Sometimes abandoning sex stereotypes altogether, General Motors addressed readers of the *Ladies' Home Journal* in 1926 with such messages as "Whenever motor cars are discussed, one of the first things heard is the remark, 'Buick has a wonderful engine!' " and "You will step from the wheel [of a Chevrolet] amazed that such power, speed and snap could be achieved in a car that costs so little."[82]

Other manufacturers remembered the women who had sought personal emancipation in their cars, whether motoring across the continent, racing on a track, questing after the vote, or demonstrating their patriotism in the war effort. However strongly Edward S. Jordan believed that women wanted most of all to be comfortably displayed in their autos, his company appealed to female consumers' aspirations to power and adventure. In the most famous automobile advertisement of the period, the Jordan Motor Car Company invoked the romance of the road with a highly stylized drawing of a woman driver at the wheel of an open Jordan Playboy touring car, racing a rider on horseback. The copy injected auto advertising with a new and dashing emotionality:

> Somewhere west of Laramie there's a broncho-busting, steer-roping girl who knows what I'm talking about. She can tell what a sassy pony, that's a cross between greased lightning and the place where it hits, can do with eleven hundred pounds of steel and

action when he's going high, wide, and handsome. The truth is—the Playboy was built for her. . . . She loves the cross of the wild and the tame.[83]

Even Ray Sherman, however, still contrasted women's interest in the decorative with men's purported practicality. "When man was the real buyer in the automotive field," he wrote, "a car could be a good piece of machinery and be successfully sold. That is not true any more." Sherman said that to meet the woman driver's approval, cars must "run without trouble. They must in comfort and appointments suit the woman. Accessories that appeal to her can be sold in big volume."[84] That some presumably feminine accessories, like electric signals and cloth upholstery, indeed proved popular, and others, such as crystal bud vases, faded from automotive design suggests that consumer tastes could not simply be divided, predicted, and manipulated on the basis of sex. At the same time, Sherman asserted that an automobile could be "a good piece of machinery," pleasing to the male customer, even if it did not possess the characteristic of "running without trouble." Why treat mechanical reliability as a luxury? When women like actress Julia Faye, who promoted the Crow-Elkhart, declared that they required "dependability" in a car above all things, they were not necessarily expressing a feminine taste for refinement.

And if they were? Was a handsome, comfortable car necessarily a badly built one? Christine Frederick, author of the 1929 advertising tract, *Selling Mrs. Consumer*, saw automotive decoration as neither superficial nor elitist, but rather as life-enhancing, democratic, and progressive. For Frederick, the Model T's demise in the mid-twenties represented not the triumph of General Motors' marketing and design strategies, but instead, Mrs. Consumer's victory over Henry Ford, "one of the most arbitrary of dictators. . . . While Ford arrogantly said, 'You can have any color so long as it is black,' Chrysler and General Motors supplied color and feminine luxury until Mrs. Consumer disdained to step into a Ford Model T. Even the mighty Ford was brought to his knees by Mrs. Consumer's power."[85]

Frederick differed from most commentators in arguing the

social and political worth of the ornamental. Like others, she relied on a simple sex dichotomy to explain market trends, ignoring the technological problem-solving, financial maneuvering, and corporate politics of automobile design. Ford's insistence on producing black cars stemmed in part from his masculinist bias, but it also derived from the fact that his rivals at General Motors, including Charles Kettering, working in cooperation with DuPont chemical laboratories, were able to mass-produce colorful cars because they had perfected Duco quick-drying lacquer in 1923.[86] Yet there was reason for Frederick to see GM's technical innovation as a question of gender. Even as General Motors edged away from addressing the public in purely sex-specific terms, while emphasizing the ornamental aspect of auto design, stereotyping remained part of industry ideology. GM insiders would refer to the Art and Color section, established in 1927 to make GM cars prettier, as "the beauty parlor." In 1964, Alfred Sloan would proudly claim that in the Art and Color section, "we employed women as automobile designers, to express the woman's point of view. We were the first to do so, I believe, and today we have the largest number of them in the industry."[87] In the GM beauty parlor, it seemed, woman's sphere entered the factory.

∞

In the 1920s as never before, auto manufacturers occupied themselves with the business of selling, as well as making, cars. Industry commentators' solicitude for the feminine consumer betrayed an embarrassment about male consumption patterns tantamount to anxiety about the preservation of masculine identity. Uncertain and defensive, auto makers and their marketing people both wondered what women (and men) wanted, and tried to assure themselves that indeed, they already knew.

For good or ill, the public received the industry's marketing message with enthusiasm. Budget-conscious and hard-pressed American families of the twenties often determined to sacrifice other services and goods to purchase automobiles.[88] While car manufacturers and their army of promoters contemplated the relevance of masculinity and femininity to auto marketing, some observers, notably those who sold other consumer goods, treated the act of buying a car as a threat to women's spending priorities. Textile and shoe manufacturers and retailers were said to be particularly concerned about the auto's inroads in the family budget.[89] The *New York Daily News Record,* an organ of the textile trade, declared, "It seems impossible to overlook the fact that people are buying too many automobiles and not enough washing machines."[90]

It remains to be proven that women opposed car buying, or that they should have done so. A *Ladies' Home Journal* writer, pointing out the advantages of her "conservation car," said driving her children to school saved the family money on clothing and shoe leather.[91] A Muncie, Indiana housewife told Robert and Helen Lynd that her family "would rather do without clothes than give up the car," while another explained that "I'll go without food before I'll see us give up the car."[92]

Why would women say such things? What benefits did they believe the family car brought them? Automobility meant much more to women than a chance to recline in sumptuous surroundings, just as it meant more to men than a chance to feel the wind in their hair. Buying and driving a car, not simply an end in itself, was a means of acting on personal choices, which were sometimes individualistic, but were in most instances shaped by family negotiations, responsibilities and loyalties. Acting on behalf of such values, women drivers would play a critical role in the transformation of the American way of life in the twentieth century.

CHAPTER **8**

Women at the Wheel in the 1920s

By 1920, the modern woman made her appearance on the American road. Sleek and streamlined, she had slipped the ponderous drapery of Victorian clothing. The hem of her dress no longer trailed on the ground. Often enough, now, it swung free at knee level. Some youthful female motorists, sporting the bobbed hair and daring demeanor of the flapper, even abandoned dresses altogether in favor of suits with knickers.[1] The cumbersome picture hats and veils of the early motoring period had given way to snug-fitting cloches, and tailored motoring coats replaced heavy dusters. Whether a sedate housewife or a high-spirited jazz baby, the woman motorist of the twenties announced with her very clothing that she took mobility for granted.

The automobile, more than any of the other consumer goods Americans adopted so enthusiastically in the 1920s, offered women new possibilities for excitement, for leisure and for sociability. During the twenties, many would travel further and further from home, from woman's vaunted place, in pursuit of pleasure. Social critics of the period worried that women would be so beguiled by the era's new entertainments, motoring not least among them, that they would neglect home, family, and morality. As much fun as they had with motorcars, however, women generally did not abandon hearth and duty in favor of the road, which posed perils of its own. Instead, they reconciled mobility and domesticity, using the automobile to fulfill their family roles as well as to enjoy themselves. In that process of reconciliation, they not only transformed woman's place, but also played a subtle yet important part in reshaping the American landscape.

∞

Amid the multitudes of automobile tourists who took off on cross-country vacations in the 1920s, adventurous American women carried on the legacy of the emancipated women drivers of earlier years. "Dilettantes, debutantes, and even dowagers are falling under the spell of western touring," wrote motorist Laura B. McClintock. "Mothers with their children are seen as frequently as college girls out for a lark, and schoolteachers and business women in increasing numbers are seeking this form of relaxation."[2]

Some female tourists, traveling alone or with women friends, saw themselves as modern pioneers. Winifred Hawkridge Dixon embarked from Boston in 1921 with her friend Katherine Thaxter, bound to see the American West, to "follow the old trails, immigrant trails, cattle trails, traders' routes." Determined to prove that they could cope with the rigors of the journey without male companionship, they "mutually divided the labor as our tastes and talents dictated." Dixon claimed plenty of experience as a mechanic, declaring that "I love to tinker!" and proclaimed her friend Thaxter a wizard at tire changing: "The jack holds no mysteries for her, and tire rims click into place at the sound of her voice." Like their emigrant forerunners, faced with oozing mud and roadbed craters, Dixon and Thaxter sometimes relied on the good will of benevolent strangers. They had to ask a man with a mule team to extricate the car from sticky Texas gumbo, and were sometimes reduced to trying to attract aid by "fix[ing] smiles fairly dripping with saccharine on our faces." Yet they were less embarrassed at needing on occasion to ask for help than at the fact that wherever they went, men remarked that they were "a long way from home, ain't you?"[3]

Far from home as they were, these two self-described "ladies from Boston" fended for themselves to a remarkable degree. They gloried in fixing their ignition fifty miles from the nearest garage, and were thrilled when a Montana cowboy observed, "They ain't helpless." They clearly regarded their Western motoring adventure as a journey to personal liberation. As they approached the Rocky Mountains, Dixon observed, "for the first time in my life, I felt I had all the room I wanted." Navigating rugged mountain and desert roads strengthened her fingers and made her wrists "like iron." Confronting the rawness and vastness of the western landscape, they rejoiced at their newfound confidence and vision: "We had a sense of courage toward life new to us all." Returning home, they lamented leaving "the great, free West, 'where a man can be a man and a woman can be a woman.' "[4]

For many other American women, cross-country auto touring was less a personal quest than a family undertaking. Employing a fantastic array of camping equipment, from elaborate "homes on wheels" to pup tents and bedrolls mounted on running boards, "gasoline gypsies" by the thousands spent summer vacations on the road.[5] Motorists had enjoyed picnics and other outdoor entertainments since the beginning of the automobile era, but such outings became both more commonplace and more ambitious in the twenties, as western towns and cities welcomed tourists to municipal auto camps. Twenties tourists celebrated the democracy of the camp, a place where strangers mingled companionably, exchanging information on road conditions and scenic attractions, borrowing supplies, and helping one another with repairs.

For men, autocamping was a way to "get away from it all," to commune with nature and leave the workaday world behind. Women also enjoyed the chance to see the country, and to dress for comfort rather than fashion, but putting the family on wheels did not necessarily mean getting away from housework. Domestic routines, transferred to the road, could still be elaborate, and jobs that had been performed with familiar equipment in customary surroundings could become problems requiring extra energy and creativity. Buying food and keeping it from spoiling, doing laundry, and keeping passengers and gear clean and dry taxed women's ingenuity and their patience. Men might lend a hand with cooking, but other traditionally female tasks, from dishwashing to laundry to child care, remained women's work. As writer Mary Roberts Rinehart observed, "The difference between the men I have camped with and myself, generally speaking, has been this: they have called it sport; I have known it was work."[6]

If women found motor camping a form of fun well mixed with labor, surely not all automotive entertainments entailed drudgery. There was such a thing as joy riding, a fancy supposed to be particularly appealing to that most visible and boldest symbol of American womanhood in the 1920s, the flapper. Her appetite for self-display, for pretty objects, and for reckless fun made her seem a perfect customer for the "pleasure car."

To be sure, some social critics, contemplating the flapper, worried that the attractions and diversions of modern life would seduce young women away from home and duty. Dr. French Oliver of the Los Angeles Bible Institute referred to the auto, the movies, and the dance hall as a "triumvirate of hell" for American youth.[7] Like ragtime, jazz, and motion pictures, and the new public spaces associated with popular entertainments, the auto seemed to embody an attractive and dangerous modern "freedom in manners and morals" for those previously socially constrained.[8] The pleasures of motoring ranged, after all, from a few minutes away from mundane responsibilities, to a stolen kiss away from prying eyes, to the utter abandonment of family and reputation in the name of love or adventure. The seemingly innocent Sunday drive might erode a family's attendance at church; how much more threatening the spectre of Saturday night roadhouse escapades, far from community censure. Would motor-mad men throw over their jobs in wild pursuit of distance and velocity? Would women drive so far and fast that they would forget to come home? Would children appropriate the family car only to wreck it and the familial future?

No idea seemed more alarming or more irresistible to observers than the notion that, instruments of hedonism that they were, motorcars would make people more sexually demonstrative. From the earliest days of the car culture, automobiles had been expected to provide a new space for courtship and sex.[9] Magazine

covers, stories, jokes, and popular songs linked cars with romance, and experts ranging from sociologists to ministers offered
varied opinions of the auto's effect on Americans' sex lives.[10]

Some women doubtless took advantage of the motorcar as
a means to sexual ends. F. Scott Fitzgerald's picture of the flapper
as a girl who considered the automobile an ideal place to pet
had its basis in fact, and such activities were not limited to the
wellborn or the young or the unmarried. Magazine writer Eleanor
Wembridge reported:

> Every evening in the city, "gas hawks" or roving young men in
> automobiles, pick up the young girls as they come out from work,
> and "pet" them even in the streets. They have done it outside
> my window with an enthusiasm which even two large paper
> bags filled with water and hurled against their windshield by
> an interested spectator failed to cool.[11]

Some also viewed the motorcar as a threat to marital fidelity.
An aggrieved husband, suing for divorce, told a Los Angeles
judge that he had followed his wife and another man to a lonely
spot, then hidden in a ditch and watched as "his wife and the
man climbed into the back seat."[12]

Yet if sexually adventuresome women made use of the auto
for their own purposes, the Jazz Age was also the era of enforce-
ment of the Mann Act of 1910. That law, intended to combat
"white slavery," was designed to safeguard female purity by
prohibiting men from transporting women across state lines "for
immoral purposes."[13] Such protective legislation, predicated on
the notion of woman as passenger rather than pilot, at once
denied women the right to, and the responsibility for, control
over both sexuality and transportation technology, regardless
of women's own wishes or capacities.

Where women sought openly to seize sensual or mobile
pleasure, they risked placing themselves outside the protection
of public opinion, if not the law. Parents cautioned their daughters not to get in cars with boys, and the newspapers rushed to
point out the dire consequences when such warnings were ignored. In Los Angeles, some members of the California Congress

of Mothers and PTAs insisted that "school boys' and girls' promiscuous use of the auto is one of the greatest menaces of the age."[14] Girls who gave in to the temptation to take a joyride received little sympathy when things turned out badly.

There was, of course, truth in the notion that men in cars endangered women. Women who sought sexual pleasure risked loss of reputation and unwanted pregnancy, whereas men's participation in sex, if discovered, generally enhanced their peer standing. Getting into a car added a dimension to men's relative power in sexual encounters, since more men than women drove, more men than women owned cars, and even where both were qualified, men usually took the wheel. When, in 1920, Los Angeles police cracked down on "mashers" (men who made unwelcome sexual overtures to women), a member of the police "Purity Squad" commented, "We seem to have men in this town who have no sense of decency and will brazenly stop a woman anywhere on the streets."[15] Frightening on foot, such men became even scarier when they drove automobiles. The Los Angeles Record noted that "girls complained these men have lurked around with autos inviting them to 'come and have a good time,' " and that "parents of two little girls claim [an] old man has tried to lure little girls into his car with offers of chocolate."[16]

While in many areas the police made a concentrated effort to prevent male drivers from harming female pedestrians, sometimes even making arrests without asking women to testify against those accused, drivers' numbers grew faster than did police capacity to prevent abuses.[17] In Los Angeles, at New Year's 1919–1920, one Mary Gelso, described by the Los Angeles Record as "a beautiful girl living at the Continental Hotel," had felt "lonely last night and dressed up to go to a dance somewhere." Accosted by a "gentlemanly, very well-dressed stranger" in downtown L.A., she agreed to take a short ride down Broadway "to see the New Year crowd." Another man was at the wheel of the automobile. "Before she realized it," the Record reported, they were speeding to Vernon, a remote suburb. When they reached a lonely point on the road, the man who had originally engaged her in conversation sexually assaulted her and beat her severely, finally hurling her out of the car.

While the police declared their outrage at "this detestable mashing nuisance," and promised to arrest any man caught "ogling, or winking, or [making] obscene remarks," the inclusion of details about the victim in the story cast doubt on her character, depicting Gelso as a loose woman who only got what she deserved.[18] Mary Gelso's ordeal, and the implicit criticism of her behavior, offered a typical moral lesson to young American women of the 1920s. Hedonistic flappers might find temporary pleasures, but danger lurked too. The wise girl would temper her behavior in the interest of personal safety, and discard wild ways upon assuming the responsibilities of marriage. The motorcar could provide young women with almost unlimited potential for entertainment, but America's daughters knew they went joyriding at their own risk.

Presented thus with the manifold fascinations and hazards of motoring, American women were urged to accept a compromise. If they had to forsake the fiery delights of youthful adventure for the soberer satisfactions of adult womanhood, the auto, they learned, might enable them to salvage some fun, to claim pleasure as well as security, mobility as well as domesticity. Few contemporary observers doubted that household pursuits would (and should) define women's days and identities.[19] Ideas such as female responsibility for domestic activities (including child rearing, cooking, housekeeping, and managing consumption) so pervaded American thinking that they remained powerful in the face of even so potent a technological force as the automobile. These vital concepts would shape women's car travel, distorting and widening woman's sphere without exploding it.[20]

Auto manufacturers, advertising in such publications as *The Ladies' Home Journal* and *Good Housekeeping*, depicted the motorcar as the key to reconciling women's household business and personal pleasure.[21] The ads featured smiling groups of well-dressed women enjoying each other's company in Cadillacs and Chevrolets and Overland Sixes, and frequently set the dry comfort of the closed car against a backdrop of rainy weather outside. Ford Motor Company, in its first ever large-scale advertising campaign, promised readers of *The Ladies' Home Journal* that a Ford would be "An 'Open Door' to Wider Contacts," asserting that "By owning a Ford car a woman can with ease widen her sphere of interests without extra time or effort. She can accomplish more daily, yet easily keep pace with her usual schedule of domestic pursuits."[22] Ford ads showed women in a variety of situations—vacationing, going shopping, visiting, and even conducting business—but always emphasized the social aspect of the product. No woman need feel lonesome, Ford implied, because "the car is so easy to drive that it constantly suggests thoughtful services to her friends. She can call for them without effort and share pleasantly their companionship."[23]

Auto advertisements that made driving appear perfectly effortless and enjoyable claimed far more for their products than they could deliver. Cars were not always reliable; road conditions left much to be desired; the noise, congestion, and dirt of traffic was on the rise in many places. Yet for at least one group of women, the motorcar offered the noteworthy benefit of diminished social isolation. Rural Americans of the 1920s, experiencing the enormity of the American landscape to a far greater degree than their urban compatriots, regarded the automobile as a solution to the problem of distance from community life.[24]

In 1919, U.S. Department of Agriculture home demonstration agents conducted a survey of over 10,000 women in rural homes to determine farm women's attitudes toward their situation. The survey suggested that "the farm woman feels her isolation from neighbors as well as from libraries and other means of keeping in touch with outside life." Given an average distance from the farm of 5.9 miles to the nearest high school, 2.9 miles to the nearest church, and 4.8 miles to the nearest market,

> country people are far enough from the centers of trade, social, and religious activities to tempt the spirit of individualism and to put their neighborliness and piety to the test. . . . The automobile contributes materially to community life by reducing the distance factor.[25]

Not surprisingly, farm families had taken to the motorcar with relish. Sixty-two percent of farms in the USDA study reported owning cars, with the highest percentage in the Midwest

(seventy-three percent), next highest in the West (sixty-two percent), and lowest in the East (forty-eight percent).[26] An article
in the *Rural New Yorker* based on 1920 Commerce Department
records indicated that more than 166,000 farms (or eight percent
of all farms in the country) might have had more than one car.[27]

Even those who lived on carless farms felt the influence
of the automobile when they received visits from home demonstration agents. By 1914, after the passage of the Smith-Lever
Act providing for federal support of farm extension programs,
such agents, chiefly women educated in college home economics
programs, criss-crossed the country.[28] If climate, ethnic traditions
and antagonisms, rural poverty and communication problems
limited their effectiveness, the automobile made their work
possible.[29] In Colorado, for example, according to a 1920 article
in *Popular Mechanics,* a home demonstration team did some
150 canning demonstrations in one year, traveling a thousand
miles in a specially equipped vehicle which served both as home
and mobile kitchen.[30]

Most extension agents employed more modest motor vehicles in their efforts to bring domestic science to the provinces.
Agent Florence Carvin wrote an enthusiastic description of her
four years' experience in the field. Extolling the freedom of the
home demonstration agent's mobile vocation—"She is not bound
by bells, hours, and four walls . . . she has the whole countryside
for her classroom"—she saw automobility as the key to personal
fulfillment. "Why should I like to leave a country like this one?"
she asked. "I am 8 miles from a city of three hundred thousand,
where I can hear and see the best things that come to the middle
west. . . . I have 500 miles of hard surface road over which to
drive my Ford, and above all, I am beginning to know my people
and they to believe in me."[31]

To be sure, not all rural housewives welcomed the extension
agent. And even if they were glad of the company, some doubted
the agents' claims that their programs would make housework
easier and more efficient. Extension agents' domestic techniques
were not necessarily less arduous or more productive than those
they sought to supplant, and in any case, many farm wives could
not afford the equipment necessary to carry out demonstration

programs.[32] Carvin admitted that farm women were likely to
start out resisting the extension agent's ideas about how to increase domestic efficiency and enhance family life, but insisted
that the competent home demonstration agent quickly learned
what rural housewives wanted and needed. For the farm woman,
Carvin believed, the skillful agent was "a friend, a neighbor,
an advisor, a playmate. She is 'A little bit of heaven come down
to earth in a Tin Lizzie.' "[33]

If they brought more visitors to the farmstead, automobiles
also enabled rural women to participate in town life much more
frequently than they had in the days of horse and foot transportation, to more easily combine household duties with sociability.
They used cars to attend meetings, visit friends, shop for items
formerly produced at home, and generally to relieve the monot-
ony of the household routine. One farm woman expressed her
preference for the auto over other modern conveniences quite
simply, telling an interviewer, "You can't go to town in a
bathtub."[34] Many rural housewives expressed great satisfaction
in attending homemakers' extension clubs, organizations intended not only to introduce them to new consumer goods and
techniques, but also to enhance both social life and domesticity.
A Montana woman told an oral history interviewer, "We looked
forward to the meetings—the information they gave there, and
the sociability that was involved. It was really the social life of
the community."[35] Getting there might nevertheless require both
creativity and cooperation. Just having a car did not guarantee
the access to the consumer goods and social resources which
farm women saw as the chief benefit of automobility. Mechanical
difficulties, lack of driving ability or experience, and wretched
roads sometimes barred the door to wider contacts.

Country women devised ingenious solutions to their transportation problems.[36] Posey County, Indiana farm woman Vernell
Saltzman recalled a meeting at which extension agents taught
club members how to preserve food by the coldpacking method:

> I drove a horse and buggy halfway, and I met up with Carlena
> Cowan Ramsey. She had a car. I could drive a car straight forward,
> but I could not back one. So I picked her up and Lena Thompson

Holler up and Lena had one of those newfangled coldpackers, and I drove the car up to Farmersville School, and we worked all day canning.

When we got ready to go home, Carlena couldn't drive that car straight, but she could back it, so she backs it up, and we loaded Lena in with her precious coldpacker, and I drove the car home, and got my horse and buggy and come on home.[37]

Vernell Saltzman's anecdote reveals not only that farm wives sometimes used technology with remarkable imagination, but also that country women, in any case, did not necessarily regard domesticity and sociability as contradictory, even when the two endeavors were spatially segregated.

Paradoxically, the notion that women needed to stay at home to meet the demands of domestic work persisted as a cultural fiction. A 1916 article in *Motor Age* accused rural women of gadding about in autos and neglecting their laying hens.[38] Woman's place, if still defined by domesticity, was less than ever strictly confined to the household, but not everyone was happy about the fact. As housewives used the auto to change the way they made use of time and space, they inadvertently fueled long-standing confusion about whether American women were doing their familial duty.

As deeply as Americans believed in women's domestic mission, they had a hard time visualizing what women did in the home as real work. The homemaker's vocation had changed radically since preindustrial times. Where housewives had once had to make much of what their families used, occupying themselves with spinning and weaving and sewing, butchering and rendering and cooking, their modern counterparts could go to a department store and buy ready-to-wear clothes, then stop off at a grocery and purchase whatever they needed for the evening's meal. Social scientists of the time referred to this change as the departure of "economic functions" from the home, and they tended to cast a disapproving eye on the modern homemaker, celebrating earlier commodity production as "real" work and at least implicitly denigrating the contemporary woman's activities as profligate idleness.[39]

Certainly the modern middle-class housewife produced fewer commodities than had her preindustrial predecessor. Instead, she invested her energies and time in emotionally intense child rearing and husband nurturing, in purchasing the things her family needed, and in providing the services that made goods usable and family members productive—cooking complicated meals, keeping up with rising standards of cleanliness for household and clothing.[40] Such changes in the domestic vocation reflected a wider transition in the United States, from a country grown wealthy by producing commodities, to a nation investing more and more of its resources in providing services. They also meant that domestic work tended more and more to be self-erasing. Shopping, cooking, cleaning, accommodating husbands, and cuddling and disciplining children could be emotionally and physically taxing, but those activities were seldom considered as labor, especially since the most successful practitioners were those who called least attention to their efforts. Groceries purchased were consumed. The process of shopping, cooking, and washing dishes was designed to create an impression that no meal had ever been served. Cleaning meant eradicating messes before anyone perceived disorder. The job of delivering children to school and husbands to commuter trains reversed itself when housewives returned to pick up family members and bring them home. The woman who worked hardest, who succeeded most brilliantly in creating a relaxing "haven in a heartless world," labored mightily to obscure her own exertions.[41] No wonder she could be accused of indulging herself with bonbons and trashy novels while others toiled. In a cultural climate where women's domestic work achieved fruition only when it reached the vanishing point, the distinction between labor and leisure was far from obvious.

The job of driving embodied the difficulty of distinguishing between women's work and play. As American cities grew, and millions of families bought automobiles, women found themselves increasingly responsible for producing transportation. By the middle of the twentieth century, as historian Ruth Schwartz Cowan noted, "the time that housewives had once spent in preserving strawberries and stitching petticoats was being spent

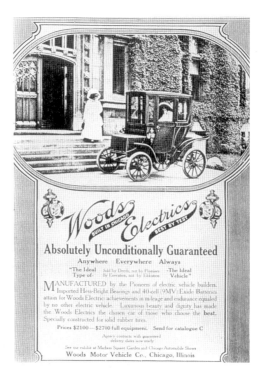

From the beginning of the motor age, some automakers geared their products to appeal to a feminine clientele, by emphasizing "beauty and dignity" for those women who could afford the luxury of automobility. *(Courtesy Motor magazine)*

Another well-off consumer demonstrates that women with children could especially benefit from the new technology. Rather than threatening the maternal role, motoring could enhance a mother's time with her child. *(Courtesy Arizona Historical Society Library)*

At the beginning of the automobile era, women traveling long distances had to be hardy enough to cope with calamity. These early motorists discovered that bad roads, unpredictable weather, and cantankerous vehicles often meant long walks and long waits. *(Courtesy Arizona Historical Society Library)*

Group motor tours not only provided a new leisure pastime, but also increased the safety and reliability of motoring, making it more appealing and accessible for women. Here, a tour group visits San Javier Mission in Arizona. *(Courtesy Arizona Historical Society Library)*

WOMEN WON'T WORRY

Women won't worry if their cars are equipped with Auto-Lite starting motors and lighting generators. They are an open-sesame which removes the last obstacles from the pleasant and successful operation of gasoline motor cars by women — eliminating muscular effort and placing completely within their control the most powerful machines.

The Auto-Lite Starting Motor will turn on ...

Many pre–World War I auto ads were pitched to women. This one emphasizes the cleanliness and ease of the electric starter and automatic generator. Although such devices were marketed to women, they assuredly proved convenient for men as well. *(Courtesy Motor magazine)*

Alice Ramsey, second from left, defied the stereotype of the fastidious and timid female driver by being the first woman to drive across America. "The journey demanded a steady crew," she wrote later, "and no invalids were invited." *(From the collections of Henry Ford Museum and Greenfield Village)*

For those with financial means, ethnicity was no barrier to enjoying the automobile. Here, three Mexican-American women pose in their elegant touring car. *(Courtesy Arizona Historical Society Library)*

Women used their "wheels" to expand their geographical horizons and seek social emancipation. These women, photographed in New Jersey, are participants in an all-woman automobile race from New York to Philadelphia and back, in 1909. *(From the collections of Henry Ford Museum and Greenfield Village)*

The Ford Model T, first sold in 1908, made the automobile available to middle- and working-class families. Though it was marketed as "Everyman's car," ordinary women like this one, shown parked in her neighborhood, also took to the Tin Lizzie. *(Courtesy Arizona Historical Society Library)*

Some women combined automobility with political concerns. Here, three NAWSA suffrage activists on a cross-country tour arrive in Berkeley, California, in 1916. *(Courtesy the Bancroft Library)*

At a Preparedness Day parade in 1916, these women transformed their car into an emblem of patriotism. The nurses in the back seat are poised to lend aid to American soldiers should the United States enter the war in Europe. *(Courtesy Arizona Historical Society Library)*

Women enthusiastically answered the call for ambulance drivers during World War I. During the course of the war, they would provide vital transportation for the armed forces overseas and on the homefront. *(From the collections of Henry Ford Museum and Greenfield Village)*

In prosperous postwar America, women were now comfortable and experienced drivers who increasingly used the auto for leisure activities. These women combined an acorn hunt with a motoring picnic in 1927. *(Courtesy Arizona Historical Society Library)*

The freedom of movement enjoyed by the flapper in her shiny convertible became the symbol of a corresponding new freedom in manners and morals in the 1920s. *(Courtesy Arizona Historical Society Library)*

Even as women have taken the wheel in an effort to widen the range of their activities, they are often still considered automotive accessories rather than independent pilots. This 1948 photo emphasizes woman's role as hood ornament. (*Courtesy Arizona Historical Society Library*)

For all American women, the auto has made its most indelible mark as a means of family transportation. Though women drivers have sometimes used the auto as a vehicle for personal empowerment, they have more often taken the wheel in service to their families. Indeed, Americans' vision of the good life has come to depend on women's role as producers of family transportation. (*H. Armstrong Roberts*)

in driving to stores, shopping, and waiting in lines. The automobile had become . . . the vehicle through which she did her most significant work."[42] Homemaking included the responsibility for negotiating the temporal, spatial, and emotional conflicts and distances between private and public life. Being a successful wife and mother meant not only attending to one's family, but connecting the household with the community.[43]

Given the division of labor between most adult female workers (who stayed at home and did not earn money) and most male workers (who left the household in order to secure paychecks), it seemed reasonable that women and men might use cars for different purposes—men generally to travel to work, women generally to shop and chauffeur other family members—though both would use the car for family outings and personal leisure.[44] The automobile, particularly the closed car, would prove to be a useful tool for homemakers, but it would not render driving visible as work. The privacy of the family car would have been notably appropriate for that 21.3 percent of the American population described in the census of 1930 as "housewives not gainfully occupied," women whose very vocation implied private solutions to social problems, but it would seclude and obscure their activities.[45] Moreover, the cultural legacy of the years when the motorcar had been designed and priced for leisure meant that even when activities like cooking and cleaning were recognized as labor, shopping or taking the children for a drive were treated as entertainment. In 1917, a husband blithely told a *Ladies' Home Journal* writer, "My wife tucked away in the car the two children every dry day last summer and scooted here and there all over the country around us."[46] Columnist Mildred Maddocks Bentley, in an article titled "The Housekeeper and Her Car," urged women, "Away, away from the kitchen stove/ And drive the car to the picnic grove."[47] Advertisers also often contrasted automobility and leisure with domesticity and work. A Westinghouse electric range ad in the October, 1920 issue of *Sunset* depicted two smiling women out for a drive, one apparently declaring, "I go anytime—I've an *Automatic Cook*." Below, the company asked, "Wouldn't *you* rather be motoring . . . or doing any one of a hundred things than standing over a hot stove in a hot kitchen?" The American Laundry Machinery Company promoted public laundries in a 1926 *Ladies' Home Journal* spread with the assertion that sending the family laundry out would "lead to motor trips and matinees, to golf links and club meetings—to all the things that keep a woman young." This advertisement featured a testimonial from a Corvallis, Oregon housewife who declared, "Since I have been sending my washing to the laundry, I am better able to do other household duties, look after my family, and get out in the car during the late afternoon hours to enjoy our beautiful Oregon scenery, or to visit with my friends."[48]

Such statements contributed to the mystification of middle-class women's work. No matter how much women enjoyed the company of their offspring, the combination of children and automobiles contributed to the increased time and effort devoted to shopping and driving.[49] A New York woman wrote the *Woman's Home Companion* describing a money-making scheme in which she offered to chauffeur "tired out mothers with small children" on country picnics," portraying the outings as "a day of loafing for the parents."[50] At the same time, she advised her customers to "get a big lunch ready," and mentioned the fact that once the right spot was found, "out go the blankets, cushions, and lunch baskets," all of which the housewife would have to clear up, wash, and put away upon returning home. In offering advice on what to pack when taking the children for a motor outing, Mildred Bentley unwittingly provided a glimpse of the work involved in pursuing leisure. She suggested that housewives prepare sandwiches and pack drinks in thermos bottles, "since children do not take kindly to a strange water or a strange milk," taking along "plenty" of white enameled dishes and cups and silverware, all in carefully labeled customized containers. She also outlined the new disciplinary strategies mothers would have to learn in order to teach their children to "ride acceptably":

> At the first sign of restless moving or noise, draw to the side of the road and stop. Turn around and assure the small offenders that the car will not start again until they are all quiet. . . . It takes but a few similar stops before they develop good riding manners, provided the discipline is begun early enough.[51]

Bentley went on to note the perils of leaving children in a parked car while mothers went about their business. "It is a nuisance, I know, to let the children out at every stop, but actually it is the only safe procedure." The danger that curious children might play at driving, injuring themselves or damaging the car, was compounded by the possibility of other drivers' carelessness. Bentley explained that she had herself returned from shopping one morning to find that a truck had bashed in the back end of her car, and pointed out that "any child if left in the car would have been badly frightened, if not thrown about and bruised."[52] Insuring child safety was unquestionably part of a mother's job, but most Americans would have classed such activity as caretaking rather than employment.

Conventional language helped to obscure women's work as family chauffeurs. A Los Angeles auto dealer advertised a National coupe as "the ideal woman's car," referring to a seating arrangement designed for child safety and compartments to store large and small parcels as "conveniences" for mothers and shoppers, rather than as engineering innovations designed to make the tasks of mothering and purchasing more efficient. We might describe an object or plan intended to minimize waste of time and energy as either "convenient" or "efficient," but these terms came to have gendered meanings as the sites of domestic life and paid labor diverged. Outside the home, in increasingly centralized and specialized workplaces, the advocates of scientific management had begun to refine the process of translating time and motion into money.[53] Although professional promoters of domestic science sought to apply the principles of economics and engineering to the home, most Americans tended increasingly to define work as activity performed for cash remuneration. Since "efficiency" was presumed to promote money-saving by improving wage workers' productivity, that which was seen as efficient was regarded as worth promoting. The housewife's activities, not compensated in cash, were often considered valueless. Whatever saved her time and energy was trivialized as optional and somehow frivolous "convenience," rather than celebrated as "efficiency."[54]

Such assumptions concealed female drivers' exertions, but women would still play a role in reshaping the American landscape. Automobiles enabled people to forge new ways of using time and occupying space; cars also reshaped the city and the countryside, and altered the politics of everyday experience.[55] This multifaceted social transformation served ideological goals, the overt as well as the hidden. As more and more people moved from country to metropolis, urban Americans expressed their hope for some middle ground, some compromise between the isolation of the rural world and the dirty clamor of the city. That middle ground, sought after by consumers in search of household refuges, and provided by real estate developers in search of profits, was suburbia.[56] To be sure, the new suburbs of the 1920s lay beyond the reach of millions of Americans, including African-Americans and other people restricted by income, harassment, and legal segregation to rural poverty and urban ghettos. Yet even among those hardest pressed, the suburban ideal beckoned. Many poor people still assumed that single-family dwellings in the suburban environment combined the best features of city and country, and hoped to own a car to help them achieve the American dream.[57] In the utopian vision of the suburban Good Life, home-owning families, residing in detached houses surrounded by verdant lawns, could remain sequestered from the frustrating, competitive, messy domains of commerce and industry, while still having access to the income that connection with the city would bring. While the automobile did not create suburbia, it would provide a flexible means to bridge the space between residential neighborhoods and business districts.

The notion of the Good Life encompassed presumptions about gender as well as geography. It linked an idea of the proper roles of women and men with the separation of leisure and work, of domesticity from commercial life.[58] Yet such distinctions, tenuous to begin with, were not always easy to maintain, particularly as American women took the wheel. If a man's home was his castle and sanctuary, it was a woman's workplace too. Even as it brought new entertainments within their compass, the automobile extended the realm of women's labor. Indeed, domestic work would come to require car travel, and more and more of women's time would be spent driving to or around town.[59] Non-rural homemakers found themselves even more likely than rural housewives to spend time in the car. A United States Bureau of Home Economics Study found that housewives in urban areas spent an average of fifty-six hours and thirty-nine minutes per week doing their work, while their counterparts in farm households averaged fifty-three hours and fifty minutes each week performing domestic work. The home economists who conducted the study, unlike most commentators of the day, counted women's driving time as work time. Nonrural women reported spending about thirteen percent of their housework time in driving, or about seven and one-half hours per week, while driving accounted for about seven percent of farm women's work time, or about three and three-quarters hours each week.[60] These numbers suggest that automobility, like other twentieth-century innovations, did not make housewives' jobs less time-consuming, since according to these figures, the greater amount of time city women spent driving accounted for their spending more time than farm women did in activities denoted as work.[61]

No city better embodied the emerging metropolitan car culture of the 1920s than Los Angeles. Though observers from the East dismissed Los Angeles as "not a city," or as a "Midwestern town," this great, diffuse urban agglomeration, indeed something novel under the sun, would prove to be the prototype for twentieth-century American cities.[62] In new cities like Los Angeles, emigrants tended for a time to be relatively affluent and native-born, rather than poor and foreign-born, and suburbanization often meant that people moved from the country and from towns and small cities to the suburbs, rather than from the city's center to its periphery.[63] Such individuals peopled the growing suburbs in search of what Elaine Tyler May has called "a middle ground between tradition and experimentation . . . provid[ing] urban advantages without urban problems . . . and high-level consumption in an egalitarian environment."[64] Real estate advertising in the *Los Angeles Times* typically made a personal appeal to the individual whose view of the Good Life incorporated the amenities of the farm and the city:

> Confess that you don't like the crowded Los Angeles street cars, the muddy crossings, the gas bills, the telephone service, the noise, the smoke, and 'shut-in' feeling. . . .

You DO like Los Angeles for its life, its theaters, its cafes, its business opportunities.

Then why not move your home to Monrovia, where you are within comfortable distance of your office and the city's attractions—right in touch with the city's life and yet removed from the objectionable features. Come to the City Beautiful, Monrovia, a city designed for homes, not for commerce.[65]

Of course, even in the 1920s, a time of rising real incomes, the affluence necessary to afford suburbia eluded many; in 1929, some forty-two percent of American families (twelve million out of twenty-seven million) had annual incomes under $1,500, putting them below what the government considered the "comfort minimum."[66] Assuredly, Los Angeles was plagued by widespread racism toward Mexican and Asian immigrants, and many people who came to find stardom in Hollywood ended up parking cars or waiting tables. Yet the power of consumerism in the United States has rested in part on widespread faith in upward mobility. Americans like to act as if their dreams will come true. At least on a material level, Los Angeles in the twenties was a place where people realized their aspirations to a remarkable degree.[67] Not only did the city feature the nation's highest per capita incidence of home ownership, but it also claimed the highest number of automobiles per capita of any city in the nation—some 65,000 in Los Angeles proper, and 110,000 in the city and county combined, or about one for every five inhabitants.[68] Author Kathleen Norris held that California's benign climate made motoring "an adventure in optimism," observing that "wherever you go you pass loaded automobiles bearing ecstatic children and beaming mothers to some sort of merrymaking. . . . the dear little dusty, shabby cars that we have come to love, because each one stands for so much happiness."[69]

According to historian Scott Bottles, "southern California residents quickly accepted the automobile because they saw it as a democratic and progressive alternative to the seeming corruption and inadequacies of the area's electric traction companies."[70] Without doubt, a host of technological, economic, ideological, and geographical factors, including the capture and diversion of rivers and groundwater, the spread of the telephone, real estate prices, the preference for detached single-family dwellings, and the availability of suburban land suitable for development, contributed to the emergence of the decentralized metropolis. But if not quite as omnipotent as has often been thought, the private automobile certainly contributed to the process of decentralization, and it could not have triumphed over other forms of urban transportation had not drivers sometimes acted as a group. In the following intriguing case, Los Angeles area women drivers, confronting the problems of parking and worsening city traffic, made themselves remarkably visible and demonstrated the worth of their consumption work. Using their cars for shopping, they became a crucial factor in establishing both Mrs. Consumer's and the automobile's right to occupy the very heart of the city, or transplant that heart to a more convenient location.

In 1920, the city of Los Angeles faced up to the fact that its downtown business district had become so congested that traffic generally moved at an excruciating crawl, if at all. Streetcars bursting with passengers backed up for blocks while pedestrians, accustomed to the "walking city," crossed the tracks wherever and whenever they pleased.[71] Automobile parking was similarly chaotic; double parking was common.

After considering a variety of alternatives, the Los Angeles City Council decided that since some ninety percent of those who entered the downtown area did so by streetcar, the best solution to overcrowding on the streets was to ban private automobile parking downtown.[72] Between the hours of 11:00 A.M. and 6:15 P.M., passenger cars would only be allowed to stop for two minutes to load and unload. A section restricting delivery vehicles to fifteen-minute stops until 4:00 P.M. and no stops at all between 4:00 and 6:15 P.M. was eliminated from the ordinance before it went into effect, to placate the Linen Supply Men's Association. That group, angered at not being able to deliver clean linen to hotels at the end of the day, collected enough signatures on petitions to force a referendum on the ban.[73] Thus the no parking law that went into effect on April 10, 1920 restricted only those who wanted to park private vehicles in the downtown commercial district.[74]

As the traction railway companies pointed out and the City Council acknowledged, the vast majority of people who went into downtown Los Angeles traveled by streetcar, many working-class and affluent women consumers among the riders. People went downtown not only to work, but to do their banking, to shop at major grocery stores, and to patronize department stores like Bullock's, Hamburger's, Jacoby Brothers, the Broadway, and the Emporium Cloak and Suit House. The City Council and the California State Railroad Commission, which backed the ban, had assumed that most women would support regulating the auto in order to accommodate the street cars, and the Council and the Commission tried to enlist the support of local women's groups.[75]

But discontent with street railway service was longstanding, bitter, and widespread. In January and February of 1920, the *Los Angeles Record*, a working-class newspaper, reported almost daily on scandalous streetcar conditions. Passengers complained that the cars made too few runs, consistently ran late, and always seemed to be packed to the point of suffocation. Moreover, the street railway companies had responded to a 1919 strike for higher wages by motormen and conductors by bringing in poorly trained strikebreaking workers, seen by many riders as dangerous incompetents who "often endanger the lives of passengers, particularly elderly women."[76] The *Record* suggested that pickpockets plagued riders, and that the conductors were no better than thugs and criminals, reporting that passengers had been thrown off moving streetcars, beaten by conductors, and on one occasion even stabbed by the motorman. One woman who angrily recalled being "deliberately pitched off the car" by a motorman who was in a bad mood broke her arm, lost her purse, and claimed to have been "handicapped for the rest of my life through the viciousness and cruelty of a heartless corporation."[77]

Passengers who avoided assault still had to put up with overcrowding. The *Record* frequently invoked the image of men, women, and children "jammed indiscriminately together with elbows sticking in one another's ribs." A woman rider told a reporter, "I have grown ten years older waiting at corners for cars that do not come, being indecently jammed into other people."[78] Some passengers worried about health risks. A woman wrote the *Record* that on one occasion she had "felt suffocated and almost fainting. I felt somebody breathe right in my face and could not move away. The next day I had a bad sore throat, the result of the over-heated condition when we were packed so close."[79] A 1920 visitor to Los Angeles asked:

> What is the matter with the Los Angeles street car service? Monday evening when I was a passenger on a South Pasadena car a little girl made us all miserable crying at the loss of her coat, which had been dragged out of the car by a woman passenger when leaving the car, the jam being so great that she came near tearing everybody's clothes off their backs in her exit. The little girl . . . had hard work to keep from being crushed to death and in the excitement did not know that her coat was gone until other passengers called attention to the fact that the woman was standing at the corner vainly waving the garment after the receding car.[80]

Frequent delays, economically threatening to male workers who risked their jobs if they were late, could be doubly dangerous for women who stood alone in some neighborhoods. One woman reported waiting twenty minutes for a streetcar on a notorious corner. When the car eventually came, it passed her by, with the motorman blowing his whistle for her to get out of the way. "I was all alone in a district like that," she wrote to the *Record*, "and he had no more sense of decency than to go right on. I had to wait another twenty minutes for a car."[81] Women who managed to catch the streetcar were also subjected to sexual advances, sometimes welcome, sometimes not. The *Record*'s sports page featured a cartoon called "The Boys in the Other Car," depicting men's rowdy enjoyments on commuter trains, including "flirting with a doll in the rear coach."[82]

Because of crowding, the streetcars offered a setting for a struggle between men and women for scarce space that was often treated as a conflict between workers and ladies of leisure. In response to a resolution by the Women's Christian Temperance Union to ban smoking on the streetcars, a male passenger wrote the *Record*, "Why not have the ladies pass a resolution or two agreeing that all ladies keep out of the space allotted to smokers and there will be no need for smokers to smoke in other parts of the car. [Men] like this one little boon on their way home after a day of real work."[83]

There were, of course, many women who worked for pay, just as there were men who shopped. As a type, however, the popular press depicted the shopper as female. One woman consumer, a Mrs. Haun, took issue with the idea that only male wage-earners performed "real work." Following the *Record's* publication of a letter from a man who advised women shoppers to get off the streetcar and "give way to the tired laborers," she unleashed a tirade rare in its detailed description of women's time. Observing that "no doubt this man has never shopped or he would realize shopping is no recreation," she continued:

> The woman is jostled in the crowds, pushed from one counter to another, oftentimes having to stand from 10 to 15 minutes waiting for the services of a clerk.
>
> When her shopping is done she stands on the crowded corners with her arms full of packages, waiting for a street car, and then usually stands all the way home.
>
> Women cannot always leave their homes and do the shopping when they would choose to do so. There is often washing and an ironing to be done, a house to clean, dinner to get for hungry children, and then dishes to clear away and many other things you men never seem to consider.[84]

The writer concluded with a blast at men's unwillingness to help make dinner or clean up afterward, instead sitting and smoking and letting "little wifie, who hasn't done a thing all day, clean the kitchen. Wake up, Mr. Man, this is America, not Russia."[85]

Given domestic duties and crammed streetcars, any woman who had access to a private automobile might understandably have preferred her own vehicle over riding the street railway to get to the shopping district, particularly if she were going to take children along. For women who planned to shop with friends, private autos provided an environment for sociability far more pleasant than overcrowded streetcars. Many women shoppers by this time lived in suburban areas remote from streetcar service, and others, doubtless, simply preferred the auto's flexibility to the railway's scheduled journeys and fixed routes.[86]

Though the 1920 parking ban was not explicitly directed against them, women who used their cars to shop were strongly affected by the ordinance. Local evidence suggests a deep ambivalence toward the presence of such women in the center of public commercial life. The writer of one letter to the *Los Angeles Times* complained that the chief problem with allowing motor vehicles in the "congested" area was the practice of double-parking. "The worst offenders," this writer said, "are delivery vehicles and women shoppers who have chauffeurs to attend the car."[87] The ordinance prohibited only the latter abuse. On the one hand, the *Times* campaigned against the ban, branding it "a retrogressive jump and a vital blow at the business life of the city" and insisting that "motor cars have come to occupy the highest position of usefulness in every-day business life." Eager to promote the virtues of Los Angeles, the newspaper also praised the supposedly happy bustle of the downtown streets, painting a rosy picture of "the shopping crowds. Women, young and beautiful, women with the gait of health and joy."[88] On the other hand, despite the number of downtown businesses that relied on women customers, humorous squibs in the *Times* ridiculed the naivete, corruptibility, and vanity of women who went downtown. One piece bore the title "Problems in Parking," saying:

> The problem in parking is one that bobs up in some form almost every day. If a man parks his wife in a downtown tea room, he is liable to find her smoking perfumed cigarettes and talking Yogi stuff with a copper-colored Mahatma.[89]

A letter signed "H. FORDE" poked fun at women motorists, allowing that

> as regards parking, lately Henrietta and I notice other women as well, like to sit in their cars on the sunny side of the street and do their knitting or embroidery work. It gives them the feeling of being in the midst of things. They are where the busy wheels of industry are whirring. They are away from the hum-drum things of life, such as sweeping the parlor or washing the dishes. And most important of all, they are where they can be seen.[90]

Women were also presumed to be irresponsible about managing their time. A joke in the automotive and sports section featured a citizen asking a policeman, "Would you mind compelling me to move on, officer? I've been waiting on this corner three hours for my wife."[91]

These examples of newspaper humor suggest that Mrs. Consumer, and Mrs. Motorist, seemed somehow incongruous and fatuous presences in the hub of commercial activity. Yet however much women enjoyed shopping (a point difficult to estimate), they could take pleasure in consumption and still be working. Buying things for themselves and their families was part of their job. Finding a parking space and walking to and from stores required time and effort, particularly when there were packages to carry and children to herd. There was reason to believe that women consumers hated to waste time. As the Los Angeles City Council pondered what to do about traffic congestion, a Mrs. Lee Freese of Pasadena wrote to the *Times* suggesting that elevated sidewalks might improve conditions downtown, since "most of the large dry goods houses now have all their yardage goods, ready-to-wear clothing and other departments on the second and third floors. And in order to reach these departments a full block has to be wasted in walking from the store entrance back to the elevator and then forward again, usually to the front of the building—not mentioning the time spent at the elevator."[92]

Still, women's desire for time- and energy-saving measures including proximate parking, like the use of the auto itself, was often treated as a form of laziness.[93] When the no parking ordinance went into effect, the *Record* ran the headline, "NO PARKING Law Plays Havoc With Leisure-Loving Habits of Milady Autoist; Learning to Walk."[94] In a later edition of the *Record*, a cartoon featured a confrontation between a woman shopper who claimed she had only been in a store ten minutes and a policeman who maintained her car had been parked for two hours. The caption read, "Time means nothing to most women shoppers."[95]

Businesses in the area covered by the parking ban soon discovered how much they depended on women who used automobiles to go shopping. By the second day the ordinance was in force, the *Los Angeles Examiner* remarked that "Broadway yesterday afternoon looked like Hickville at midnight. . . . The motorists, many of them, didn't come downtown at all, because they didn't want to park a car at Fifteenth Street and Western Avenue in order to buy a ham at a downtown grocery."[96] An advertising manager for Jacoby Brothers, a store in the area covered by the ban, reported that business was down fifteen percent by the third day of parking prohibition, explaining, "I believe there are many more women who use automobiles for shopping in Los Angeles than any other place in the country."[97] By April 18, L. R. Davis of the Emporium Cloak and Suit House was quoted as saying that downtown business was down forty percent.[98] Stores just outside the area of the ban reported increased business, while those within the area announced steep declines in trade, except in the hours before the ban took effect.[99] The fact that downtown businesses reported *increased* patronage in the morning, during the hours before parking was prohibited, suggests that housewife-shoppers were primarily responsible for changes in business activity downtown as a result of the ban, since most of those who worked for pay would presumably not have been able to change their schedules to accommodate the parking ban.[100]

More than anything else, downtown Los Angeles merchants feared competition from retailers in other parts of the metropolitan area. In a January 1, 1920 letter to the *Times*, one writer had predicted what passage of a no parking law for the downtown "congested area" would mean:

> Our law makers will have to pass an ordinance prohibiting auto users from shopping anywhere in Los Angeles, for no sane person could expect one who has become accustomed to the comfort and convenience of going to his business or doing her shopping in an auto to revert to the ancient horrors of street-car inconveniences.[101]

Stores outside the area to be covered by the restrictions took advantage of the ban, and began to feature access to parking in their advertisements. One establishment promoted a January clearance sale with the claim, "This Great Store Is Very Easy to Reach. . . . If you drive your car, you can park on Grand Avenue south of Seventh Street indefinitely."[102] By the time the ordinance went into effect, the Times was predicting that shoppers would avoid not only the part of downtown actually off limits to parking, but the entire central commercial district. An April 11 cartoon about the parking ban depicted a mass flight to the suburbs. In the next day's edition of the paper, the Pasadena Furniture Company asked, "Why Not Come Here for Your Home Furnishings? . . . No matter where you live, we can give you good service—your auto places the splendid facilities of our big organization at your command. Home makers from all over Southern California come here."[103]

Downtown merchants were demanding the law's repeal or amendment within days of its going into effect. William Chamberlain of Hamburger's, a department store in the affected district, insisted, "What we need . . . is to keep the street hog off our streets. If we allow forty-five minutes it will give the women time enough to do their shopping, and accommodate all except those who want to use our streets as garages." Merchants voiced a reasonable concern that women drivers, denied convenient auto access to businesses already remote from their homes, might simply shop elsewhere. A rumor had already swept the downtown business community that "one Los Angeles woman went to Pasadena and bought a $23,000 bill of furniture because the police made her remove her car from the vicinity of Barker Bros. store a few days ago when she was inspecting goods there."[104]

The Automobile Club of Southern California had originally opposed the parking ban on the grounds that "the ordinance is discriminatory because it prohibits parking in the congested district by passenger vehicles, but allows it by truck and delivery wagons."[105] A protest by an advertising manager for one of the downtown stores, on the third day of the ban, revealed the arbitrariness of the legal distinction between working vehicles and pleasure cars. He parked, ordered one dollar worth of bulky merchandise, and when he returned to his car fourteen minutes later, was arrested. He planned to argue in court that "anyone who buys legitimate purchases at stores and takes them away in his car is making his car a delivery vehicle for the moment, and hence is entitled to fifteen minutes at the curb." Clarifying his motives, the advertising manager pointed out that if the courts upheld his contention, "women will have at least fifteen minutes in which to purchase necessaries, without having to walk to the store."[106]

Some City Council members argued that the merchants were considering only their own interest and that the parking ban ought to be given a fair chance to succeed. In a *Record* story on April 21, councilman Bert L. Farmer asserted that "among women's clubs there is a sentiment in favor of this ordinance as it stands now. They will resent any serious changes in it." Another councilman, warning against hasty action, made a more ambiguous claim: "Every man, woman and child in the city is interested in this ordinance. If a woman goes downtown with a baby she is interested in this ordinance." The formal political process did not, however, provide evidence of any female consensus on the parking problem. The only woman quoted in the local press, a member of the City Planning Association (a private civic group) had gone on record opposing the ban, stating that "autos are here to stay and cannot be banished from the streets." The *Times* reported, "She declared that some solution must be found to permit them to move fast, but the . . . law was worse than the congestion." When public hearings on the ordinance were held, attracting many speakers, no woman or representative of any women's group spoke.[107]

Instead of using formal political structures, women expressed themselves by staying out of the stores and taking, briefly and spectacularly, to the streets. The no parking ordinance was all but dead when Hollywood film actress Clara Kimball Young called a meeting of merchants to organize an automobile parade through downtown to demonstrate opposition to the ban. The *Times* reported that "no less than 200 protests have been received this week by Miss Young from admirers who assert they have been unable to attend matinees at the film houses owing to the parking law, and that they live too far away to come downtown at night," and that the movie star "and a committee of Los Angeles women drivers will attempt to visit every merchant in the city today with petitions, asking participation."[108] The *Examiner* and the *Record* reported on April 23 that "committees of girls canvassed the downtown district yesterday," signing up businessmen to participate in the parade.[109] The following day, a Saturday, hundreds of vehicles assembled to form a parade several miles long.[110]

On April 26, 1920, the Los Angeles City Council admitted that its no parking experiment had failed, and voted to amend the ordinance, allowing passenger car parking downtown for forty-five minutes between the hours of 10 A.M. and 4 P.M.[111] According to the *Times*, the city had learned the lesson that "Los Angeles people, and it is just as true of any other metropolitan city of any size, depend on their motor cars for shopping. When their cars were barred from the downtown streets, they either went someplace else to shop or they put their money in the family sock and didn't spend it at all."[112]

This effort to resist decentralization was ultimately in vain. By 1920, Los Angeles retailers had already begun to locate outside the central business district to be nearer to consumers. Advertisements for the Unity grocery chain claimed, "In whatever neighborhood you live you'll find a UNITY store" and sometimes featured a map showing Unity stores in Pasadena and Long Beach as well as in Los Angeles proper.[113] The department stores would follow; by 1929, Bullock's would open a branch on Wilshire Boulevard.[114] That year, writer Christine Frederick explained in *Selling Mrs. Consumer:*

> Traffic conditions in large cities point clearly to a decentralizing tendency, and as a consumer I loudly applaud. Women, like men, are coming to hate rather than to love "shopping" under modern crowded city conditions, and have already cut down the average time they spend in a store from about three hours to one hour. . . . We consumers want desperately to cut down our shopping time on standard goods. We fume with impatience—setting as we do a real value upon a woman's time these days.[115]

Merchants had learned their lesson; they could not assume that "time means nothing to most women shoppers;" they would also learn that space meant something. Partly in response to consumer preferences, Los Angeles was quickly coming to embody the new American city, one no longer characterized by a central business district surrounded by a radial pattern of residential areas.

While the claim that shoppers in all metropolitan cities depended on their cars was certainly exaggerated in 1920, Mrs. Consumer's future belonged to the automobile. By 1930, 222 cities with at least 10,000 residents were entirely dependent on motor transportation.[116] The automobile, which had made the transition from toy to tool, was in the process of becoming a necessity, and sometimes a burden, for women as well as men. The motorcar would enable American women of the 1920s to respond to the allures of modern leisure life while carrying on their responsibilities as homemakers. Automobility did not lead middle-class housewives to challenge openly their domestic vocation. Instead, those who drove found themselves more often using their cars as extensions of the family home than as paths to public power. The motoring housewives of the 1920s played a role in the transformation of American domesticity, but their legacy looks not so much like breaking new ground as reinventing the wheel.

At the same time, it would be a mistake to see American women in suburbanizing America as passive pawns of cynical men, whether politicians, real estate developers, retail merchants, advertising executives, auto manufacturers, or domineering husbands. During the 1920s, women who were privileged to have access to automobiles availed themselves of the power of the machine to explore new territory. Female tourists laid claim to a wider terrain, some finding a new breadth of personal vision and endeavor even as most carted along a full load of domestic responsibilities. Thrill-seeking flappers found new possibilities for fun in the driver's seat as well as the back seat, encountering new dangers as well as pleasures. Rural women forged new ways of combining domesticity and sociability. And automobility for middle-class metropolitan housewives meant that when public agencies prohibited what women drivers regarded as easy, or convenient, or efficient access to commercial concerns, they had the purchasing power to play a major role in diffusing the center of commerce. These motoring women, employing the multiple possibilities of the automobile, gave new meanings to the notion of "woman's place."

CHAPTER **9**

Reinventing the Wheel

I̶N massive and trivial ways, culture and technology propel and inhibit one another. The automobile, long blamed and enshrined for its transformation of American life, conformed to and reified existing patterns of belief and behavior. The mechanics who squabbled over paternity rights to the horseless carriage surely shared a sense of what fathering the auto would mean. For these automotive pioneers, for those who would promote and profit from the motorcar, and for a public which took the wheel with excitement and trepidation, the critical cultural categories of masculinity and femininity penetrated, applied to, and organized the dawning car culture.[1]

The early years of the motor age, which coincided with the Progressive Era and the rosy morning of consumerism, represented a time when the field for invention, mechanical and social, seemed wide open. In the realm of transportation, gasoline, electric, and steam power—no less than the auto makers who invested hope and fortune in such systems—competed and converged. Social engineers, like their counterparts in overalls, believed they could solve the nation's problems, ensuring progress and prosperity, through the application of reason and good will. Entrepreneurs like Henry Ford imagined that they could make capitalism just and beautiful, could perfect the free enterprise system, by giving workers the means to buy all the wonderful things they produced.

Innovative as they were in some ways, Ford and his automotive colleagues were generally conservative when it came to gender. To them and to most Americans, "driver" meant male; the modifier "woman" meant interloper. The well-to-do women who shrugged off feminine immobility and presumed to take the wheel, celebrated as daredevils or dismissed as dilettantes, burst on the road as a surprise to their contemporaries. The prospect of unleashing women on the American landscape deeply disturbed many observers, who worried that mobile women would be beyond control, socially, spatially, sexually. By way of reassuring themselves and containing the new technology's potential for disruption, Americans invoked standing myths, including ideas about masculinity and femininity. Indeed, the popular search for *comfort* in traditional gender ideology underlines the cultural cruciality of the search for physical and psychological ease at a time when social life was changing fast. While the auto transformed the particular places men and women went and the things they did, people remained, at the general level, embedded in their gendered identities, just as gender remained a critical category of American culture.

For nearly a century, then, the auto has been identified with masculinity and male mobility, and women's right and ability to use cars has been disputed. Although class status, age, geographical location, occupation, race, and ethnicity profoundly affected people's access to and control over cars, sex always outdistanced these other social factors as a focus of public debate about who could and should use motorcars. According to long-standing popular mythology, men enjoy a sympathetic relation with cars, mastering their machines as skillful and fearless drivers, knowing their engines as adept mechanics, rising to the physical challenge of driving on miserable roads or in bad weather, deftly negotiating heavy traffic. Indeed, the connection between men and cars has often been described as a "love affair," encompassing all the erotic and emotional complexity the metaphor conveys.

On the other hand, in advertisements, popular songs, movies, and novels, women have typically appeared as passive figures, seated next to driving husbands or boyfriends, or draped over auto bodies like hood ornaments, almost becoming automotive accessories. As drivers, women have been characterized as antipathetic to automobiles. They have often been depicted as incompetent and flighty behind the wheel, helplessly ignorant in the face of mechanical problems, terrified of the rigors of motoring over mud holes or in storms, and timid (though dangerous) on crowded city streets.

Of course, women and men sometimes did use their automobiles in ways consistent with widespread beliefs about gender. One such belief, the presumption of female passivity, further obscured women's part in creating the car culture. To the extent that their activities could be veiled and trivialized, women motorists were less threatening symbols of motorized modernity, of life in the machine era.

The American gender system, after all, was no egalitarian cultural construct; what was seen as feminine, or as belonging to women, seemed trivial at best, dangerous at worst. Car makers and many car buyers were uneasy about qualities associated with femininity—convenience, safety, comfort, style—and their ideas about gender affected the very nuts and bolts of automotive design, as well as the way new designs and devices would be seen by the industry, offered to the public, and adopted by the populace. Even as Victorian femininity was considered something of an encumbrance to the use of the motorcar, female automobility seemed to signal women's emancipation, a promising and ominous social development.

Paradoxically, references to women's desires and demands, as well as their capabilities, sometimes served as a way of preserving masculine identity by obscuring men's and women's common wishes and aptitudes. Introducing a powerful device like the electric starter as a gallant concession to feeble females may have indeed made driving more attractive to women who had learned to cultivate feminine weakness. It also preserved the fiction that real men, invariably muscle-bound, relished the inconvenience and danger of cranking. Certainly, that labor-intensive task impeded both male drivers' enjoyment of automobility and the usefulness of the family car as a way of getting to work. Combining cultural conservatism with mechanical innovation, automakers altered yet perpetuated a gendered view of the consumer and the machine.

After the Great War, the image of the woman driver would more than ever epitomize the new American consumer culture, variously dedicated to fun, to family, to affluence, to display, to personal exploration. Auto industry commentators responded to the visibility of women's driving by announcing the advent of the feminine automobile market, a morally suspect clientele supposedly concerned more with leisure than labor. As the auto-buying public expanded in the twenties, and the closed car triumphed over the open vehicles of an earlier time, many observers relied on a gendered view of human nature to explain why male breadwinners, who purportedly, qua men, had once embraced the rigors of open-air motoring, would spend their hard-earned wages on shut-in sedans and coupes. Rather than emphasizing the gender-neutral practical advantages of mobile shelter, many attributed men's behavior to the wasteful influence of luxury-loving women.

Still, while manufacturers and publicists were reassuring themselves that women wanted comfort and glamour and men wanted adventure, they were reluctant to bank on such assumptions. They did not, after all, build separate cars for women and men, but instead built cars they believed would please both. General Motors insiders might refer to the company's the "Art and Color" section as "the beauty parlor," a place where women designers might express "the woman's point of view." But they also knew, as Alfred Sloan wrote, that "the future of General Motors [would] be measured by the attractiveness that we put in the bodies."[2] Men were buying closed cars; might women not buy power and adventure? Might modern men even prefer a bold woman to a simpering sybarite?

However deeply mired in cultural patterns, the auto arrived on the national scene as a new technological force boding unpredictable and immense possibilities for social change. As a complicated and powerful piece of machinery, it embodied new possibilities not only in transportation, but also in consumption. To its creators and purveyors, it represented uncountable hours spent problem-solving, monkey-wrenching, strategizing, arguing, and cajoling. To its users, it meant both new freedoms and new burdens, the lure of the open road and the anchor of the chauffeur's job. More broadly, it embodied potent and potentially contradictory cultural forces. The motorcar stood for power over space and time; for control over wealth; for luxury, waste, and leisure; for sex. Driving was in itself a complicated act, encompassing at once service and authority, skill and ease, choice and responsibility.

If traditional beliefs proved tenacious and flexible enough to affect the changes the auto brought, even the most powerful ideas could not completely contain social transformation. When automobiles first appeared on American streets, few families could afford to own a car, and even fewer questioned the idea that men would hold sway in the driver's seat. As women claimed the right to travel by automobile, first as passengers and then as drivers, they influenced the development of automotive technology, shaped the car culture, and adapted to changes in the automobile.

Women's role in the making of the car culture was assuredly as important in the instances where they refused to conform as when they acted according to conventional thinking. As manufacturers responded to female driving by making cars easier to operate, they did so, ironically, because numerous women motorists set out to prove that they could master any difficulty the car or the road had to offer, asking no special consideration. Some took the wheel in the name of personal pleasure, avoiding any identification with women's rights advocacy. Others, animated by the political spirit and the organizing fervor of Progressivism, saw automobility as both emblem of female freedom and feminist political tool. By World War I, still others would come to use their driving skills on behalf of patriotism and humanitarian endeavor, demonstrating the physical, emotional, and mental fitness necessary to do what had been regarded as men's work, as well as the allegiance to family and nation signifying that their self-assertion would not go too far. Breaching traditional gender boundaries for the duration, they would help to redraw the map of masculine and feminine domains. A few would choose to remain in No Man's Land; most opted for a return to something that the President of the United States called "normalcy."

Going home again was, however, as much a venture into new terrain as a return to the familiar. Motor transportation promoted postwar suburbanization, disrupting the traditional radial pattern of urban development, and increasing the distance between housewives' scattered domiciles and traditional centers of public affairs. The auto, in women's hands, would prove both a means of mediating new distances and a centrifugal force in the transformation of the urban landscape. While it extended and distorted woman's geographical sphere, the motorcar did little to reduce women's domestic responsibilities, or to put their work in plain sight. The middle-class housewife roamed farther from home, but home was always within range. Millions of women took the wheel, cheered on by Detroit and Madison Avenue, while the man in the street ridiculed their legitimacy as drivers, and much of the work they did remained invisible.

Putting wheels on woman's sphere meant contesting gender stereotypes, muddying the distinction between public and private, redesigning the landscape, decentralizing the American city, and creating new forms of control and vulnerability for American women. As historical figures, the women drivers of the first third of the century seem to us at once exotic and familiar. Often mystified or misunderstood by their contemporaries, they struggled for access to the motorcar and all it conveyed on their own terms. They expected the auto to transport them to new and exciting places and to bring the fruits of the consumer economy to their kitchen doors. To onlookers and auto makers, women represented at once a predictable feminine public and, paradoxically, a vast, mysterious, and unsettling force in the marketplace and the landscape.

However baffling to their contemporaries, their presence was undeniable. By 1928, Herbert Hoover would campaign for the presidency promising that under his leadership, Americans could look forward to "two cars in every garage." This vision of utopian consumerism, domestic and mobile, suggested that both security and independence were within the reach of all citizens, male and female. The automotive class market had been supplanted by a mass market; the presumption of male driving had given way to reckoning with the consequences of female automobility. Within the space of three decades, the car culture had moved a long way toward what philosopher of science Thomas Kuhn might call a paradigm shift.[3] Observers could no longer explain or predict what automobiles would bring by referring only to what men did or where they went.

The new and intrepid, if reassuringly domestic, vision of womanhood reflected the social reality of the woman driver. Where the auto was concerned, American women had always seen and wanted more than a cushy place to sit. Automobility, to the diverse women who sought its power, meant access to a wider social life, new possibilities in where and how to live, new leisure practices, new goods and information. To many, driving a car offered a new way of organizing domestic activities and family life. As it had from the beginning of the automotive era, control over an automobile also signified new and flexible possibilities for women's independent entry into the public realm, a spatial and cultural innovation that seemed, to many, at once inconsequential and revolutionary. In a nation where middle-class people had long believed women belonged literally at home, female automobility seemed, in Motor editor Ray Sherman's words, a real threat to the order of things.

By the mid-1920s, many American women possessed a freedom of movement which would have astonished and horrified their forerunners. Millions of families found some way to buy automobiles, and both the pleasures of the household and the job of housekeeping hit the road. Gone were the days when people of modest means put their financial limitations on display in spartan, rattling Model Ts, and the wealthy declared their automotive privileges from the car roof down. In the diversified, price-segmented market first introduced in the twenties, car owners might aspire, unwisely, to more expensive models than they could afford, but innovations like installment financing meant that they could purchase more automotive features and more mobile privacy than ever before. For more people than ever, the auto had become both a means to and a measure of sensual gratification, as well as a tool of workaday life.

The stock market crash of 1929, and the long Depression

that followed, provided a bitter refutation of the idea that consumerism, buying things, could eradicate inequality and injustice. Americans clung to the heartrending promise of the Good Life nonetheless. The Joad family piled into their Ford truck and headed down Route 66, bound for California, dreaming of oranges you could pick right off the tree. Not only did Americans' attachment to the auto survive even the destruction of home and livelihood; for some very desperate people, the car represented the best chance of keeping the family going.

As we near the end of the first century of car culture, women can be found at the wheel wherever automobiles go. Women's driving has become essential to our economy and our way of life. Yet the suspect figure of the woman driver remains part of our folklore and popular literature. When *Redbook* magazine writer Bonnie Remsberg looked at the woman driver question in 1973, she found statistics indicating that women were safer drivers than men and, moreover, that they appeared to have more stamina than male drivers on long-distance trips. Nevertheless, for at least some people, putting women at the wheel of automobiles held as much peril as promise. "One charming male chauvinist safety statistician I talked to insisted on having the last word," Remsberg noted. "Saying that some things never change, he contends that the one traffic violation women commit more often than men is the failure to yield."[4]

The failure to yield, whether regarding the matter of female driving aptitude or the question of women's automotive access to public space, had profound consequences for American women's lives and for the society at large in the twentieth century. The safety statistician's cavalier disquietude alerts us to the historical contest behind the woman driver stereotype, a struggle over access not only to cars, but to the material resources cars exemplify, to the behavior cars make possible, and to the places automobiles can go. The enduring figure of the woman driver continues to embody fears about what women might do with plenty of money, big powerful machines, and relatively unrestricted freedom of movement.

From the turn of the century to this day, women have seized the potential of the pleasure car. Some, from Joan Cuneo to Janet

Guthrie, the nation's most recent woman auto racing champion, have thrilled to the automobile's speed and power. Innumerable others have sought sexual adventure in back seats, truck beds, van bunks, and even, in testimony to human ingenuity, the bucket seats of sports cars. Still others have hoped simply to get away from home for a few hours, days, or weeks.

By refusing to be relegated permanently to the passenger seat, women helped to determine what shape their lives and landscapes would take in twentieth-century America. Their presence at the wheel did not disrupt fundamental patterns of gender; indeed, as the car culture absorbed and adapted to popular notions about what masculinity and femininity decreed, developers and planners would map a new landscape of separate spheres. Still, the automobile provided an unpredictable vehicle for contests over women's access to public space, control over their time, and right to technological power. The tension between greater female mobility and the sex-segregated terrain of the car culture would continue to simmer.

Today, traffic jams are full of women on their way to work, or to the grocery store, or to pick up children. Indeed, in the preponderance of American cities and towns today, women keep family life moving, and their ability to manage both domesticity and paid work depends on their access to cars. The auto, for better or worse, is the only way most women can get where they must go. Their cars are not "second cars" to be dismissed as frivolous conveniences; their daily driving keeps their families going and the economy moving.

Nevertheless, the tendency to trivialize women's driving remains strong among Americans, and continues not only to denigrate women but also to inhibit the creative possibilities of the car culture. When the men and women of the car-buying public insisted on behaving contrary to prescribed sex roles, traditional expectations about the consequences of womanhood (and manhood) for automobile use proved reductive, contradictory, often misleading, and sometimes simply wrong. But these ideas remained powerful.

The connections between women's status and female automobility illustrate a larger set of links between the ways women operate in modern society and women's acquaintance with material objects and machines. Ignoring women's part in technological change distorts our understanding of that change, just as belittling what is perceived as feminine handicaps us in seeing the present and planning for the future. Many Americans continue to assume that women's time and effort are not worth saving.

There is, however, reason to believe that accounting for cultural influences on technology can yield concrete benefits. A few thoughtful planners have grappled with the gendering of automobility and have begun to account for women's temporal and geographical obligations in their visions of model communities. Why waste people's time and the nation's scarce petroleum, they ask, poisoning the air and fouling millions of motorists' moods by insisting on distance between (women at) home and (men at) work? By building bedroom communities remote from business districts we map gender onto our landscape and continue to perpetuate misleading zones of labor and leisure, safety and danger, manicured pastoralism and cacophonous ugliness.[5] Recognizing and questioning the concepts that underlie the land, we make new urban visions possible.

As we contemplate redesigning the city, we also begin to reinvent the wheel. Automotive characteristics associated with "comfort," historically trivialized as feminine, demand serious attention. As long as we continue to imagine drivers as he-men who are solely concerned with speed and display, scoffing at safety, convenience, and cleanliness, we will misinterpret what motorists, male and female, might want, and be slow to design automobiles that get all of us where we want to go with a minimum of damage to ourselves and our world. Women as well as men will hesitate to adopt features deemed feminine, denigrating such innovations even when they prove valuable. We have to develop a more pluralistic view of who uses cars, and how, and why; we may see new ways to make our car culture cities livable for everyone.

Clearly, technology is powerful, but even so potent a machine as the auto cannot quite absorb the central dilemmas of culture, including the ambiguities of gender. Trying to tailor technological change to human needs would mean asking more general cultural questions like: What is the relation between masculinity and femininity? Are these two categories contradictory? Can they be reconciled? If so, how? Might we find instances in which the cultural forces of masculine and feminine, and the social needs of women and men, are complementary? The tendency to develop his-and-hers technologies, from cars to cities, will always raise these issues. And to further complicate the picture, often as not, human beings will defy gender expectations.

There is nothing inevitable about the masculinity of technology, even where the automobile, often considered a kind of metallic phallus, is concerned. Whatever else it is by way of bane or blessing, the private motorcar is a form of transportation that gives the driver enormous latitude in choosing where to go, and when to make the trip. Women today use cars to go to work, to make endless expeditions to the "Pay and Save," to drive thousands of miles for fun or politics or profit, to escape from abusive husbands. Since the beginning of the motor age, the woman at the wheel has challenged Americans to reinvent assumptions, machines, cities. These days, for better or worse, by obligation or choice, in the name of desire and the presence of danger, anywhere the road leads is woman's place.

Notes

1   The Lady and the Mechanic

1. Barbara Ehrenreich and Deirdre English, *For Her Own Good: 150 Years of the Experts' Advice to Women* (Garden City, N.Y.: Anchor Books, 1979), p. 111.

2. Edward Clarke, *Sex in Education: Or, a Fair Chance for the Girls* (Boston: Osgood and Co., 1873), p. 127, quoted in Rosalind Rosenberg, *Beyond Separate Spheres: Intellectual Roots of Modern Feminism* (New Haven: Yale University Press, 1982), pp. 11–12.

3. Quoted in Aileen S. Kraditor, *The Ideas of the Woman Suffrage Movement, 1890–1920* (New York: W. W. Norton, 1981), p. 20.

4. Ibid., p. 26.

5. John B. Rae, *The Road and Car in American Life* (Cambridge: M.I.T. Press, 1971), p. 197.

6. *The Oxford English Dictionary*, vol. 11 (Oxford, England: Clarendon Press, 1933), pp. 228–229.

7. Ibid.

8. Ibid.

9. Ibid.

10. Ibid.

11. Ellen Willis has suggested that leftist thinkers have shared mistrust of women's ability to manage consumption. See A Redstocking Sister (Ellen Willis), "Consumerism and Women," in Vivian Gornick and Barbara K. Moran, eds., *Woman in Sexist Society: Studies in Power and Powerlessness* (New York: Basic Books, 1971), pp. 658–664.

12. On women in New York City, see Christine Stansell, *City of Women: Sex and Class in New York, 1789–1860* (Urbana: University of Illinois Press, 1987), for the Jacksonian period; see also Kathy Peiss, *Cheap Amusements: Working Women and Leisure in Turn-of-the-Century New York* (Philadelphia: Temple University Press, 1986).

13. Howard N. Rabinowitz, *Race Relations in the Urban South*,

177

1865–1890 (New York: Oxford University Press, 1978), pp. 182–184, 192–196, 218, 334–336.

14. Clay McShane, "American Cities and the Coming of the Automobile, 1890–1915" (Ph.D. dissertation, University of Wisconsin, 1975), p. 26.

15. On changes in the metropolitan landscape and transportation innovation, see Scott L. Bottles, "The Making of the Modern City: Los Angeles and the Automobile, 1900–1950" (Ph.D. dissertation, University of California at Los Angeles, 1984); Scott L. Bottles, *Los Angeles and the Automobile* (Berkeley: University of California Press, 1987); Joseph Interrante, "The Road to Autopia: The Automobile and the Spatial Transformation of American Culture," in David L. Lewis and Laurence Goldstein, eds., *The Automobile and American Culture* (Ann Arbor: University of Michigan Press, 1983); Kenneth T. Jackson, *The Crabgrass Frontier* (New York: Oxford University Press, 1985); Sam Bass Warner, Jr., *Streetcar Suburbs: The Process of Growth in Boston, 1870–1900* (Cambridge: Harvard University Press, 1962).

16. Diary of Mrs. Ernest T. Emery, Division of Special Collections, University Research Library, University of California at Los Angeles.

17. Emery diary, November 11, 1905. On long-running public disaffection with the traction companies in Los Angeles, see Scott Bottles, "The Making of the Modern City," pp. 23–52.

18. "Women Will War on Car Evils," *New York Times*, April 2, 1907. Conditions in the Los Angeles system will be discussed in Chapter 7.

19. *Los Angeles Record*, December 10, 1912, quoted in Bottles, "The Making of the Modern City," p. 23.

20. On women and the Chicago transit system, see Paul Barrett, *The Automobile and Urban Transit: The Formation of Public Policy in Chicago, 1900–1930* (Philadelphia: Temple University Press, 1983), pp. 110–114; 197–199. On Los Angeles, see Chapter 8 below.

21. John B. Rae, *The American Automobile* (Chicago: University of Chicago Press, 1965), pp. 3–5.

22. Rae, pp. 7–11; Motor Vehicle Manufacturers Association, *Automobiles of America* (Detroit: Wayne State University Press, 1974), p. 11; Frank Donovan, *Wheels for a Nation* (New York: Thomas Y. Crowell, 1965), p. 44; M. M. Musselman, *Get a Horse! The Story of the Automobile in America* (New York: J. B. Lippincott, 1950), pp. 35–37.

23. Rae, p. 9; Motor Vehicle Manufacturers Association, pp. 13–14; Donovan, pp. 46–47; Musselman, pp. 37–38.

24. Motor Vehicle Manufacturers Association, p. 12; Rae, pp. 9–10; Musselman, pp. 40–42; Donovan, pp. 48–49.

25. Donovan's and Musselman's accounts are typical; Rae, pp. 21–

29, offers a concise and useful collective biography of "pioneer producers." See also Hiram Percy Maxim, *Horseless Carriage Days* (New York: Harper and Brothers, 1937); Theodore F. MacManus and Norman Beasley, *Men, Money, and Motors: The Drama of the Automobile* (New York: Harper and Brothers, 1930).

26. Alfred P. Sloan, Jr. and Boyden Sparks, *Adventures of a White-Collar Man* (New York: Doubleday, Doran, and Company, 1941), p. 69.

27. Rae, pp. 23–25; Donovan, pp. 62–63; Motor Vehicle Manufacturers Association, pp. 24–26; Musselman, 70–73.

28. Among the almost numberless biographies of Henry Ford see Allan Nevins and Frank Ernest Hill, *Ford: The Times, the Man, the Company*, vol. 1 (New York: Charles Scribner's Sons, 1954); Allan Nevins and Frank Ernest Hill, *Ford: Expansion and Challenge, 1915–1933* vol. 2 (New York: Charles Scribner's Sons, 1957); Allan Nevins and Frank Ernest Hill, *Ford: Decline and Rebirth, 1933–1962*, vol. 3 (New York: Charles Scribner's Sons, 1963); Robert Lacey, *Ford: The Men and the Machine* (Boston: Little, Brown and Company, 1986); Keith Sward, *The Legend of Henry Ford* (New York: Russell and Russell, 1948); Reynold M. Wik, *Henry Ford and Grass-Roots America* (Ann Arbor: University of Michigan Press, 1973).

29. Lacey, pp. 51–64; Donovan, 59–61; Musselman, pp. 50–65.

30. Sloan and Sparks, pp. 71–72. See also MacManus and Beasley, and Musselman, for enthusiastic portrayals of the early auto manufacturers as competitive, risk-taking pioneers.

31. Lacey, p. 64.

32. Maxim, pp. 174–175.

33. Dolores Hayden, *Redesigning the American Dream: The Future of Housing, Work, and Family Life* (New York: W. W. Norton, 1984), pp. 210–211.

2   From Passenger to Driver

1. "What the Motor Girl Is Wearing," *Motor*, November 1903, p. 30.

2. Helena Smith, "The Frivolous Girl Goes Motoring," *Motor*, May 1905, p. 43.

3. "What the Motor Girl Is Wearing," p. 30.

4. "Fashions for Her Motoring Ladyship," *Motor*, December 1904, p. 38.

5. "Motorists Don't Make Socialists, They Say," *New York Times*, March 4, 1906.

6. "Diana" [pseudonym], "A Motor Leap Year Dance," *Motor*, February 1904, p. 33.

7. S. E. Lasher, "Society and the Motor Car," *Motor*, December 1910, p. 67. See also "Diana," "A Motor Leap Year Dance," p. 33; John B. Rae, *The Road and Car in American Life* (Cambridge: M.I.T. Press, 1971), p. 43; Thorstein Veblen, *Theory of the Leisure Class* (New York: Mentor, 1953), pp. 121, 125.

8. On the social and economic importance of habits of deference, see E. P. Thompson, *The Making of the English Working Class* (New York: Vintage Books, 1966), pp. 184–185, 202–203, 605–607, 672, 677–679, 681–682.

9. J. E. Mansion, ed., *Harrap's Standard French and English Dictionary*, part 1 (London: George E. Harrap and Company, 1956), p. 150; R. W. Burchfield, ed., *A Supplement to the Oxford English Dictionary*, vol. 1 (Oxford: Clarendon Press, 1972), p. 487.

10. C. P. Berry, *A Treatise on the Law Relating to Automobiles* (Chicago: Callaghan and Company, 1909) p. 119.

11. "Meanings of Auto Terms," *Popular Mechanics*, January 1927, p. 74.

12. *New York Times*, October 3, 1904.

13. *New York Times*, March 18, 1905; November 19, 1905.

14. *New York Times*, August 12, 1906. James J. Flink, *America Adopts the Automobile* (Cambridge: M.I.T. Press, 1970), pp. 176–177, cites a similar example of early concern over chauffeurs' mechanical qualifications, without noting the moral issue.

15. *New York Times*, April 6, 1913.

16. Frank Donovan, *Wheels for a Nation* (New York: Thomas Y. Crowell Company, 1965), p. 14.

17. Rosalind Delmar, "What is Feminism?" in Juliet Mitchell and Ann Oakley, eds., *What is Feminism? A Re-examination* (New York: Pantheon, 1986), p. 26, notes a connection between fire imagery and protests against sexual constraint in the Paris Commune and the twentieth-century suffrage movement.

18. The authors of the serial describe Lady Beeston's relation with the car in rhetoric that reminds the modern reader of Harlequin romances. For an insightful analysis of this popular genre, see Ann Barr Snitow, "Mass Market Romance: Pornography for Women Is Different," in Ann Snitow, Christine Stansell, and Sharon Thompson, eds., *Powers of Desire: The Politics of Sexuality* (New York: Monthly Review Press, 1983), pp. 245–263.

19. "Rita" [pseudonym], "The Wonderful Monster," *Motor*, January 1905, p. 45.

20. Ibid.

21. Max Pemberton, "The Wonderful Monster," *Motor*, May 1905, p. 64.

22. Ibid., pp. 64, 66, 68.

23. Sociologist Anthony Giddens refers to such power as the ability to transcend sequestration. See Anthony Giddens, *A Contemporary Critique of Historical Materialism* (New York: Macmillan, 1981), p. 174.

24. Pemberton, p. 64.

25. Numerous historians have analyzed the early twentieth-century arguments against higher education for women and woman suffrage, including Rosalind Rosenberg, *Beyond Separate Spheres: Intellectual Roots of Modern Feminism* (New Haven: Yale University Press, 1982); Barbara Miller Solomon, *In the Company of Educated Women: A History of Women and Higher Education* (New Haven: Yale University Press, 1986); Margaret Rossiter, *Women Scientists in America: Struggles and Strategies to 1940* (Baltimore: Johns Hopkins University Press, 1982); Eleanor Flexner, *Century of Struggle: The Woman's Rights Movement in the United States* (Cambridge: The Belknap Press of Harvard University Press, 1975); Aileen Kraditor, *The Ideas of the Woman Suffrage Movement, 1890–1920* (New York: W. W. Norton, 1981).

26. "Many Women Automobilists," *New York Times*, July 8, 1906.

27. Edith Wharton, *A Backward Glance* (New York: D. Appleton-Century Company, 1934), pp. 136–137.

28. R. W. B. Lewis, *Edith Wharton: A Biography* (New York: Harper and Row, 1975), pp. 128–131; Wharton, *A Backward Glance*, p. 244.

29. Lewis, p. 166; Edith Wharton, *A Motor-Flight Through France* (New York: Charles Scribner's Sons, 1908), p. 1.

30. Motor Vehicle Manufacturers' Association, *Automobiles of America* (Detroit: Wayne State University Press, 1974), p. 21.

31. *Statistical Abstract of the United States* (Washington, D.C.: Government Printing Office, 1931), p. 403.

32. "Motor Car Law," *Motor*, June 1909, pp. 40–45.

33. See issues of *Motor* for April 1904; July 1904; and October 1905 for reports on women motorists at fashionable resorts.

34. Marlou Belyea, "The Joy Ride and the Silver Screen: Commercial Leisure, Delinquency, and Play Reform in Los Angeles, 1900–1980" (Ph.D. dissertation, Boston University, 1983), pp. 165, 173.

35. *Tucson Automobile Directory* (Tucson: J. A. Scott, 1914); *Houston Automobile Directory* (Houston: C. L. and Theo Bering, Jr., 1915). One woman driver not listed in the Tucson directory was Edith S. Kitt, a resident of that city, who later published her diary of a 1914 auto trip. See Edith S. Kitt, "Motoring in Arizona in 1914," *Journal of Arizona History* 11, no. 1 (Spring 1970):32–65.

36. There were many articles on the woman driver question in early twentieth-century American popular magazines. Michael Berger, in two essays, "Women Drivers: How a Stereotype Kept Distaff Drivers in Their Place," *Road and Track* 36, no. 9 (May 1985):56–60, and "Women Drivers! The Emergence of Folklore and Stereotypic Opinions Concerning Feminine Automotive Behavior," *Women's Studies International Forum* 9, no. 3 (1986):257–263, has insightfully analyzed a number of those sources, and I agree with his conclusions in many regards. On the woman driver image in recent times, see Beth Kraig, "Driving Toward the Future: Images of Women Drivers in Liberated America" (paper presented to the Berkshire Conference on Women's History, Wellesley, Mass., June 1987).

37. Flexner, pp. 304–318; Kraditor, pp. 14–42; Rosenberg, pp. 1–27; Rossiter, pp. 73–99.

38. "Why Women Are, or Are Not, Good Chauffeuses," *Outing*, May 1904, p. 154.

39. Ibid., pp. 156–158.

40. Ibid., p. 159.

41. Mrs. A. Sherman Hitchcock, "A Woman's Viewpoint of Motoring," *Motor*, April 1904, p. 19.

42. Ibid.

43. Ibid.

44. Ibid.

45. Ibid.

46. Mary Mullett, "Women and the Automobile," *Outing* 48 (July 1906):500–502; *Statistical Abstract of the United States*, p. 403.

47. Ibid.

48. Rosenberg, pp. 84–113; Kraditor, pp. 43–75. Victoria Brown, "Golden Girls: Female Socialization in Los Angeles, 1880–1910" (Ph.D. dissertation, University of California at San Diego, 1985), has exhaustively documented Progressive Era scientists' and educators' arguments emphasizing gender difference.

49. Mrs. Andrew Cuneo, "Why There Are So Few Women Automobilists," *Country Life in America*, March 1908, pp. 515–516.

50. This issue will be addressed more fully in Chapter 3.

51. Cuneo, p. 516.

52. Margaret R. Burlingame, "When Woman Drives, Man Jumps," *Motor*, August 1913, pp. 48, 172.

53. Ibid., p. 48.

54. Ibid.

55. Ibid.

56. Ibid.

57. "Do Women Make Good Drivers?" *Motor*, May 1914, pp. 61–62.

58. Ibid., 61.
59. Ibid.
60. Ibid., 62.
61. Ibid.
62. F. G. Moorhead, "Women Drive to Fortune," *Illustrated World*, November 1915, p. 334.
63. Diana, "Modes in Motoring," *Motor*, January 1904, p. 35.

3 Femininity and the Electric Car

1. John B. Rae, *The American Automobile* (Chicago: University of Chicago Press, 1965), pp. 11–13; and Theodore F. MacManus and Norman Beasley, *Men, Money, and Motors: The Drama of the Automobile* (New York: Harper and Brothers, 1930), p. 6.
2. *Motor* December 1903.
3. On early women racing and rally drivers, see Chapter 5.
4. Frank Donovan, *Wheels for a Nation* (New York: Thomas Y. Crowell, 1965), pp. 1–12; S. E. Lasher, "Society and the Motor Car," *Motor*, December 1910, p. 67.
5. The first electric vehicle to run on American city streets was built by William Morrison of Des Moines, Iowa in 1891. Bonnie Remsberg, "Women Behind the Wheel," *Redbook*, September 1973, reprinted in the Motor Vehicle Manufacturers' Association, *News Review*, September 12, 1973, p. 1; Allan Nevins and F. E. Hill, *Ford: The Times, the Man, the Company, 1865–1915*, vol. 1 (New York: Charles Scribner's Sons, 1954), pp. 197–198.
6. "Chicago Warns Women Automobilists," *Horseless Age*, September 12, 1900, p. 24.
7. Electric car manufacturers adopted closed vehicle design earlier and with more frequency than did makers of most gasoline cars. One magazine writer reported that "gasoline cars set the style, in open cars, although they have borrowed many of the closed car ideas from the electric town car." See "Trend in Electric Car Construction," *Motor*, December 1910, p. 101.
8. "Motoring in Society," *Motor*, April 1904, pp. 22–23.
9. Joseph B. Baker, "The Care of the Electric Vehicle," *Motor* (May 1910):79–80; C. H. Claudy, "The Electric as a Convenience and a Necessity," *Motor*, April 1907, pp. 47–48; also C. H. Claudy, "The Lady and the Electric," *Country Life in America*, July 15, 1912, pp. 36, 44, 46, 48; C. H. Claudy, "The Woman and Her Car," *Country Life in America*, January 1913, pp. 41–42; "Establishing the Electric," *Motor*, October 1915, pp. 58–59, 132; Wilhelm Nassau, "The Number of Electrics in Use," *Motor*, July 1908, p. 54; Phil M. Riley, "What an Electric

Car Can Do," *Country Life in America,* January 1913, pp. 23–36, 70–76. I have also surveyed advertising in all issues of *Motor,* from 1903 through 1929.

10. *Motor,* June 1912, p. xxiii.

11. *Motor,* June 1911.

12. *Motor,* December 1910.

13. James J. Flink, *America Adopts the Automobile* (Cambridge: M.I.T. Press, 1970), p. 45.

14. See articles on Edison's scheme to develop such a battery, *New York Times,* July 29, 1905; August 4, 1905; October 21, 1906; October 23, 1906.

15. Herbert H. Rice, "The Electric of Today," *Motor,* July 1908, p. 49.

16. Ibid., p. 50.

17. Ibid., p. 49.

18. *Motor,* June 1914, p. 186.

19. Riley, pp. 23–36, 70–76.

20. Historians have identified "woman's sphere" as both a source of female subordination and a force in the creation of an autonomous women's culture. Assessing the costs, benefits, and significance of separate spheres for women and men has been a central task of women's history. See Barbara Welter, "The Cult of True Womanhood," *American Quarterly* 18 (1966):151–174; Kathryn Kish Sklar, *Catharine Beecher: A Study in American Domesticity* (New Haven: Yale University Press, 1973); Carroll Smith-Rosenberg, "The Female World of Love and Ritual: Relations Between Women in Nineteenth-Century America," *SIGNS: Journal of Women in Culture and Society* 1 (1975):1–30; Nancy F. Cott, *The Bonds of Womanhood: "Woman's Sphere" in New England, 1780–1835* (New Haven: Yale University Press, 1977); Estelle Freedman, "Separatism as Strategy: Female Institution Building and American Feminism, 1870–1930," *Feminist Studies* 5, no. 3 (Fall 1979):512–529. Victoria Brown has richly documented the use of similar language to describe woman's nature and prescribe sex role socialization in the United States in the Progressive Era. See Victoria Brown, "Golden Girls: Female Socialization in Los Angeles, 1880–1910" (Ph.D. dissertation, University of California at San Diego, 1985), especially pp. 93–153.

21. Linda K. Kerber, "Separate Spheres, Female Worlds, Woman's Place: The Rhetoric of Women's History," *Journal of American History* 75, no. 1 (June 1988):9–39. Historian Nancy Woloch's description of woman's sphere as "not merely a place or even a vocation, but a values system," reflects the ways in which this term has been used to locate women spatially, occupationally, and morally, conflating social factors that should be kept separate in order to see their interactions. Nancy

Woloch, *Women and the American Experience* (New York: Alfred A. Knopf, 1984), p. 101.

22. For analyses of such revisions in American women's history see Myra H. Strober and Audri Gordon Lanford, "The Feminization of Public School Teaching: Cross-Sectional Analysis, 1850–1880," *SIGNS: Journal of Women in Culture and Society* 11 (Winter 1986):212–235; Virginia Drachman, *Hospital with a Heart: Women Doctors and the Paradox of Separatism at the New England Hospital, 1862–1969* (Ithaca, N.Y.: Cornell University Press, 1984). On the process of social change, see Anthony Giddens, *A Contemporary Critique of Historical Materialism* (New York: Macmillan, 1981).

23. Claudy, "The Electric as a Convenience and a Necessity," p. 47.

24. Ibid., p. 48.

25. Ibid., pp. 47–48.

26. Ibid.

27. Montgomery Rollins, "Sane Motoring—Or Insane?" *The Outlook*, May 29, 1909, p. 279.

28. Rice, p. 50; C. H. Claudy, "The Electric as a Convenience and a Necessity," pp. 47–48. An advertisement for the Argo electric in *Motor*, June 1912, pointed out that the car was "easily handled by a lady, yet any man who motors feels 'right at home' with it." See also ads for the Detroit (*Motor*, December 1910), the Argo (*Motor*, June 1913), and the "Exide" Electric Storage Battery (*Country Life in America*, n.d.).

29. *Motor*, December 1910.

30. By 1922, electric vehicle promoters had even given up on doctors, though they continued to press women to buy electrics. See Dingman Lewis, "The Modern Electric," *Motor*, September 1922, pp. 31, 96.

31. Claudy, "The Lady and the Electric," p. 36.

32. Ibid.

33. Ibid.

34. Ibid., pp. 36, 44.

35. As of 1915, *Motor* magazine reported that there were some six thousand charging stations in the nation, and that other schemes for expanding the electric's range, such as battery exchanges, were being tried. See "Establishing the Electric," p. 59.

36. Claudy, "The Lady and the Electric," p. 44.

37. *Tucson Automobile Directory* (Tucson: J. A. Scott, 1914), Arizona Historical Society, Tucson, Arizona.

38. The 7,732 auto owners listed in the *Houston Automobile Directory, 1915* (Houston: C. L. and Theo Bering, Jr., 1915) appear to have been assigned numbers in chronological order of vehicle registration, judging from the makes of cars listed for each owner. As the numbers

got higher, more and more people (women included) were listed as owning Fords. Twenty-six out of the thirty women listed as owning electrics had numbers under 2500. In this same numerical subset, 102 women were listed as owners of gas-powered vehicles.

39. Rae, pp. 65–67.

40. Claudy, "The Woman and Her Car," p. 41.

41. Ibid., p. 41–42.

42. C. H. Claudy, "Some Points on Good Driving for the Woman Motorist," *Woman's Home Companion*, February 1917, p. 33; "Putting the Car in Order," *Woman's Home Companion*, March 1917, p. 33.

43. C. H. Claudy, "The Nervous Driver and How She May Acquire Confidence," *Woman's Home Companion*, February 1920, pp. 130–131.

44. *Motor*, June 1905, back cover.

45. Ibid.

46. Ibid.

47. See Alice Huyler Ramsey, *Veil, Duster, and Tire Iron* (Covina, Calif.: Castle Press, 1961), p. 1.

48. *Motor*, December 1909, p. 11. James S. Couzens, business manager at Ford, calculated that auto manufacturers could reach a mass market by selling a car for $600, but at the time the Ford Motor Company had not managed to achieve that objective. A 1909 Model T touring car sold for $950. By 1912, because of innovations in production technique anticipating the revolutionary moving assembly line, the same car would be available at the target price of $600. See Rae, pp. 60–61.

49. *Motor*, December 1911, p. 11.

50. *Motor*, December 1910.

51. Ibid.

52. "Casual Cutouts," *Vanity Fair*, September 1913, p. 54.

53. F. G. Moorhead, "Women Drive to Fortune," *Illustrated World*, November 1915, p. 334.

54. See, for example, B. McManus, "The Woman Who Drives Her Own Car," *Harper's Bazaar*, July 1912, p. 354; Mrs. A. Sherman Hitchcock, "Woman at the Motor Wheel," *American Home* 10 (April 1913):sup. 6; Ann Murdock, "The Girl Who Drives a Car," *Ladies' Home Journal*, July 1915, p. 11; "Little Things About a Car That Every Woman Who Means to Drive One Ought to Know," *Ladies' Home Journal*, March 1917, p. 32.

55. James J. Flink, *The Car Culture* (Cambridge: M.I.T. Press, 1975) p. 46; Rae, pp. 35–38.

56. *Historical Statistics of the United States, Colonial Times to 1970* (Washington, D.C.: U.S. Bureau of the Census, 1976), p. 716.

57. "Establishing the Electric," p. 58; *Historical Statistics of the United States,* p. 716.

58. G. Marshall Naul, ed., *The Specification Book for U.S. Cars, 1920–1929; A Complete Guide to the Passenger Automobiles of the Decade* (Osceoloa, Wisconsin: Motorbooks International, 1978):92. Rae, p. 106, notes that the 1924 National Automobile Show in New York featured gasoline cars exclusively. Auto shows, then as now, were intended to present state-of-the-art design in motorcars, as well as to publicize new models.

4   Power and Comfort

1. The story of their exploits will be detailed in Chapter 5 below.

2. *Los Angeles Times,* May 21, 1905.

3. John B. Rae, *The American Automobile* (Chicago: University of Chicago Press, 1965), p. 57; *Motor,* December 1909.

4. Reynold Wik's *Henry Ford and Grass-roots America* (Ann Arbor: University of Michigan Press, 1972) is a detailed and affectionate tribute to the Model T. On Model T sales figures see Rae, p. 61.

5. Allan Nevins and F. E. Hill, *Ford: The Times, the Man, the Company, 1865–1915* (New York: Charles Scribner's Sons, 1954), pp. 373–374; Robert Lacey, *Ford: The Men and the Machine* (Boston: Little, Brown and Company, 1986), p. 150.

6. *Tucson Automobile Directory* (Tucson: J. A. Scott, 1914); *Houston Automobile Directory, 1915* (Houston: C. L. and Theo Bering, Jr., 1915).

7. *The Woman and the Ford* (Detroit: Ford Motor Company, n.d.), p. 3.

8. Lacey, pp. 160, 195.

9. Ibid., p. 38.

10. Ibid., pp. 122, 126. On the Five Dollar Day and the family wage, see Martha May, "The Historical Problem of the Family Wage: The Ford Motor Company and the Five Dollar Day," *Feminist Studies* 8, no. 2 (Summer 1982):399–424.

11. Lacey, p. 234.

12. On farm women's work and technological competence, see Katherine Jensen, "Mother Calls Herself a Housewife, But She Buys Bulls," in Jan Zimmerman, ed., *The Technological Woman: Interfacing with Tomorrow* (New York: Praeger, 1983), pp. 136–144.

13. Frank Donovan, *Wheels for a Nation* (New York: Thomas Y. Crowell, 1965), p. 110; Gertrude Stein, *The Autobiography of Alice B. Toklas* (New York: Vintage Books, 1960), p. 172. On the combination of women and Fords in the Southern textile mill strikes of the 1920s,

see Jacquelyn Dowd Hall, "Disorderly Women: Gender and Labor Militancy in the Appalachian South," *Journal of American History* 73, no. 2 (September 1986):354–382.

14. Rae, pp. 61, 88. James Gould Couzens deserves credit for Ford Motor Company's creation of an efficient national sales force; see Lacey, p. 76.

15. Lacey, p. 96; "Make Santa Claus Your Salesman for Christmas," *Ford Dealer and Service Field*, December 1926, p. 43 (Box 5, Stuart A. Work Collection, Division of Special Collections, University Research Library, University of California at Los Angeles). See also the voluminous "Ford Supplement," a regular feature of *Motor* magazine after the introduction of the Model T.

16. Charles E. Duryea, "More Comforts for Women in Autos," *New York Times*, December 11, 1910. For more on Duryea, see James J. Flink, *The Car Culture* (Cambridge: M.I.T. Press, 1975), pp.1, 13–15; James J. Flink, *America Adopts the Automobile* (Cambridge: M.I.T. Press, 1970), pp. 19, 25, 51, 144, 156, 296; Rae, *The American Automobile*, pp. 6, 9, 10; and John B. Rae, *The Road and Car in American Life* (Cambridge: M.I.T. Press, 1971), p. 41; Theodore F. MacManus and Norman Beasley, *Men, Money, and Motors: The Drama of the Automobile* (New York: Harper and Brothers, 1930), p. xii.

17. Duryea.

18. Ibid.

19. Flink, *America Adopts the Automobile*, p. 238. Interestingly, Flink illustrated this contention with a picture of a 1906 Woods Electric "Surrey," a model that did not reflect the trend in electric vehicles toward boxiness and enclosed design apparent to contemporary observers as early as 1910. See also "Trend in Electric Car Construction," *Motor*, December 1910, p. 101.

20. Rae, *The American Automobile*, p. 47.

21. E. B. White, cited in Lacey, p. 95.

22. C. Wright Mills, *White Collar; The American Middle Classes* (London: Oxford University Press, 1971) is a classic study of the emergence of corporate bureaucracies and the particular habits and behaviors such institutions elicit.

23. *Motor*, July 1906.

24. *Motor*, January 1907, p. 238.

25. Harry Wilkin Perry, "The Retirement of the Crank," *Motor*, October 1911, p. 13.

26. Rae, *The American Automobile*, p. 48. Rae also noted that solving the starting problem cemented the triumph of the gasoline car over the steam-powered auto.

27. Ibid., pp. 47–48.

28. M. M. Musselman, *Get a Horse! The Story of the Automobile in America* (Philadelphia: J. B. Lippincott, 1950), p. 243, recalled his mother's determination to crank and drive the family car, despite the danger which, in one instance, earned her a badly bruised face.

29. Donovan, p. 138.

30. MacManus and Beasley, pp. 126–127.

31. Stuart W. Leslie, *Boss Kettering* (New York: Columbia University Press, 1983).

32. Ibid., p. 20.

33. Ibid., p. 29.

34. Lacey, p. 43; MacManus and Beasley, pp. 126–128; Leslie, p. 51.

35. Leslie, p. 48; Rae, *The American Automobile*, p. 48.

36. Nevins and Hill, p. 481.

37. "The Question of a Starter," *Motor*, December 1916, Ford Supplement.

38. In Houston in 1915, 97 out of 425 female car owners, or 22.8 percent, had Fords.

39. *Motor*, June 1915, Ford Supplement.

40. *Motor*, October 1915, Ford Supplement.

41. *Motor*, December 1915, Ford Supplement.

42. *Motor*, August 1916, Ford Supplement.

43. *Motor*, January 1917.

44. *Motor* (April 1917).

5 *Spectacle and Emancipation*

1. The American debate over protection as a strategy for empowering women was particularly significant in the first third of the twentieth century. See Alice Kessler-Harris, *Out to Work: A History of Wage-Earning Women in the United States* (New York: Oxford University Press, 1982), pp. 180–214; also J. Stanley Lemons, *The Woman Citizen: Social Feminism in the 1920's* (Urbana: University of Illinois Press, 1975).

2. Christine McGaffey Frederick, "The Commuter's Wife and the Motorcar," *Suburban Life*, July 1912, p. 13.

3. *New York Times*, November 10, 1903.

4. These cosmopolitan socialites, many of them members of a women's auto club in London, planned to pattern their organization on the British model. *New York Times*, November 10, 1903. The term "licenses" here refers to vehicle registration, and not to operators' permits.

5. Luellen Cass Teters, "Fair Woman as a Motorist," *Motor*, January 1907, p. 19.

6. "Mme. Du Gast Seeks American Fame," *Motor*, May 1904, p. 16.

7. *New York Times*, April 15, 1914.

8. *New York Times*, September 29, 1907; *The Hartford A.A.A. Automobiler*, February/March 1986. I thank Kate Swift for bringing this information to my attention.

9. An advertisement in an early issue of *Motor*, illustrated with a picture of four women in an auto, bore the caption, "The pleasures of motoring are enhanced by the knowledge that the dust and dirt of the road are quickly removed from the hair and scalp by a shampoo with CRANITONIC SOAP." *Motor*, October 1910, p. 11.

10. Teters, p. 19.

11. Ibid. See also James Brough, *Princess Alice: A Biography of Alice Roosevelt Longworth* (Boston: Little, Brown and Company, 1975), 148–149, 157; Michael Teague, *Mrs. L.: Conversations with Alice Roosevelt Longworth* (Garden City, N.Y.: Doubleday and Company, 1981), p. 82; Howard Teichmann, *Alice: The Life and Times of Alice Roosevelt Longworth* (Englewood Cliffs, N.J.: Prentice-Hall, 1979), 38–39.

12. See James R. McGovern, "The American Woman's Pre-World War I Freedom in Manners and Morals," *Journal of American History* 55 (September 1968):315–33.

13. On Roosevelt's views on "race suicide," see David M. Kennedy, *Birth Control in America: The Career of Margaret Sanger* (New Haven: Yale University Press, 1971), pp. 42–43.

14. Teague, p. 82.

15. *New York Times*, August 26, 1905.

16. *New York Times*, July 12, 1905.

17. *New York Times*, September 29, 1907.

18. *New York Times*, July 17, 1908.

19. *Motor*, August 1908, p. 37. On the Glidden tours, held between 1905 and 1913, see James J. Flink, *America Adopts the Automobile, 1895–1910* (Cambridge: M.I.T. Press, 1970), pp. 41–42,51; James J. Flink, *The Car Culture* (Cambridge: M.I.T. Press, 1975), pp. 23–24; John B. Rae, *The American Automobile* (Chicago: University of Chicago Press, 1965), pp. 31, 32, 218. For more on Cuneo, see M. M. Musselman, *Get a Horse! The Story of the Automobile in America* (New York: J. B. Lippincott, 1950), pp. 242–243.

20. *New York Times*, December 20, 1908.

21. *New York Times*, January 12, 1909; January 13, 1909; January 16, 1909; *Motor*, February 1909, p. 89.

22. *New York Times*, February 21, 1909.

23. *The Hartford A.A.A. Automobiler,* February/March 1986.

24. Musselman, p. 242.

25. Joan Newton Cuneo, "A Woman's Automobile Racing Record," *Country Life in America,* November 15, 1910, p. 127.

26. Charles J. Glidden's wife almost invariably accompanied him on auto tours in the United States and the Pacific, and evidently did some of the driving, since she reportedly taught the Queen of the Fiji Islands to drive and recalled that she "had the pleasure of giving many other native women of the Far East their first ride in a motor car." *New York Times,* September 29, 1907.

27. Flink, *The Car Culture,* pp. 22–23.

28. Among numerous studies of family journeys across the United States, see John Mack Faragher, *Women and Men on the Overland Trail* (New Haven: Yale University Press, 1979), and Lillian Schlissel, *Women's Diaries of the Westward Journey* (New York: Schocken Books, 1982.

29. Alice Huyler Ramsey, *Veil, Duster, and Tire Iron* (Covina, Calif.: Castle Press, 1961), pp. 1, 11–12.

30. Ibid., pp. 4, 9, 102–103; Lenora Berson, "What a Thrill to Take the Wheel," *Ms.,* February 1975, p. 17; David Holstrom, "With a Woman at the Wheel," *Exxon USA* 25, no. 2 (2nd Quarter, 1986):12–15.

31. Musselman, pp. 246–249.

32. *New York Times,* May 15, 1910.

33. Ibid., *New York Times,* May 17, 1910.

34. Emily Post, *By Motor to the Golden Gate* (New York: D. Appleton and Company, 1916); Harriet White Fisher, *A Woman's World Tour in a Motor* (Philadelphia and London: J. B. Lippincott, 1911); *Motor,* August 1909, p. 3; and May 1910, p. 71.

35. Jane De Hart Matthews, "The New Feminism and the Dynamics of Social Change," in Linda K. Kerber and Jane De Hart Matthews, eds., *Women's America: Refocusing the Past* (New York: Oxford University Press, 1982), p. 421, cites a similar "free rider" effect for late twentieth-century feminism.

36. On the American woman suffrage movement in the twentieth century, see Eleanor Flexner, *Century of Struggle: The Woman's Rights Movement in the United States* (Cambridge: Harvard University Press, 1975); and Aileen Kraditor, *The Ideas of the Woman Suffrage Movement, 1890–1920* (New York: W. W. Norton, 1981).

37. Ellen Carol DuBois, "Working Women, Class Relations, and Suffrage Militance: Harriot Stanton Blatch and the New York Woman Suffrage Movement, 1894–1909," *Journal of American History* 74, no. 1 (June 1987):54. In this article, DuBois explores militant suffragists' challenge to traditional notions of femininity.

38. Catherine Waugh McCulloch, "The 1910 Illinois Suffrage Auto Tours," Mary E. Dillon Collection, Arthur and Elizabeth Schlesinger Library, Radcliffe College, Cambridge, Mass. Hereafter cited as Dillon Collection, SL. See also Catherine W. McCulloch, "How to Conduct Automobile Trips," *The Woman's Journal,* July 30, 1910, p. 121.

39. McCulloch, "How to Conduct Automobile Trips," p. 121.

40. Mary E. Miller to the Illinois Equal Suffrage Association, August 4, 1910, Dillon Collection, SL.

41. McCulloch, "The 1910 Illinois Suffrage Auto Tours."

42. "Work of California's College Women," *The Woman's Journal,* October 28, 1911, p. 340.

43. Ada James to Catherine McCulloch, April 4, 1912, Dillon Collection, SL; McCulloch, "The 1910 Suffrage Auto Tours" and "How to Conduct Automobile Trips."

44. Quoted in DuBois, p. 57; these words are found in both of McCulloch's articles cited above.

45. DuBois has described working class suffragists' role in creating publicity-seeking tactics characteristic of suffrage militance. *Motor* magazine's early society column was devoted to chronicling the motoring escapades of Alva Belmont's social set, and she herself first appeared in *Motor*'s pages in May, 1911, arriving by auto at New York suffrage headquarters. On Belmont, see Frank Donovan, *Wheels for a Nation* (New York: Thomas Y. Crowell, 1965), p. 11; Allen Churchill, *The Upper Crust: An Informal History of New York's Highest Society* (Englewood Cliffs, N.J.: Prentice-Hall, 1970), p. 182.

46. *New York Times,* May 5, 1912. DuBois, pp. 53–55, discusses the treatment of suffrage actions in the popular press.

47. *New York Times,* October 3, 1913.

48. Ibid. Thanks to Ellen Dubois.

49. *New York Times,* December 16, 1914.

50. *Motor,* October 1903, p. 14. More than any other writer of her time, Edith Wharton captured the contradiction between the purportedly protected status of American women of the leisure class and the real financial insecurity such women faced. In *The House of Mirth* (New York: New American Library, 1964), Wharton told the story of Lily Bart, an American socialite who came to a pitiful end because she was unable to keep up with either the financial burden of high living or the cost of maintaining the illusion of affluence.

51. For a general introduction to Eastman's view of the feminist project, see Blanche Wiesen Cook, ed., *Crystal Eastman on Women and Revolution* (New York: Oxford University Press, 1978).

52. *New York Times,* December 16, 1914.

53. *New York Times,* January 23, 1916.

54. *New York Times,* November 29, 1914.

55. *New York Times,* January 2, 1915.
56. *New York Times,* April 23, 1916.
57. *New York Times,* July 30, 1914.
58. *New York Times,* April 29, 1915; July 4, 1915.
59. Ann Bail Howard, *The Long Campaign: A Biography of Anne Martin* (Reno: University of Nevada Press, 1985), pp. 103, 107.
60. *New York Times,* April 2, 1916; April 6, 1916; April 7, 1916; October 1, 1916. See also Margaret R. Burlingame, "The Motor Car Pays Its Debt to Woman," *Motor,* July 1919, p. 39.
61. Burlingame, p. 38. For a discussion of the crank as an embodiment of the relation between gender ideology and automotive design, see Chapter 2.
62. Joseph J. Corn, *The Winged Gospel; America's Romance with Aviation, 1900–1950* (New York: Oxford University Press, 1983), pp. 71–90, details a similar role for women in aviation, in his terms, "making flying 'thinkable.' "

6   Women Drivers in World War I

1. The phenomenon scholars have called a "crisis of masculinity" (which, to be sure, implied a complementary crisis of femininity) encompassed both collective planning for the war emergency and sudden events that exploded certainty and identity all at once. See Eric Leed, *No Man's Land: Combat and Identity in World War I* (Cambridge: Cambridge University Press, 1979); Elaine Showalter, "Rivers and Sassoon: The Inscription of Male Gender Anxieties," in Margaret R. Higonnet, Jane Jenson, Sonya Michel, and Margaret Collins Weitz, eds., *Behind the Lines: Gender and the Two World Wars* (New Haven: Yale University Press, 1987), pp. 61–69; Sandra Gilbert, "Soldier's Heart: Literary Men, Literary Women, and the Great War," in Higonnet et al., pp. 197–226.
2. For a general survey of American women's work in World War I, see Ida Clyde Clarke, *American Women and the World War* (New York: D. Appleton and Company, 1918). On American women workers, see Maureen Weiner Greenwald, *Women, War, and Work: The Impact of World War I on Women Workers in the United States* (Westport, Conn.: Greenwood Press, 1981). On the place of women's unpaid work in capitalist patriarchal economies, see Natalie Sokoloff, *Between Money and Love* (New York: Praeger, 1980), pp. 200–201. Karen Anderson, *Wartime Women: Sex Roles, Family Relations, and the Status of Women during World War II* (Westport, Conn.: Greenwood Press, 1981), pp. 88–93, deals with women's volunteer work in World War II. For an insightful case study of the place of volunteer work in Ameri-

can social and economic life, see Cheryl Knott Malone, "Labor Without Pay: Women's Volunteer Work in American Hospitals, 1945–1965" (M.A. thesis, University of Arizona, 1985), especially pp. 1–12.

3. Jenny Gould, "Women's Military Services in First World War Britain," in Higonnet et al., pp. 115–116.

4. Helen Fraser, *Women and War Work* (New York: G. Arnold Shaw, 1918), p. 56.

5. Fraser, p. 217; Harriot Stanton Blatch, *Mobilizing Woman-Power* (New York: Woman's Press, 1918), p. 42.

6. Blatch, pp. 52–53. See also Barbara McLaren, *Women of the War* (New York: George H. Doran Company, 1918), pp. 125–128; 148–150; David Mitchell, *Monstrous Regiment: The Story of the Women of the First World War* (New York: Macmillan, 1965), pp. 128–139.

7. *New York Times*, March 7, 1915. On British women's agricultural work during the war, see "Britain's Cupboard No Longer Bare," *Motor*, September 1918, pp. 54–55.

8. *New York Times*, February 27, 1916. See also Blatch, pp. 41–42; McLaren, p. 150; Mitchell, p. 128.

9. Fraser, p. 102; Blanche McManus, "The War-Time Chauffeuse," *Motor*, July 1917, pp. 78–79, 148; Nancy Woods Walburn, "Crusaders of Mercy," *Motor*, May 1918, p. 65; "Britain's Cupboards No Longer Bare."

10. Fraser, p. 103; Blatch, p. 96.

11. "Introduction," Higonnet et al., p. 17. Blatch presents a more sanguine view of the French government's response to women's willingness to volunteer, pp. 52, 60–62.

12. McManus, p. 150; *New York Times*, February 24, 1916.

13. McManus, pp. 148, 150.

14. Ibid., p. 150.

15. Clarke, pp. 466–467.

16. Blanche McManus, " 'Who's Who' of Willing Workers," *Motor*, June 1918, p. 78.

17. Gilbert, p. 214.

18. McManus, " 'Who's Who,' " p. 78; Walburn, p. 68.

19. Gilbert, p. 212.

20. Radclyffe Hall, *The Well of Loneliness* (New York: Pocket Books, 1974), p. 283.

21. Clarke, p. 468; Walburn, p. 68.

22. Walburn, p. 108.

23. Gertrude Stein, *The Autobiography of Alice B. Toklas* (New York: Vintage, 1960), p. 168.

24. Stein, pp. 168–172; James R. Mellow, *The Charmed Circle: Ger-*

trude *Stein and Company* (New York: Avon Books, 1974), pp. 275, 279. Toklas never did learn to drive, but instead performed the tedious task of keeping records and issuing supplies. She recorded many of their wartime experiences in *The Alice B. Toklas Cookbook* (New York: Perennial Library, 1984), pp. 59–94.

25. Stein, p. 174; Mellow, pp. 275–287; Toklas, pp. 63–67.

26. Clarke, 468–487; Walburn, p. 66.

27. Walburn, pp. 67, 108.

28. *New York Times*, April 25, 1916; April 27, 1916.

29. Walburn; "Society Motorists in Wartime," *Motor*, November 1917, p. 81. See also Mitchell, pp. 128–139, on Mairi Chisholm and Mrs. Knocker, two volunteers known as "the women of Pervyse."

30. McManus, " 'Who's Who,' " p. 79.

31. Clarke, pp. 181–185.

32. *New York Times*, June 3, 1917.

33. *New York Times*, April 24, 1918.

34. "Women's Work for You and Me to 'Carry On,' " *Good Housekeeping* (July 1918):39.

35. *New York Times*, April 7, 1918; July 14, 1918.

36. *New York Times*, April 7, 1918; November 3, 1918; *New York Times*, December 4, 1918.

37. *New York Times*, October 1, 1918.

38. *New York Times*, April 7, 1918. Gould, pp. 118–120, describes British resistance to putting women in uniform.

39. Hamblin Rossiter, "The Woman and the Car," *Harper's Weekly*, January 8, 1910, pp. 26.

40. Burr C. Cook, "Women as Auto Mechanics," *Illustrated World*, June 1916, p. 503.

41. H. G. Parsons, "Women Motor Mechanics for War-time Work," *Illustrated World*, May 1918, p. 363. *Automobile Digest*, August 1918, p. 44, also featured a photograph of a woman who, with her sister, ran a 250-car garage in the Bronx, with the caption, "Who Said That Women Are Not Mechanical?"

42. *New York Times*, October 1, 1918. On athleticism and femininity, see Victoria Brown, "Golder Girls: Female Socialization in Los Angeles, 1880 to 1910" (Ph. D. dissertation, University of California at San Diego, 1985).

43. "From Buds to Buddies," *Motor*, November 1918, p. 58.

44. Arthur L. Drew, "The Car in Community Service," *Motor*, October 1918, pp. 49–51.

45. Clarke, p.p. 88–89.

46. Zelda Fitzgerald, *Save Me the Waltz* (New York: Signet, 1968), p. 43.

47. Clarke, pp. 85–87. On regulation of sexuality and moral policing during World War I, see John D'Emilio and Estelle B. Freedman, *Intimate Matters: A History of Sexuality in America* (New York: Harper and Row, 1988), pp. 211–213.

48. Clarke, pp. 185–187.

49. Clarke, pp. 252–253.

50. Stein, p. 174.

51. *New York Times*, July 28, 1918.

52. Grace Bartlett, "The Red Cross Motor Corps Girl," *Motor*, January 1919, pp. 59–60, 142; Waldon Fawcett, "The Motor's Part in Red Cross Work," *American Automobile Digest*, May 1926, pp. 17–19.

53. On Anne Morgan, see Barbara Sicherman, Carol Hurd Green, Ilene Kantrov, and Harriette Walker, eds., *Notable American Women: The Modern Period* (Cambridge: The Belknap Press of Harvard University Press, 1980), pp. 498–499. On the American Committee for Devastated France, see "Friends of France; How American Girls in American Camionettes are Carrying On in Devastated France," *Motor*, February 1921, pp. 43, 66; Miriam P. Blagden, "In Humanity's Service," *Motor*, March 1922, pp. 30, 84.

54. Elizabeth O. Toombs, "A Peace-Time Motor Corps; An Aftermath of the War That Is Working for the Motoring Public," *Motor*, February 1921, pp. 41, 66.

55. Alexander Johnston, "Knights and Ladies; 'Casey' Establishes Training School for Ex-Service Women in Washington with Full Attendance," *Motor*, July 1920, pp. 56–57.

56. For a general discussion of the relation between women's status and female participation in public activities, particularly with regard to "defense," see Peggy R. Sanday, "Female Status in the Public Domain," in Michelle Zimbalist Rosaldo and Louise Lamphere, eds., *Woman, Culture, and Society* (Stanford, Calif.: Stanford University Press, 1974), pp. 189–206.

57. Gilbert, p. 217, notes the connection between lesbian eroticism and war service in Radclyffe Hall's *The Well of Loneliness* and Gertrude Stein's wartime poetry. Hall's Stephen Gordon meets her lover, Mary Llewellyn, in an ambulance unit.

58. Anita Loos, *Gentlemen Prefer Blondes* (New York: Liveright, 1973), pp. 193, 195.

59. *Motor*, December 1918.

60. "The Order of the Winged Wheel," *Motor*, December 1921, p. 35.

61. Stein, pp. 189, 190.

7   *Corporate Masculinity and the "Feminine" Market*

1. On the complexity of the emerging feminist movement and its relation to the woman suffrage campaign, see Nancy F. Cott, *The Grounding of Modern Feminism* (New Haven: Yale University Press, 1987), pp. 49–50.

2. Robert Wiebe, *The Search for Order, 1877–1920* (New York: Hill and Wang, 1967), pp. 294–296.

3. *Statistical Abstract of the United States* (Washington, D.C.: Department of Commerce, 1931), p. 403.

4. John B. Rae, *The American Automobile* (Cambridge: M.I.T. Press, 1965, pp. 87–91, summarizes the economic expansion and predominance of the industry in the 1920s. See also Alfred D. Chandler, Jr., *Giant Enterprise: Ford, General Motors, and the Automobile Industry* (New York: Harcourt, Brace and World, 1964), pp. 13–16.

5. Harold Livesay, *American Made: Men Who Shaped the American Economy* (Boston: Little, Brown and Company, 1979), pp. 5–14, 159–161, 230–232; Rae, pp. 56–57; Chandler, p. 150; James J. Flink, *The Car Culture* (Cambridge: M.I.T. Press, 1971), pp. 49, 75; Frank Donovan, *Wheels for a Nation* (New York: Thomas Y. Crowell, 1965), pp. 1–12, 99–100; Donald Finlay Davis, *Conspicuous Production: Automobiles and Elites in Detroit, 1899–1933* (Philadelphia: Temple University Press, 1988).

6. Chandler, p. 95.

7. Chandler, p. 149.

8. Turner outlined his view of the American character in "The Significance of the Frontier in American History," an address to the Mississippi Valley Historical Society, Chicago, 1893, reprinted in George Rogers Taylor, ed., *The Turner Thesis: Concerning the Role of the Frontier in American History* (Lexington, Mass.: D. C. Heath and Company, 1972), pp. 3–27. David Potter questioned the applicability of Turner's generalizations to women's character and experience in "American Women and the American Character," in Don E. Fehrenbacher, ed., *History and American Society: Essays of David M. Potter* (New York: Oxford University Press, 1973), pp. 277–303. The feminist critique, rejection, and revision of Turner's assumptions about American history have fruitfully occupied historians of women in the American West. See Susan Armitage and Elizabeth Jameson, eds., *The Women's West* (Norman: University of Oklahoma Press, 1987).

Theodore F. MacManus and Norman Beasley, *Men, Money, and Motors: the Drama of the Automobile* (New York: Harper and Brothers, 1930); and M. M. Musselman, *Get a Horse! The Story of the Automobile in America* (Philadelphia: J. B. Lippincott, 1950), offer enthusiastic portrayals of the early successful automobile manufacturers as competitive, risk-taking pioneers.

9. MacManus and Beasley, pp. vii–viii.

10. Alfred P. Sloan, Jr. and Boyden Sparks, *Adventures of a White-Collar Man* (New York: Doubleday, Doran, and Company, 1941), pp. 64, 68, 69, 71–72.

11. On Ford's halting and belated capitulation to pressure to advertise, see Roland Marchand, *Advertising the American Dream: Making Way for Modernity* (Berkeley: University of California Press, 1985), p. 7.

12. *Los Angeles Times*, January 26, 1920.

13. Though Ford held out against advertising until the mid-1920s, makers of this stunning variety of accessories possessed no similar aversion. Many advertised in *Motor's* "Ford Supplement."

14. Rae, pp. 87–88, 97; Chandler, p. 95; Donovan, p. 122; Sloan, *My Years with General Motors* (Garden City, N.Y.: Doubleday and Company, 1964), pp. 150, 162.

15. Livesay, pp. 217, 221; Sloan, quoted in Donovan, p. 121.

16. Sloan, *My Years with General Motors*, p. 164.

17. Sloan and Sparks, *Adventures of a White-Collar Man*, p. 137.

18. Ray W. Sherman, "The New Buyer," *Motor* (January 1927):306.

19. In 1922, GM led the way by contracting with Bruce Barton, of Barton, Durstine, and Osborn (now BBD&O), to coordinate corporate advertising. See Sloan, *My Years with General Motors*, pp. 104–105.

20. Marchand, pp. 1, 6–7, 33–35, 66–69. Erving Goffman discussed the social relation between sex, gender, and advertising in *Gender Advertisements* (New York: Harper and Row, 1979), pp. 1–9.

21. Marchand, pp. 6, 40–41, 46.

22. Ibid., pp. 35–36.

23. Ray W. Sherman, "The New Buyer," *Motor*, January 1927, pp. 68–69, 306, 308. See also Ray W. Sherman, "Our Next Great Development Is the Woman Driver," *Motor*, September 1925, p. 27.

24. "Where Women Motorists Excel Mere Men," *Literary Digest*, December 4, 1920, p. 74. It is not clear whether this figure reflected female automobile ownership or driver's licensing.

25. *Los Angeles Times*, April 11, 1920.

26. *Facts and Figures of the Automobile Industry* (New York: National Automobile Chamber of Commerce, 1923), p. 12.

27. Male drivers' numerical predominance and greater access to cars continues to prevail. See Mary K. Cichocki, "Women's Travel Patterns in a Suburban Development," in Gerda Wekerle, Rebecca Peterson, and David Morley, eds., *New Space for Women* (Boulder, Colo.: Westview Press, 1980), p. 158; also Jo Freeman, "Women and Urban Policy," in Catharine R. Stimpson, Elsa Dixler, Martha J. Nelson, and

Kathryn B. Yatrakis, eds., *Women and the American City* (Chicago and London: University of Chicago Press, 1981), p. 9.

28. Henry Ford recognized in the early twenties that families might buy more than one car. See Chandler, p. 103. By 1927, several manufacturers had begun to stress the theme of two-car families in their advertising. See Marchand, p. 161. For a contemporary insider's view of the female market for cars, see Sherman, "The New Buyer."

29. *Recent Social Trends in the United States: Report of the President's Research Committee on Social Trends* (New York and London: McGraw-Hill Book Company, 1933), vol. 1, p. 307; Hildegard Kneeland, "Women's Economic Contribution in the Home," *Annals of the American Academy of Political and Social Science* 143 (1929): p.33.

30. Winifred Wandersee, *Women's Work and Family Values* (Cambridge: Harvard University Press, 1981), p. 82.

31. The question of women's influence on men's car buying was not entirely new. As early as 1913, *Motor* writer Margaret R. Burlingame had asserted that "it is beginning to be a recognized fact in the marketing of automobiles that women must be taken into consideration in almost every sale." Margaret R. Burlingame, "Needs Must, When—Woman Asks," *Motor*, May 1913, p. 50.

By 1915, *Harper's Bazaar*, eager for auto advertising, was running ads in *Motor* magazine claiming that at least seventy-five percent of car sales were influenced by women, and citing a *Printer's Ink* article from that year quoting a "well-known" car salesman's remark that in ninety-nine percent of all auto transactions, "the women *close*, or *queer* the sale." Appealing to manufacturers of high-priced vehicles, a more select group than Burlingame appeared to address, *Harper's Bazaar* assured potential advertisers that it was "edited for and read by a class of women whose station in life makes their approval or disapproval the deciding factor in the purchase of automobiles." *Motor*, June 1915. Donovan, p. 14, reported that Oldsmobile had advertised in the *Ladies' Home Journal* as early as 1903. By January 1927, *Good Housekeeping* was running ads in *Motor* claiming that "the Woman Appeal is selling automobiles today."

32. *Los Angeles Times*, April 25, 1920; *Los Angeles Examiner*, April 25, 1920.

33. Edward S. Jordan, "Man Pays But Woman Chooses," *Motor*, February 1920, p. 35.

34. Elizabeth Hallam Bohn, "How to Sell the Woman," *Motor*, August 1922, pp. 60, 96.

35. O. O. McIntyre, "Enter Madame!" *Motor*, January 1927, p. 119.

36. Historian Frank Donovan would make the same connection in 1965, pp. 13–14, 99. On working women's automobility in this period,

see Jacquelyn Dowd Hall, "Disorderly Women: Gender and Labor Militancy in the Appalachian South," *Journal of American History* 73, no. 2 (September 1986):354, 360, 362, 366, 377, 379.

37. Frank J. Arkins, "Fitting Your Car to Your Fancy," *Motor*, September 1912, pp. 58–59.

38. Burlingame, "Needs Must," p. 50.

39. Clifford B. Knight, "The Women Decide," *Motor* (October 1923):96.

40. Jordan, "Man Pays," pp. 35, 86.

41. "More or Less Feminine," *Motor*, December 1921, p. 44; "Dainty Accessories for Women Motorists," *Motor*, May 1922, p. 28; "Appealing Particularly to Women Motorists," *Motor*, October 1923, p. 50.

42. Monte W. Sohn, "Would Women Buy This Car?" *Motor*, September 1924, pp. 29, 74, 88. See also John Chapman Hilder, "Who Says the Woman Pays," *Motor*, July 1921, pp. 37, 82, 84.

43. Bohn, p. 60.

44. Janice Doane and Devon Hodges explore the relation between nostalgia and gender ideology in *Nostalgia and Sexual Difference* (New York: Methuen, 1987).

45. *Los Angeles Record*, February 12, 1920. Other sources also mention nagging wives: Robert S. Hall, "Why People Buy Motor Cars," *Touring Topics*, May 1925, p. 26; Hilder, "Who Says the Woman Pays?"; "The High Cost of Women," *Motor*, August 1921, p. 73.

46. "What's On Your Mind?", *Motor*, October 1923, p. 53.

47. Roscoe Peacock, "I Want a Man's Car," *Motor*, January 1929, pp. 86–87.

48. *Statistical Abstract of the United States* (Washington, D.C.: Government Printing Office, 1930), p. 385.

49. Sloan, *My Years with General Motors*, p. 162.

50. "Closed Car Types Are More Popular; Indispensable for All Year Use in the City or Country—Favored by Women Motorists," *New York Times*, January 6, 1918; "The Triumph of the Sedan," *Motor*, February 1922, p. 19; Bohn, p. 62; John C. Long, "Ask Mother—She Knows," *Motor*, September 1923, pp. 92, 98, 100; "Distinguished Cars for Distinguished Women," *Motor*, March 1923, pp. 26–27; H. C. Wendt, "Meeting Woman's Taste in Body Style," *Automobile Topics* June 20, 1925, pp. 531–533.

51. See advertisements for the Grant Six, Buick, and Morse Chain Company in *Motor*, January 1920; for the Overland, *Motor*, February 1920; and for the American, *Motor*, January 1921.

52. Rae, p. 75; Sloan, *My Years with General Motors*, p. 160; The open car's springtime maintenance was no small matter. C. H. Claudy described the process in "Putting the Car in Order," *Woman's Home Companion*, March 1917, p. 33.

53. *Motor*, October 1920, p. 95.

54. Peacock, "I Want a Man's Car," p. 87.

55. Long, "Ask Mother—She Knows," p. 92.

56. Ibid.; Rae, p. 74; Donovan, p. 151; "The Triumph of the Sedan," p. 19.

57. *Motor*, October 1916.

58. Martha May, "The Historical Problem of the Family Wage: The Ford Motor Company and the Five Dollar Day," *Feminist Studies* 8, no. 2 (Summer 1982):399–424.

59. *Motor*, November 1920; Sloan, *My Years with General Motors*, pp. 158–159.

60. Donovan, p. 151.

61. *Statistical Abstract of the United States*, p. 385.

62. Sloan, *My Years at General Motors*, p. 266.

63. Ibid.

64. Long, "Ask Mother—She Knows," p. 92.

65. The phrases are found in "All the Comforts of Home," *Motor*, December 1919, p. 58; "Closed Car Types Are More Popular"; advertisement for the Moon, *Motor*, February 1920; Harold F. Blanchard, "Mr. Designer—Come Out of the Kitchen," *Motor*, October 1925, pp. 32–33, 128, 136.

66. Ibid.

67. Lady Duff-Gordon (Lucile), "The Philosophy of Automobile Decoration," *Motor*, September 1919, p. 39.

68. Edith M. Garfield, "As the Woman Buyer Sees You," *Motor*, January 1925, pp. 84–85, 156. The Lanchester vibration dampener, a device intended to provide a smoother ride, was introduced by Packard in 1920. See Motor Vehicle Manufacturers Association of the United States, *Automobiles of America*, 4th ed. (Detroit: Wayne State University Press, 1974), p. 70.

69. See advertisements for Houdaille shock absorbers, *Motor*, August 1921, and *Motor*, September 1923; for the smooth-riding Paige car, *Motor*, March 1924; also seat cover advertisements in the June 1915, April 1916, June 1917, December 1919, and January 1920 issues of *Motor*. Auto heaters were depicted as boons to women, children, and the elderly in "The Heater for Your Closed Car," *Motor*, September 1922, pp. 76, 104, 106, and in advertisements in *Motor*, December 1916, December 1917, November 1921, and June 1925. For ads emphasizing the advantages of windshields, windshield wipers, side windows, and window curtains to women drivers and passengers, see *Motor*, December 1909, January 1910, January 1917, December 1919, April 1920, August 1920, and September 1920. For examples of advertising stressing the benefit to women of reliable tires and tire-changing equipment including jacks and inflating devices, see ads in *Motor* in March

1904, February 1907, January 1910, January 1920, February 1920, July 1920, August 1920, September 1920, May 1921, June 1921, August 1921, and October 1921.

70. "Comfort in Motor Travel," *Motor*, September 1920, p. 94.

71. Teresa Madeline Tarantous, "Make Yourself Comfortable," *Motor*, August 1920, pp. 40–41.

72. As of 1987, many states had passed mandatory child car seat laws in an effort to insure safe transportation for small children. In Arizona, for example, motorists need not suffer financial hardship complying with the law; car seats are available on loan through programs administered by hospitals.

73. Arkins, "Fitting Your Car to Your Fancy," p. 58.

74. "New Things for the Motorist," *Motor*, July 1918, pp. 98–99. Similar devices appeared in *Motor*, April 1917, August 1920, and May 1921.

75. Tarantous, "Make Yourself Comfortable," p. 41.

76. J. L. Wilson, "The Feminine Influence," *Motor*, February 1921, p. 28.

77. Ray W. Sherman, "Our Next Great Development," *Motor*, September 1925, p. 27.

78. *Sunset*, May 1920, p. 63; *New York Times*, January 8, 1929.

79. *Good Housekeeping*, May 1924, p. 107.

80. *Ladies' Home Journal*, April 1925.

81. *Ladies' Home Journal*, February 1926.

82. *Ladies' Home Journal*, February 1926, p. 65; March 1926, p. 116.

83. Rae, illustration facing p. 49.

84. Sherman, "A New Buyer," pp. 68–69, 306, 308.

85. Christine Frederick, *Selling Mrs. Consumer* (New York: Business Bourse, 1929), p. 6.

86. Donovan, pp. 150–151; Rae, p. 90.

87. Sloan, *My Years with General Motors*, pp. 272–273.

88. Wandersee, p. 20.

89. Frederick, p. 35.

90. "Can Every Family Own a Car?" *Literary Digest*, February 3, 1923, p. 60.

91. Marjorie Davis, "Our Conservation Car," *Ladies' Home Journal*, April 1920, p. 113.

92. Robert S. Lynd and Helen M. Lynd, *Middletown: A Study in Contemporary American Culture* (New York: Harcourt, Brace and Company, 1929), pp. 256, 260.

8   Women at the Wheel in the 1920s

1. "New *Convertible* Body Model," *Motor* (August 1922):37, described an automobile body called "The Flapper," and featured an illustration of a young woman in a military-style knicker suit with riding crop, standing in front of the car. The Flapper model was equipped with a folding bed, side curtains, an ice box, and a variety of devices to facilitate cross-country touring. See also Laura B. McClintock, "Knickers and Smiles," *Motor*, September 1923, pp. 32–33, 94, 96; "Hitting the High Spots," *Sunset*, August 1920, p. 15.

2. McClintock, pp. 33, 94; see also "Lucky Ladies Who Motor Alone," *Literary Digest*, August 11, 1923, pp. 50, 52, 54.

3. Winifred Hawkridge Dixon, *Westward Hoboes: Ups and Downs of Frontier Motoring* (New York: Charles Scribner's Sons, 1922), pp. 2–4, 17, 30–31, 37, 45.

4. Dixon, pp. 49, 249, 274, 339, 352, 357.

5. Warren James Belasco, *Americans on the Road: From Autocamp to Motel, 1910–1945* (Cambridge: M.I.T. Press, 1981).

6. Quoted in Belasco, p. 85. On women's work and motor camping in the 1920s, see also Harriet Wilkin Johnson, "Housekeeping on Wheels," *Motor*, May 1922, pp. 26, 82, 84; pictorial feature, *Motor*, May 1924, pp. 33–34; "A Woman's Advice on Motor Camping" *Literary Digest*, April 4, 1925, pp. 82–86; F. E. Brimmer, "The Motor Camping Commissary," *Motor*, August 1922, pp. 50, 92; L. W. C. Tuthill, "Camping in Home Comfort," *Motor*, May 1924, pp. 44–45, 94; Frederick F. van de Water, "Discovering America in a Flivver," Part 1, *Ladies' Home Journal*, February 1926, pp. 6–7, 82; Frederick F. Van de Water, "Discovering America in a Flivver," Part 2, *Ladies' Home Journal*, May 1926, p. 27.

7. *Los Angeles Record*, January 12, 1920.

8. James R. McGovern, "The American Woman's Pre-World War I Freedom in Manners and Morals," in Jean E. Friedman and William G. Shade, eds., *Our American Sisters: Women in American Life and Thought*, 3rd ed. (Lexington, Mass.: D. C. Heath and Company, 1982), pp. 479–499. See also John C. Burnham, "The Progressive Era Revolution in American Attitudes Toward Sex," *Journal of American History* 59, no. 4 (March 1973):885–908. On dance halls, night spots, and motion pictures, see Lewis A. Ehrenberg, *Steppin' Out: New York Nightlife and the Transformation of American Culture* (Chicago: University of Chicago Press, 1981); Kathy Peiss, *Cheap Amusements: Working Women and Leisure in Turn-of-the-Century New York* (Philadelphia: Temple University Press, 1986); Mary P. Ryan, "The Projection of a New Womanhood: The Movie Moderns in the 1920's," in Friedman and Shade, pp. 500–518.

9. On the relation between the auto, morality, and sexuality, see John B. Rae, *The Road and Car in American Life* (Cambridge: M.I.T. Press, 1971), p. 150; Marlou Belyea, "The Joy Ride and the Silver Screen: Commercial Leisure, Delinquency, and Play Reform in Los Angeles, 1900–1980" (Ph.D. dissertation, Boston University, 1983); Michael L. Berger, *The Devil Wagon in God's Country: The Automobile and Social Change in Rural America, 1893–1929* (Hamden, Conn.: Archon Books, 1979), pp. 138–142; Ashleigh Brilliant, "The Social Effects of the Automobile in Southern California During the 1920's" (Ph.D. dissertation, University of California, 1964), pp. 36–91; Glen Jeansonne, "The Automobile and American Morality," *Journal of Popular Culture* 8 (1974):128; David L. Lewis, "Sex and the Automobile: From Rumble Seats to Rockin' Vans," in David L. Lewis and Laurence Goldstein, eds., *The Automobile and American Culture* (Ann Arbor: University of Michigan Press, 1983), pp. 123–133. The best-known treatment of the subject is in Robert S. and Helen M. Lynd, *Middletown: A Study in Contemporary Culture* (New York: Harcourt, Brace and Company, 1929).

10. Among the innumerable examples of the linking of automobility with courtship, see Harold McGrath, "Love in the Motor Car," *Motor*, November 1903, pp. 27–29; Elizabeth A. Moore, "The Hay Motor and the Bubble," *Motor*, January 1904, pp. 36–37; and Marion Gregory, "The Maid and the Motor Car," *Motor*, October 1904, pp. 35, 74. For expert opinions, see Niles Carpenter, "Courtship Practices and Contemporary Social Change," *Annals of the American Academy of Political and Social Science* 160 (March 1932):41. The most widely cited statement of the auto as sexual peril is the 1925 remark by a resident of Muncie, Indiana that automobiles were "houses of prostitution on wheels." See Lynd and Lynd, p. 114.

11. Eleanor Rowland Wembridge, "Petting and the Campus," *Survey* 54 (July 1, 1925):395. On the culture of petting see Paula Fass, *The Damned and the Beautiful: American Youth in the 1920's* (New York: Oxford University Press, 1977), pp. 262–278.

12. *Los Angeles Examiner*, February 1, 1920.

13. Burnham, p. 887.

14. *Los Angeles Record*, May 10, 1920.

15. *Los Angeles Examiner*, February 7, 1920.

16. *Los Angeles Record*, January 8, 1920.

17. *Los Angeles Times*, January 8, 1920. In one case, a woman walking along a street in a thickly populated residential area was abducted by two men who threw a blanket over her head, poured "drugs" over the blanket, and stuffed her in the rear of an automobile, robbing and abandoning her in the Hollywood foothills. *Los Angeles Record*, July 31, 1919. In another instance, a young Oakland, California woman

who had walked a friend to a streetcar was kidnapped by two men in an automobile and strangled to death. *Los Angeles Record*, March 13, 1920.

18. *Los Angeles Record*, January 2, 1920. For similar treatment of women who claimed a right to public pleasures, see Karen Anderson's analysis of "Victory Girls" in World War II, in *Wartime Women: Sex Roles, Family Relations, and the Status of Women During World War II* (Westport, Conn.: Greenwood Press, 1982), pp. 103–111.

19. On the tenacity of domestic ideology, see Alice Kessler-Harris, "Independence and Virtue in the Lives of Wage-Earning Women: The United States, 1870–1930," in Judith Friedlander, Blanche Wiesen Cook, Alice Kessler-Harris, and Carroll Smith-Rosenberg, eds., *Women in Culture and Politics: A Century of Change* (Bloomington: Indiana University Press, 1986), pp. 3–17.

20. On this point, my argument is similar to Martin Wachs, "Men, Women, and Wheels: The Historical Basis of Gender Differences in Travel Patterns" (paper presented to the 66th Annual Meeting of the Transportation Research Board, Washington, D.C., January 1987, in author's possession).

21. For a similarly sanguine assessment of the auto's impact on women's social life, see James J. Flink, *The Car Culture* (Cambridge: M.I.T. Press, 1975), p. 87.

22. *Ladies' Home Journal*, March 1925, p. 70.

23. *Good Housekeeping*, March 1924, p. 99.

24. Berger, p. 57. On the auto's impact on rural life, see also Joseph Interrante, "You Can't Go to Town in a Bathtub: Automobile Movement and the Reorganization of Rural American Space, 1900–1930," *Radical History Review* 21 (Fall 1979):151–168; Reynold M. Wik, *Henry Ford and Grass-Roots America* (Ann Arbor: University of Michigan Press, 1972); and Reynold M. Wik, "The Early Automobile and the American Farmer," in Lewis and Goldstein, eds., pp. 37–47.

25. Florence E. Ward, "The Farm Woman's Problems," *Journal of Home Economics* 12, no. 10 (October 1920):445–446.

26. Ibid.

27. Cited in Berger, p. 52.

28. Ward, p. 450.

29. Joan M. Jensen, "Canning Comes to New Mexico: Women and the Agricultural Extension Service, 1914–1919," in Joan M. Jensen and Darlis A. Miller, eds., *New Mexico Women: Intercultural Perspectives* (Albuquerque: University of New Mexico Press, 1986), pp. 201–226.

30. "Canning Club Leader Uses Remarkably Equipped Car," *Popular Mechanics*, April 1920, p. 567. I am indebted to Martin Wachs for bringing this article to my attention.

31. Florence Carvin, "My Four Years in Jackson County, Missouri, as a Home Demonstration Agent," *Journal of Home Economics* 13, no. 11 (November 1921):543–544.

32. Jensen, "Canning Comes to New Mexico," p. 221, points out that urban women were at this time abandoning many of the practices home demonstration agents were trying to encourage among rural women. Anna Gilbert, "The Extensionized Farm Woman," *Journal of Home Economics* 13, no. 7 (July 1921):303.

33. Carvin, p. 544.

34. Berger, pp. 65–66.

35. Eleanor Arnold, ed., *Voices of American Homemakers* (Washington, D.C.: National Extension Homemakers' Council, 1985), p. 210.

36. Sociologist Katherine Jensen argues that "rural women's relation to economic production demands that they gain a higher level of skills and more diverse technological competence than is usually expected of urban women (and most urban men)." See Katherine R. Jensen, "Mother Calls Herself a Housewife, But She Buys Bulls," in Jan Zimmerman, ed., *The Technological Woman: Interfacing with Tomorrow* (New York: Praeger Books, 1983), p. 136.

37. Eleanor Arnold, ed., *Buggies and Bad Times* (Indianapolis: Indiana Extension Homemakers' Association, 1985), pp. 43–44.

38. Berger, p. 66.

39. For a representative statement of early twentieth-century social science commentary on the transformation of the household, see *Recent Social Trends in the United States,* vol. 1 (New York: McGraw-Hill Book Company, 1933), pp. 292, 664–666. William H. Sewell, Jr., "Abbe Sieyès and the Rhetoric of Revolution," in *Proceedings of the 14th Consortium on Revolutionary Europe* (Durham: University of North Carolina Press, 1984), traces the origins of the valorization of production in an examination of Sieyès' pamphlet, "What Is the Third Estate?" E. P. Thompson, "The Moral Economy of the Crowd in Eighteenth-Century England," *Past and Present* 50 (February 1971):76–136, offered a path-breaking analysis of the social and political role of consumption in England before the formulation of liberal political economy.

Some contemporary social scientists share the anticonsumerist perspective. See especially Stewart Ewen, *Captains of Consciousness: Advertising and the Social Roots of the Consumer Culture* (New York: McGraw-Hill, 1976). For a critique of this perspective, see "A Redstocking Sister" (Ellen Willis), "Consumerism and Women," in Vivian Gornick and Barbara K. Moran, eds., *Woman in Sexist Society: Studies in Power and Powerlessness* (New York: Basic Books, 1971), pp. 658–664.

40. Ruth Schwartz Cowan, *More Work for Mother: The Ironies of*

Household Technology from the Open Hearth to the Microwave (New York: Basic Books, 1983).

41. This phrase comes from Christopher Lasch, *Haven in a Heartless World: The Family Besieged* (New York: Basic Books, 1979).

42. Cowan, p. 85.

43. Laura Balbo, "The Servicing Work of Women and the Capitalist State," *Political Power and Social Theory* 3 (1982):251–270; Cowan, *More Work for Mother*; Marjorie DeVault, "The Logic of Housework: Feeding and Family Life" (paper presented to the National Women's Studies Association, Seattle, June 1985); Micaela Di Leonardo, "The Female World of Cards and Holidays: Women, Families, and the Work of Kinship," *SIGNS: Journal of Women in Culture and Society* 12, no. 3 (Spring 1987):440–453; Alison Griffith, "Mothering and Schooling" (paper presented to the National Women's Studies Association, Seattle, June 1985); Ann Oakley, *The Sociology of Housework* (London: Martin Robinson, 1974), and Ann Oakley, *Subject Women* (New York: Pantheon Books, 1981), pp. 163–187; Rayna Rapp, "Family and Class in Contemporary America: Notes Toward an Understanding of Ideology," in Barrie Thorne and Marilyn Yalom, eds., *Rethinking the Family* (New York: Longman, 1982), pp. 25–39.

44. Wachs, "Men, Women, and Wheels"; Sandra Rosenbloom, "Why Working Families Need a Car" (paper presented to a conference on "The Car and the City: Los Angeles, The Automobile, and the Built Environment," Los Angeles, April 1988); "What Do Folks Use Their Cars For?" *Literary Digest*, November 17, 1923, pp. 66–69.

45. *Recent Social Trends*, vol. 1, p. 274. The automobile, as historian Joseph Interrante has noted, particularly appealed to American women because it "was a *private* vehicle, and that characteristic made it safer and more acceptable than public streetcars or trains." Joseph Interrante, "The Road to Autopia: The Automobile and the Spatial Transformation of American Culture," in Lewis and Goldstein, eds., p. 99.

46. "What Does Your Car Cost You?" *Ladies' Home Journal*, February 1917, p. 24.

47. Mildred Maddocks Bentley, "The Housekeeper and Her Car," *Ladies' Home Journal*, June 1926, p. 141.

48. *Ladies' Home Journal*, May 1926.

49. Ruth Schwartz Cowan, "From Virginia Dare to Virginia Slims: Women and Technology in American Life," *Technology and Culture* 20, no. 1 (January 1979):59–60.

50. "Driving a Car," *Woman's Home Companion*, May 1919, p. 52.

51. Bentley, p. 141.

52. Ibid.

53. Harry Braverman, *Labor and Monopoly Capital: The Degradation*

of Work in the Twentieth Century (New York: Monthly Review Press, 1974).

54. Christine E. Bose, Philip L. Bereano, and Mary Malloy, "Household Technology and the Social Construction of Housework," *Technology and Culture* 25, no. 1 (January 1984):53–82, cited and critiqued home economics literature, arguing that housework, involving labor-intensive personal service in a small-scale, decentralized setting, is to some degree inherently inefficient. The importance of this insight notwithstanding, I would argue for further inquiry into the gender-laden term "efficiency."

55. Sociologist Anthony Giddens has called attention to the problem of "how societies 'bind' time and space." Anthony Giddens, *A Contemporary Critique of Historical Materialism* (New York: Macmillan, 1981), pp. 3, 90. Contests over time-space relations have had profound consequences for twentieth-century American history. The process of suburbanization involved continual conflict over, and negotiation of, control over metropolitan space. *Radical History Review* 21 (Fall 1979) was devoted to an examination of the significance of space in history. See especially Interrante, "You Can't Go to Town in a Bathtub," pp. 151–168; Susan Porter Benson, "Palace of Consumption and Machine for Selling: The American Department Store, 1880–1940," pp. 199–224; and Dolores Hayden, "Charlotte Perkins Gilman and the Kitchenless House," pp. 225–247. See also Interrante, "The Road to Autopia."

56. Kenneth T. Jackson, *The Crabgrass Frontier* (New York: Oxford University Press, 1985), provides a useful synthesis of the literature on suburbanization, including a particularly insightful analysis of the role of racial antagonism in structuring urban space. Eric H. Monkkonen, *America Becomes Urban: The Development of U.S. Cities and Towns, 1780–1980* (Berkeley: University of California Press, 1988), offers an insightful analysis of American urbanization.

57. Blaine A. Brownell, "A Symbol of Modernity: Attitudes Toward the Automobile in Southern Cities in the 1920's," *American Quarterly* 24 (March 1972):20–44; Robert M. Fogelson, *The Fragmented Metropolis* (Cambridge: Harvard University Press, 1967), p. 146; Mark Foster, "The Decentralization of Los Angeles" (Ph.D. dissertation, University of Southern California, 1971), p. 58. As Joseph Interrante and others have noted, such factors as class, race, and age structured automobile use in complicated ways. See Interrante, "The Road to Autopia," p. 103; Michael L. Berger, "The Great White Hope on Wheels," in Lewis and Goldstein, eds., pp. 59–70; Robert E. Paaswell, *Problems of the Carless* (New York: Praeger, 1978); and Howard L. Preston, *Automobile Age Atlanta: The Making of a Southern Metropolis* (Athens: University of Georgia Press, 1979).

58. Dolores Hayden, *Redesigning the American Dream: The Future of Housing, Work, and Family Life* (New York: W. W. Norton and

Company, 1984); Martin Wachs, "Mass Transit and the Early Suburbs" (unpublished manuscript, in author's possession).

59. Interrante, "You Can't Go to Town in a Bathtub," p. 159.

60. *Recent Social Trends*, vol. 1, p. 669.

61. Ibid. On housewives' time, see Joann Vanek, "Time Spent in Housework," *Scientific American*, November 1974, pp. 116–121.

62. Fogelson, *The Fragmented Metropolis*; Robert B. Riley, "Urban Myths and the New Cities of the Southwest," *Landscape* 17 (Autumn 1967):21–23; Arthur J. Krim, "Imagery in Search of a City: The Geosophy of Los Angeles, 1921–1971" (Ph.D. dissertation, Clark University, 1980), pp. 215–219, 267, 289; Mark S. Foster, "The Model T, the Hard Sell, and Los Angeles' Urban Growth: The Decentralization of Los Angeles in the 1920's," *Pacific Historical Review* 44, no. 4 (1975):459–484; Reyner Banham, *Los Angeles; The Architecture of Four Ecologies* (New York: Harper and Row, 1971), p. 91; Elaine Tyler May, *Great Expectations: Marriage and Divorce in Post-Victorian America* (Chicago: University of Chicago Press, 1980), pp. 8–9. Kenneth Jackson describes the processes that made other cities more like Los Angeles in the course of the twentieth century. Los Angeles and Southern California, moreover, anticipated changing patterns in the ethnic composition of American society, particularly with regard to the increasing importance of Hispanic Americans. See Albert Camarillo, *Chicanos in a Changing Society: From Mexican Pueblos to American Barrios in Santa Barbara and Southern California, 1848–1930* (Cambridge: Harvard University Press, 1979.)

63. On the growth of Los Angeles, see Foster, "The Model T, The Hard Sell, and Los Angeles' Urban Growth," p. 483; and Fogelson, pp. 69–72.

64. May, p. 57. Fogelson has observed that "the native Americans came to Los Angeles with a conception of the good community which was embodied in single-family houses, located on large lots, surrounded by landscaped lawns, and isolated from business activities." Fogelson, p. 144.

65. *Los Angeles Times*, January 27, 1907.

66. Winifred Wandersee, *Women's Work and Family Values, 1920–1940* (Cambridge: Harvard University Press, 1981), pp. 9–11.

67. The relative affluence of those who moved to Los Angeles certainly shaped the character of that city, as well as its image as an urban utopia. See Fogelson, p. 67; Victoria Bissell Brown, "Golden Girls: Female Socialization in Los Angeles, 1880–1910" (Ph.D. dissertation, University of California, San Diego, 1985), pp. 52–55; Martin Wachs, "Autos, Transit, and the Sprawl of Los Angeles: The 1920's," *Journal of the American Planning Association* 50, no 3 (Summer 1984):297–310.

68. *Los Angeles Times*, January 1, 1920; Foster, "The Model T;"

Scott L. Bottles, "The Making of the Modern City: Los Angeles and the Automobile, 1900–1950" (Ph.D. dissertation, University of California at Los Angeles, 1984), p. 100.

69. Kathleen Norris, "Speaking of California," *Motor*, October 1923, pp. 34–35, 74.

70. Bottles, p. xii.

71. On the walking city, see Sam Bass Warner, Jr., *Streetcar Suburbs: The Process of Growth in Boston, 1870–1900* (New York: Atheneum, 1976), pp. 15–21.

72. Bottles, p. 53–103, insightfully discusses the parking ban as a struggle over urban space, without specifically addressing the contested role of women consumer/drivers in the controversy.

73. Ibid., 90–92. See also *Los Angeles Times*, February 3, 1920 and February 12, 1920.

74. *Los Angeles Time*, April 10, 1920; *Los Angeles Record*, April 10, 1920; *Los Angeles Examiner*, April 10, 1920.

75. The Council and the Commission approached women's groups including the Friday Morning Club, the Ebell Club, the Woman's City Club, the Wednesday Morning Club, and the Federation of Parent-Teacher Associations. *Los Angeles Record*, April 2, 1920; *Los Angeles Times*, April 26, 1920 and January 20, 1920.

76. *Los Angeles Record*, January 7, 1920.

77. Bottles, pp. 63, 78; *Los Angeles Record*, January 7, 1920; January 15, 1920; January 29, 1920; February 4, 1920; February 7, 1920.

78. *Los Angeles Record*, January 7, 1920; January 12, 1920; January 23, 1920.

79. *Los Angeles Record*, January 23, 1920.

80. *Los Angeles Times*, January 4, 1920.

81. *Los Angeles Record*, January 19, 1920.

82. *Los Angeles Record*, January 29, 1920.

83. *Los Angeles Record*, April 8, 1920.

84. *Los Angeles Record*, February 2, 1920. Roger Miller, "Household Activity Patterns in Nineteenth-Century Suburbs: A Time-Geographic Exploration," *Annals of the Association of American Geographers* 72, no. 3 (September 1982):355–371, notes the predominance of routine in middle-class household life.

85. *Los Angeles Record*, February 2, 1920.

86. Bottles, p. 60, observes that as early as 1917, the Los Angeles City Engineer had noted that the suburbs had spread beyond the streetcar's reach.

87. *Los Angeles Times*, January 1, 1920.

88. *Los Angeles Times*, January 23, 1920; January 1, 1920.

89. *Los Angeles Times*, January 3, 1920.

90. *Los Angeles Times*, January 11, 1920.

91. *Los Angeles Times*, January 18, 1920.

92. *Los Angeles Times*, January 25, 1920. Miller, "Household Activity Patterns," discusses the importance of time to housewives.

93. A writer in *The Medical Review of Reviews* criticized "the large number of people who drive, not because they are in a hurry or have to cover long distances, but because they are lazy. . . . Women . . . are leading exponents of a sedentary life. They hate to walk." Cited in "Are Motor Cars Making Us Lazy?" *Literary Digest*, August 11, 1923, p. 25.

94. *Los Angeles Record*, April 17, 1920.

95. *Los Angeles Record*, May 1, 1920.

96. *Los Angeles Examiner*, April 11, 1920.

97. *Los Angeles Record*, April 12, 1920.

98. *Los Angeles Examiner*, April 18, 1920.

99. *Los Angeles Examiner*, April 14, 1920.

100. *Los Angeles Times*, April 11, 1920; April 12, 1920; April 13, 1920; April 14, 1920.

101. *Los Angeles Times*, January 1, 1920.

102. *Los Angeles Times*, January 11, 1920.

103. *Los Angeles Times*, April 12, 1920.

104. *Los Angeles Times*, April 21, 1920; *Los Angeles Record*, April 21, 1920.

105. *Los Angeles Times*, January 23, 1920.

106. *Los Angeles Examiner*, April 13, 1920.

107. *Los Angeles Record*, April 21, 1920; *Los Angeles Times*, January 6, 1920; *Los Angeles Examiner*, April 24, 1920.

108. *Los Angeles Times*, April 22, 1920; Bottles, "Making of the Modern City," p. 100.

109. *Los Angeles Examiner*, April 23, 1920; *Los Angeles Record*, April 23, 1920.

110. *Los Angeles Examiner*, April 25, 1920.

111. *Los Angeles Times*, April 27, 1920.

112. *Los Angeles Times*, April 25, 1920.

113. *Los Angeles Record*, January 9, 1920; January 20, 1920.

114. Foster, "The Decentralization of Los Angeles," p. 155.

115. Christine Frederick, *Selling Mrs. Consumer* (New York: Business Bourse, 1929), pp. 311–312.

116. Interrante, "The Road to Autopia," p. 94–95.

9 Reinventing the Wheel

1. In taking this position, I join those historians of technology who affirm a "New History" position that technology is more than the prod-

uct of pure rationality. For a review of recent literature in the field, see John M. Staudenmaier, "*Comment:* Recent Trends in the History of Technology," *American Historical Review* 95, no. 3 (June 1990):715–725. I take my argument about the importance of gender as a category of historical analysis from Joan Wallach Scott, "Gender: A Useful Category of Historical Analysis," in Joan Wallach Scott, *Gender and the Politics of History* (New York: Columbia University Press, 1988), pp. 28–50.

2. Alfred P. Sloan, *My Years with General Motors* (Garden City, N.Y.: Doubleday and Company), pp. 269, 272.

3. Thomas Kuhn, *The Structure of Scientific Revolutions*, 2nd ed. (Chicago: University of Chicago Press, 1970).

4. Bonnie Remsberg, "Women Behind the Wheel," *Redbook*, September 1973, reprinted in the Motor Vehicle Manufacturers' Association of the United States, *News Review*, September 12, 1973.

5. Dolores Hayden, *Redesigning the American Dream: The Future of Housing, Work, and Family Life* (New York: W. W. Norton, 1984); Joseph Interrante, "The Road to Autopia: The Automobile and the Spatial Transformation of American Culture," in David L. Lewis and Laurence Goldstein, eds., *The Automobile and American Culture* (Ann Arbor: University of Michigan Press, 1983), pp. 89–104; Genevieve Giuliano, "Getting There: Women and Transportation," in Jan Zimmerman, ed., *The Technological Woman: Interfacing with Tomorrow* (New York: Praeger, 1983), pp. 102–112; Sandra Rosenbloom, "Why Working Families Need a Car" (paper presented to a symposium on "The Car and the City: The Automobile, the Built Environment, and Daily Life in Los Angeles," Los Angeles, April 9, 1988); Sam Bass Warner, "Services for Families" (paper presented to a symposium on "The Car and the City: The Automobile, the Built Environment, and Daily Life in Los Angeles," Los Angeles, April 9, 1988); Susan Hanson and Ibipo Johnson, "Gender Differences in Work-Trip Length: Explanations and Implications," *Urban Geography* 6 (1985):193–219; Martin Wachs, "Men, Women, and Wheels: The Historical Basis of Gender Differences in Travel Patterns" (paper presented to the Transportation Research Board, Washington, D.C., January, 1987, in author's possession).

Index

Advertising, 35–36, 38, 39, 42, 47–
  48, 58–59, 62–65, 115–116,
  129–131, 141–142
Agriculture, Department of, 142
American Automobile Asso-
  ciation (AAA), 19, 70, 75,
  77
American Committee for Devas-
  tated France, 105
American Fund for French
  Wounded (AFFW), 93–97
American Girls' Aid, 97
American Laundry Machinery
  Company, 148
American Women's Over-Seas
  Hospital, 97
Anchor Auto Top, 122
Anchor Buggy Company, 123
Ancient Rome, 3
Anderson Electric Car Company,
  38
Apperson brothers, 9, 10
Argo company, 38
Atalanta story, 69–70
Austin, Mary, 86
Autobiography of Alice B. Toklas,
  The (Stein), 96
Automobile Club of America
  (ACA), 68, 70
Automobile Club of France, 70

Automobile Club of Southern Cali-
  fornia, 160
Automobile Manufacturers' Asso-
  ciation, 77
Automotive pioneers, 7–13, 165
Automotive schools, 100, 101
Auto touring, 65, 67, 73–82, 85–
  87, 136–138, 163
Ayer, Elizabeth, 95

Baker, Newton D., 103
Barber, Flora B., 84–85
Beard, Mary, 81, 83, 84
Beasley, Norman, 61, 113
Belmont, Alva, 81
Bentley, Mildred Maddocks, 147–
  149
Benz, Karl, 8, 9
Berry, C. P., 19
Bicycling, 8, 9
Birdsall, E. T., 19
Blaine, Mrs. James G., 37
Blatch, Harriot Stanton, 81, 82, 86
Bohn, Elizabeth Hallam, 118, 120
Boston, Massachusetts, 36
Bottles, Scott, 152
Brayton, George B., 8
British Voluntary Aid Detach-
  ments (VADs), 91

British Women's Convoy Corps, 91
British Women's Reserve Ambulance Corps, 91
Brush Runabout, 52
Burke, Alice, 86–87
Burlingame, Margaret R., 29–31, 119, 120

Cadillac Motor Company, 60, 62, 115
California, 6, 7, 25, 80, 117, 139–140, 151–163
Camping, 137–138
Car saleswomen, 83–85
Carter, Byron, 60–61
Cartercar, 60
Carvin, Florence, 143, 144
Cassini, Marguerite, 71
Catt, Carrie Chapman, 86
Chamberlain, William, 160
Chapin, Roy D., 10, 11, 123
Chauffeurs, 17–22, 56, 68
Chevrolet, 130
Child's car seat, 128
Chinese women, 3
Chrysler Corp., 131
Clarke, Edward, 2
Claudy, C. H., 41–46
Closed cars, 48, 57, 114, 122–126, 168
Club Feminin Automobile, 92, 93
Colorado, 143
Comfort, 41, 42, 55–57, 60, 62, 66, 114, 119, 120, 122, 123, 127–131, 166–168, 174
Commerce Department, 143
Congressional Union (CU), 86

Convenience, 41–44, 56, 62, 66, 114, 128, 129, 149, 167, 174
Cook, Charles, 24
Country Life in America magazine, 38, 39
Couzens, James Gould, 56
Cowan, Ruth Schwartz, 146–147
Cranking, 58–61, 65, 167
Criticism of women drivers, 26–33, 167, 172
Crow-Elkhart, 131
Cuneo, Joan Newton, 29, 73–75, 80, 87, 172
Cutler-Hammer Magnetic Gear Shift, 64–65
Cutler-Hammer Manufacturing Company, 64

Daimler, Gottlieb, 8
Darwin, Charles, 2
Davis, Jennie, 31–32
Davis, L. R., 159
Dayton Engineering Laboratories Company (Delco), 62
De Palma, Ralph, 75
de Wolfe, Elsie, 105
Dike, Mrs. Norman, 105
Dixon, Winifred Hawkridge, 136–137
Dodge Brothers, 113
Domestic work, 145–150
Donovan, Frank, 60–61
Drew, Arthur L., 102
Duff-Gordon, Lucile Lady, 126
Du Gast, Camille, 70
DuPont chemical laboratories, 132
Durant, William C., 113
Duryea, Charles, 8–9, 57
Duryea, Frank, 8–9
Duryea War Relief, 97

Earl, Wheeler, 119
Eastman, Crystal, 83, 84
Edison, Thomas, 38–39
Education of women, 2, 23
Electric cars, 35–50, 57, 60, 64
Electric gear shift, 64–65
Electric starter, 59–63, 167
Electric Vehicle Company, 49
Emery, Wilhelmina, 6
Essex coach, 123–124
Evans, Bob, 118
Extension agents, 143–144

Face protectors, 15, 16
Farmer, Bert L., 161
Fashion, 15, 16, 33, 135
Faye, Julia, 131
Female automobile employees, 54
Female stereotypes, 26–33, 167, 172
Femininity, 16, 35–50, 54, 55, 60, 65, 68, 89, 101, 102, 111, 112, 115, 116, 119–122, 125, 126, 132, 165–168, 173–175
Field, Sarah Bard, 86
Fisher, Harriet White, 78
Fitler, Mrs. Clarence Cecil, 73
Fitzgerald, F. Scott, 139
Fitzgerald, Zelda, 103
Five Dollar Day (1913), 54
Flanders, Walter, 113
Flappers, 103, 105, 107, 135, 138, 139, 163
Ford, Clara, 53, 54
Ford, Edsel, 53
Ford, Henry, 11–12, 45, 52–57, 62, 63, 112–114, 131, 132, 166
Ford Motor Company, 53, 130, 141–142
Foster, S. P., 32

Fraser, Helen, 91
Frederick, Christine, 68, 131–132, 162
Freese, Mrs. Lee, 158
French Wounded Emergency Fund, 93

Gardner, E. W., 31
Garfield, Edith M., 126–127
Gelso, Mary, 140–141
Gender ideology: *see* Femininity; Masculinity
General Electric Company, 39
General Motors Corp., 112–114, 130, 131, 132, 168
Gentlemen Prefer Blondes (Loos), 107
Gilbert, Sandra, 93
Girl Scouts, 108, 109
Glidden Cup tours, 73
Good Housekeeping magazine, 130, 141
Good Life, notion of, 150–152, 172
Gould, Grace Margaret, 16
Gould, Mrs. George J., 17
Great Depression, 171–172
Guthrie, Janet, 172–173

Haldane, Richard, 90, 91
Hall, Radclyffe, 94, 107
Harding, Warren, 111, 170
Harrison Wagon Company, 58–59
Hay, Mary Garrett, 83, 84
Hayden, Dolores, 13
Haynes, Elwood, 10
Hearst, William Randolph, 17, 20
Hemingway, Ernest, 90
Hitchcock, Mrs. A. Sherman, 27–29

Hollander, Mrs. R. S., 120
Home demonstrations, 143–144
Hoover, Herbert, 170
Horse-drawn railways, 6
Horseless Age magazine, 37
Horseless carriages, 8–13
Houston, Texas, 25–26, 45, 53
Houston Automobile Directory,
    25–26, 45
Hudson Motor Company, 123–124
Hunter Auto Supply Company, 63
Hupmobile, 129

Illinois Equal Suffrage Associa-
    tion, 79–80
Illustrated World magazine, 48
Installment buying, 114, 171
Internal combustion engine, 8

James, Ada, 80–81
James, Henry, 23, 24
Jordan, Edward S., 118, 120, 130
Jordan Motor Car Company, 130–
    131
Joy riding, 138–141

Kettering, Charles, 61–62, 65, 132
King, Anita, 77
Knights of Columbus, 106
Koch, Valentine, 19
Kuhn, Thomas, 171

Lacey, Robert, 55
Ladies' Home Journal magazine,
    49, 130, 133, 141, 147, 148
League of American Wheelmen, 8
Leland, Henry F., 60–62

Lesbians, 107
Levassor, Emile Constant, 8
Lewis, Sinclair, 115
Lexington Minute Man Six, 129
Lexington Motor Company, 108
Licenses, 23, 25, 68
Long, John C., 125, 126
Longworth, Alice Roosevelt, 71–
    73
Loos, Anita, 107
Los Angeles, California, 6, 7, 25,
    117, 139–140, 151–163
*Los Angeles County Automobile
    Directory,* 25
Los Angeles Examiner, 158, 161
Los Angeles Record, 7, 121, 140,
    154–156, 158, 161, 162
Los Angeles Times, 51, 117, 151,
    157, 159–162
Lynd, Helen, 133
Lynd, Robert, 133

MacManus, Theodore F., 61, 113,
    115
Mann Act of 1910, 139
Masculinity, 10, 12, 15, 37, 40, 50,
    60, 65, 68, 89, 111–116, 119,
    121, 122, 124–126, 132, 165–
    167, 173–175
Maxim, Hiram Percy, 13
Maxwell, Jonathan D., 10
Maxwell-Briscoe Company, 47–
    48, 76, 77, 84
May, Elaine Tyler, 151
McClintock, Laura B., 136
McCulloch, Catherine Waugh, 79–
    81
McIntyre, O. O., 118
McManus, Blanche, 92–94, 98
Mechanical knowledge, 27, 29, 47

Men, Money, and Motors (Mac-Manus and Beasley), 113
Merry Oldsmobile, 11, 15
Miller, Mary E., 79–80
Millholland, Inez, 83, 84
Model AA (Maxwell-Briscoe Company), 47
Model C (Winton Company), 47
Model T (Ford Motor Company), 45, 47, 52–57, 63, 82, 113–114, 122, 131
Moehle, Jean Earl, 84
Morgan, Anne, 93, 105
Morgan, J. P., 93
Morgan, Jane, 93
Mors cars, 59
Motor Age magazine, 145
Motor magazine, 17, 20, 27, 29, 31, 33, 37, 38, 46, 49, 50, 62, 63, 87, 102, 109, 114, 116–117, 120, 125, 128, 129
Mudge, Genevera Delphine, 37
Mullett, Mary, 28, 30
Munro Corps, 91
Musselman, M. M., 75

National American Woman Suffrage Association (NAWSA), 86
National Automobile Chamber of Commerce (NACC), 117
National League for Women's Service, 99, 104, 108
Nevins, Allan, 53
New Jersey, 23, 117
Newport, Rhode Island, 25, 36, 71
New York City, 6–7, 81, 85
New York Daily News Record, 133
New York State, 81, 82, 85–86

New York State Ambulance Corps, 99–100
New York Times, 19, 23, 68, 73, 84, 85, 97–100, 102
999 model, 12
Norris, Kathleen, 152

Olcott, Jane, 85–86
Oldfield, Barney, 12, 75
Olds, Ransom E., 11, 52
Oldsmobile car, 11, 52
Olds Motor Works, 10
Oliver, French, 138
Outing magazine, 26
Outlook, The, 42
Overland Six, 130

Pallier, Jeanne, 92, 93
Peacock, Roscoe, 121, 123
Peaslee, Frances Randolph, 97–98
Perry, Harry Wilkin, 59
Philadelphia, Pennsylvania, 6, 74
Phillips, Mrs. John Howell, 25
Political Equity League of Wisconsin, 80
Pope, Albert E., 8, 35, 36, 38, 43
Pope Manufacturing Company, 35
Popular Mechanics magazine, 19, 143
Post, Daisy, 37
Post, Emily, 78
Power, 12, 43, 49
Professional Chauffeurs' Club, 20
Progressive Era, 4, 25, 67, 165
Public transit, development of, 5–7

Quadricycle, 62

Racing, 9, 11, 12, 66, 67, 70, 73, 75, 87, 173
Rae, John B., 60
Ramsey, Alice Huyler, 47, 74, 76–77, 84, 87
Ramsey, John Rathbone, 76
Red Cross, 91, 92, 97, 99, 105, 108
Reesing, Florence P., 84
Registrations, 25–26, 112, 117
Remsberg, Bonnie, 172
Rice, Herbert R., 39, 40
Richardson, Nell, 86–87
Riley, Phil M., 39–40
Rinehart, Mary Roberts, 104–105, 138
Road system, 8, 45
Rochester, Claire, 65, 66
Rollins, Montgomery, 42
Roosevelt, Theodore, 71, 72
Rossiter, Hamblin, 101
Rural women, 142–145, 151, 163
Russey, Wilma, 85

Safety, 119, 128, 149, 167, 172, 174
Saleswomen, 83–85
Saltzman, Vernell, 144–145
San Francisco, California, 117
Save Me the Waltz (Fitzgerald), 103
Schultz, Olive, 82
Scientific management, 149
Scott, Blanche Stuart, 78
Scottish Women's Hospital Unit, 91, 97, 98
Self-starter, 57–63
Selling Mrs. Consumer (Frederick), 131, 162
"Sex No Criterion" (Gardner), 31
Sexuality, 20–22, 138–140, 173

Shaw, Anna Howard, 87
Sherman, Ray W., 115, 117, 129, 131, 171
Sloan, Alfred P., 112–114, 122, 124, 132, 168
Smith, Samuel L., 11
Smith Girls' Unit, 97
Smith-Lever Act of 1914, 143
Social class, 18–22, 68–69
Society for the Protection of Passenger Rights, 6–7
Society Le Bien-Être du Blessé, 97
Speed, 10, 12, 43, 45, 47, 70, 129
Spencer, Herbert, 2
Splitdorf Electric Company, 63
Stein, Gertrude, 55, 95–97, 104, 109, 111
Stewart-Warner Speedometer Corp., 63
Stobart, Mabel St. Clair, 91
Stock market crash of 1929, 171
Streetcars, 6, 7, 153–156
Suburbia, 150, 152, 170
Subways, 6–7
Sunset magazine, 129, 147
Sutton, Veda, 81

Teague, Michael, 72
Teters, Luellen Cass, 69, 71
Thaxter, Katherine, 136–137
Toklas, Alice B., 96, 104
Tonneau, 18, 20
Tucson, Arizona, 25, 45, 53
Tucson Automobile Directory, 45
Turner, Frederick Jackson, 113

United States Bureau of Home Economics Study, 151
Used car trade-ins, 114

Valdettaro, Louis A., 32
Valley of Decision, The (Wharton), 23
Vanity Fair magazine, 48
Veblen, Thorstein, 17
Vulcan Electric Gear Shifter, 64

War Camp Community Service, 102–104
Well of Loneliness, The (Hall), 107
Wembridge, Eleanor, 139
Westinghouse Electric Corp., 63
Wharton, Edith, 23–24
"When Woman Drives, Man Jumps" (Burlingame), 30–31
White, E. B., 58
White brothers, 8
White coupe, 48
White Motor Company, 48
Whitney, Charlotte Anita, 80
Wills, C. Harold, 12
Willys-Overland Company, 130
Wilson, J. L., 129
Wilson, Woodrow, 17, 18, 86, 89
Wings of the Dove, The (James), 23
Winton Company, 47

Wisconsin, 80
"Woman and Her Car, The" (Claudy), 45
Woman's Home Companion magazine, 41, 46, 148
Woman's National Automobile Club of America (WNACA), 106
"Woman's Point of View, A" (Davis), 31–32
Woman suffrage, 2, 3, 23, 32, 54, 66, 67, 79–83, 85–87, 111
Women's Christian Temperance Union, 155
Women's Committee of the Council of National Defense, 103–104
Women's Motor Corps, 99–102, 106
Women's racing, 66, 67, 70, 73, 75, 87, 173
"Wonderful Monster, The," 20–22
World War I, 66, 88, 89–109, 169–170

YMCA, 97, 108
Young, Clara Kimball, 161